Curbing Bailouts

NEW COMPARATIVE POLITICS

Series Editor
Michael Laver, New York University

Editorial Board
Ken Benoit, Trinity College, Dublin
Gary Cox, University of California, San Diego
Simon Hix, London School of Economics
John Huber, Columbia
Herbert Kitschelt, Duke
W. Bingham Powell, Rochester
Kaare Strøm, University of California, San Diego
George Tsebelis, University of Michigan
Leonard Wantchekon, New York University

The New Comparative Politics series brings together cutting-edge work on social conflict, political economy, and institutional development. Whatever its substantive focus, each book in the series builds on solid theoretical foundations; uses rigorous empirical analysis; and deals with timely, politically relevant questions.

Curbing Bailouts: Bank Crises and Democratic Accountability in Comparative Perspective
  Guillermo Rosas

Curbing Bailouts

Bank Crises and Democratic Accountability in Comparative Perspective

Guillermo Rosas

The University of Michigan Press
Ann Arbor

Copyright © by the University of Michigan 2009
All rights reserved
Published in the United States of America by
The University of Michigan Press
Manufactured in the United States of America
⊗ Printed on acid-free paper

2012   2011   2010   2009   4   3   2   1

A CIP catalog record for this book is available from the British Library.

U.S. CIP data on file.

ISBN 978-0-472-11713-0 (cloth : alk. paper)

Para Tabea, Aitana y Emilio

Contents

List of Tables

List of Figures

List of Acronyms

AdeBA	*Asociación de Bancos de Argentina*
Banxico	*Banco de México*
BCRA	*Banco Central de la República Argentina*
BNA	*Banco de la Nación Argentina*
CAR	capital-asset ratio
CMHN	*Consejo Mexicano de Hombres de Negocios*
CNBV	*Comisión Nacional Bancaria y de Valores*
ECB	European Central Bank
FFCB	*Fondo Fiduciario de Capitalización Bancaria*
Fobaproa	*Fondo Bancario de Protección al Ahorro*
Fogade	*Fondo de Garantía de Depósitos*
IFS	International Financial Statistics
IMF	International Monetary Fund
INEGI	*Instituto Nacional de Estadística, Geografía e Informática*
IPAB	*Instituto de Protección al Ahorro Bancario*
Libor	London Interbank Offered Rate
LOLR	lender of last resort
MCMC	Markov chain Monte Carlo
MECON	*Ministerio de Economía*

NPL   non-performing loans

P&A   Purchase and Assumption

Procapte   Programa de Capitalización Permanente

SHCP   *Secretaría de Hacienda y Crédito Público*

Sedesa   *Seguro de Depósitos, S.A.*

SEF   *Superintendencia de Entidades Financieras*

Preface and Acknowledgments

As I write these words, many countries face recession following a protracted period of financial turmoil in the core economies of the world. An economic crisis of truly global proportion started as the seemingly unstoppable upward trend in home prices in the United States halted and abruptly changed direction over the past couple of years. Yet another period of unabated credit expansion ended in doubts about the ability of banks to withstand the loss of value of their assets. As these doubts deepened, banks and banking systems around the world seemed ready to succumb to financial distress, but many of them have received a new lease on life through taxpayer-sponsored bailouts. With the benefit of hindsight, it now seems obvious that the credit expansion of the past few years, based on rosy expectations about steadily-climbing home prices, could not go on forever, but in fact very few voices warned about the looming disaster. This lack of foresight is even more surprising considering that instances of boom, bust, and bailout have been plentiful over the past quarter century.

This book deals with government responses to banking crises. More often than not, the term "bailout" is used scornfully to refer to any such response. This by-now vacuous term suggests an alarming degree of uniformity in the use of policies to redress situations of insolvency in a country's banking sector. Contrary to this view, however, there is ample variation in the kind and degree of government involvement to manage banking crises. My main contention is that the political regimes within which governments operate pattern these responses. Specifically, I argue that democratic regimes are more likely than non-democracies to engineer more limited interventions in distressed banking sectors.

I have incurred many debts of gratitude over the course of writing this book. The evolution of the manuscript from my doctoral research was slow and so thorough that very little of that first effort remains in these pages. For their unyielding support and advice from those early days onward, I wish to thank Gabe Aguilera, Federico Estévez, Kirk Hawkins, Robert O.

xiii

Keohane, Herbert Kitschelt, Peter Lange, Eric Magar, Luigi Manzetti, Robert Mickey, Scott Morgenstern, Alejandro Poiré, Karen Remmer, Ethan Scheiner, Mauricio Tenorio, Jeff Weldon, and Liz Zechmeister. A large portion of this book was written while on sabbatical at the Institut Barcelona d'Estudis Internacionals; I gratefully acknowledge the help of Carles Boix and Jacint Jordana in helping me find a conducive work environment in Barcelona, and the support of Washington University in allowing me to spend this profitable year abroad. The Department of Political Science at Washington University has been my academic home over the past five years. I am grateful to my colleagues in the department, who provide an environment that blends intellectual challenge and nourishment with collegiality and encouragement. I would like to thank Brian Crisp, Matt Gabel, Nate Jensen, Andrew Martin, Sunita Parikh, and Andy Sobel for entertaining questions about methods, substance, and professional guidance, and the Weidenbaum Center on the Economy, Government and Public Policy for financial support. I would also like to thank Sam Drzymala, Jacob Gerber, and Yael Shomer for providing outstanding research assistance, and Steve Haptonstahl for his help in developing Chapter 3. Melody Herr and the editorial team at the University of Michigan Press provided invaluable help every step of the way. Finally, David Singer and Paul Vaaler read the manuscript in its entirety and provided an array of thoughtful and provocative assessments, as did two anonymous reviewers at the University of Michigan Press. I thank them wholeheartedly for helping me write a better book. Any remaining errors are, of course, mine to bear alone.

My final acknowledgments are for my family, always close to me despite geographical distance. My mother-in-law, Karin, passed away before I could finish the book. I am thankful for the many ways she and José found to give us solace and respite when Tabea and I needed time to work on our projects; above all, I deeply cherish their constant affection and unfailing support throughout the years. My parents, Marcela and Guillermo, managed to raise a family through two protracted and devastating economic meltdowns in Mexico. They made enormous sacrifices so that we would never lack shelter, care, and a good education even during harsh times. I'm happy to finally express my gratitude to them in print. To my siblings, Marcela and Mauricio, I owe the sense of community they provide me with even though we are all so far away from the home where we grew up together. Tabea, Aitana, and Emilio have seen me through many of the possible moods available to human experience with endless patience and understanding as I strove to finish this book. I feel elated to dedicate this book to them, with all my love.

Guillermo Rosas
Saint Louis, Missouri

1

Bagehot or Bailout?
Policy Responses to Banking Crises

On September 14, 2007, following the announcement that the Bank of England would provide liquidity support to Northern Rock, jittery depositors of this financial institution started long queues outside its main branches to withdraw their savings. A few months later, on February 17, 2008, British taxpayers woke up to the news that they had become the proud owners of Northern Rock after the British government's decision to nationalize the troubled bank. The bank's financial situation had taken a turn for the worse due to heavy exposure to mortgage loans in arrears; these non-performing assets saddled the bank's loan portfolio and had led the bank to the brink of insolvency. As new owners of Northern Rock, British taxpayers would be responsible for nursing the bank back to financial health or to arrange for its liquidation after paying off its creditors, in any case sinking resources into the bank without much hope of eventually making a profit. However, the decision to nationalize Northern Rock protected "the best interests of taxpayers" according to Prime Minister Gordon Brown.[1] Elsewhere, the "subprime mortgage crisis" that spelled Northern Rock's doom weakened the financial status of banks in the United States, continental Europe, and many other countries. The failure of Northern Rock was not an isolated instance, but part and parcel of a deeper crisis affecting financial markets and intermediaries—banks among them—around the world. The extent and depth of this crisis, as well as the fact that it has affected banks in countries where prudential supervision is presumably strong, has reignited policy debates about the proper role of government action in limiting risky behavior in financial markets.

---

[1] "Timeline: Northern Rock bank crisis," *BBC News online*, February 19, 2008, http://news.bbc.co.uk/1/hi/business/7007076.stm.

Banking crises are situations of widespread insolvency in a country's banking system (Sundararajan and Baliño 1991). They can be the consequence of exogenous shocks that shift the value of banks' assets and liabilities or of pressure from depositors that starts "panic runs" on banks (Calomiris 2008). The Northern Rock bank failure may have been the first event in a global crisis started in the core financial markets in recent memory, yet banking crises are nothing new: Tacitus registers one of the first banking crises—and what can be construed as a government bailout—in the year 33 A.D. (Davis 1913). In modern times, banking crises were common in the 19th century and throughout the Gold Standard era in the industrialized countries of the Atlantic basin (Bordo 1986, 2002; Calomiris 2007; Schwartz 1988). In the United States alone, Schwartz (1988) reports eleven banking panics in the antebellum period. The creation of the Federal Reserve System (1914) and of the Federal Deposit Insurance Corporation (1934)—which were instituted in the wake of banking panics—is often credited for the reduced incidence of banking crises in the United States, particularly after the Great Depression. Later on, regulatory controls, financial repression, and limited international capital flows combined to reduce the possibility of widespread insolvency in banking systems around the world. It was not until the demise of Bretton Woods that the frequency and severity of banking crises began to increase again.

Just over the past three decades, banking crises have wreaked havoc in a large number of countries at all levels of development. Over the last year, global turmoil in the wake of the subprime mortgage crisis has led to banking distress even in countries with developed financial markets and reputable systems of bank oversight and regulation. A recent tally of banking crises puts the total count at 204 events between 1975 and 2003, some of them lasting several years and affecting as many as 120 countries (Beim and Calomiris 2001; Caprio, Klingebiel, Laeven and Noguera 2005). The frequency of these events is as impressive as their economic costs. Indeed, banking crises tend to coincide with periods of depressed economic growth. In a sample of over 2,000 "country/years," mean economic growth in country/years with banking crises was −2.84%, compared to 1.36% in non-crisis country/years (Rosas 2002).[2] More importantly, the fiscal costs of restoring banks to solvency have been staggering across countries. The average fiscal cost of banking crises in a sample of 46 events exceeds 11% of GDP, with the cheapest recorded crisis exhausting 1.4% (Estonia in the early 1990s) and the most expensive one draining 55.3% of the country's product (Argentina in the early

---

[2] See Calderón and Liu (2003) for a recent empirical analysis of the broader causal connections between financial development and economic growth and Dell'Ariccia, Detragiache and Rajan (2008) for an analysis of the real economic effects of banking crises.

1980s).[3] Though these figures are per force inexact, the orders of magnitude reveal that banking crises are far from trivial events. Aside from the direct economic costs to taxpayers—indeed, perhaps as a consequence of these effects—banking crises literally break people's hearts: Systemic banking crises are associated with increases in population heart disease mortality rates of about 6% in high-income countries and as much as 26% in low-income economies (Stuckler, Meissner and King 2008).

One of the most fascinating and important aspects of banking crises—indeed one reason why fiscal costs vary so much—is that governments react differently to what are in essence very similar problems. Take the cases of Argentina and Mexico, two countries that have faced widespread insolvency in their banking systems at several points during the past decades. Their responses to banking crises have been diverse, depending as one might expect on policy tools at their governments' disposal, their degree of openness to international capital flows, and the institutional setup within which they conduct monetary policy. In the mid-1990s, these countries suffered the contemporaneous onslaught of banking crises, preceded by doubts about the extent of non-performing loans carried by domestic banks and deepened by severe capital outflows that eroded bank balance sheets. The *Tequila* crises of the mid-1990s, as these events were dubbed, had profound political, economic, and social consequences in these two countries. In the realm of banking, these crises eventually led to the total reconstruction of their systems of financial intermediation. Within five years, the process of gradual financial openness that Argentina and Mexico had started in the early 1990s was speeded up and completed. Small banks were closed and sold off to large banks; large banks, in turn, were slowly nursed back to solvency and eventually auctioned to newcomers. Among the newcomers, international banks made huge inroads into these banking systems, to an extent unprecedented in the recent history of Latin America.

But before working through the legislative changes required to carry out these momentous reforms, long before lining up potential buyers to purchase the bigger banks, governments in Argentina and Mexico had to deal with the more immediate consequences of widespread bank insolvency. Argentina's performance during the *Tequila* crisis can be portrayed as a case of market-friendly reconstruction of the banking system in which public officials avoided recourse to expensive bank bailouts. The Argentine government sorted out solvent from insolvent banks and forced shareholders and depositors of

---

[3]Based on data from Honohan and Klingebiel (2000). In fact, the cost of contemporary banking crises, as a share of a country's GDP, is much larger than it was for similar events in the 19th century. One possible explanation for this increase is the proliferation of government-sponsored safety nets, especially deposit insurance, that blunt depositors' incentives to monitor banks and permit imprudent risk-taking by banks (cf. Calomiris 2008).

insolvent banks to take their losses in a series of moves reminiscent of Sir Walter Bagehot's advice on confronting banking panics: lend freely and on good collateral to solvent banks, close down the rest (Bagehot 1873). A wealth of evidence supports this view: The government enforced the closure of a large number of banks in a relatively short period, the central government aided privatization of public provincial banks, and depositors of insolvent banks lost a fraction of their wealth. Not that these policies were cheap, but authorities still managed to restructure the Argentine banking system at meager cost to the taxpayer (0.5% of GDP, according to Honohan and Klingebiel 2000).

In contrast, the Mexican government's reaction to the *Tequila* crisis finds few apologists. In response to the debacle, Mexico engaged in an unprecedented bailout of its banking system, redistributing bank losses away from bank shareholders and big bank creditors. Liquidation of insolvent banks occurred at a very slow pace, the government sponsored a non-performing loans purchase program that was exceptionally generous to bankers, and upheld a blanket insurance scheme that protected all depositors. Years after the bank bailout, Mexico's erstwhile deposit insurance corporation (Fobaproa by its Spanish acronym) is still considered a symbol of government corruption, inefficiency, and crony capitalism. In the end, the process of bank restructuring in Mexico left a hefty bill that continues to burden public finances to this day. In 1999, government liabilities from the bank bailout were estimated at 52 bn. dollars, roughly 11.17% of GDP. This amounted to a debt of about $550.00 USD per capita.[4]

My goal in this book is to show that the political regime within which governments operate has a discernible impact on policy responses to banking crises. I argue that democratic governments, constrained as they are by links of electoral accountability, are more cautious in implementing costly policies that are ultimately shouldered by taxpayers, whereas authoritarian governments are more prone to bail out banks. Though the mechanism of electoral accountability is not airtight, it exerts enough of a constraint on policy-makers to leave noticeable effects in the way in which politicians address banking crises.

This argument may seem counterintuitive, to put it euphemistically, given that a number of governments in wealthy democracies have recently chosen to support banks and other financial intermediaries to contain the effects of the subprime mortgage crisis. Take the case of the United States itself, a country with a long and unchequered history of electoral accountability and with a relatively limited record of state intervention in the economy. This example

---

[4] Author's calculation. Per capita GDP figures are constant-dollar corrected for purchasing power parity and use 2000 as the baseline year (The World Bank 2006).

might suggest that there are no meaningful differences in the ways in which democratic and authoritarian governments choose to contain banking crises.

However, the case for or against the relevance of political regimes does not depend solely on the observation of democratic regimes that take measures to protect their financial systems, but rather on answering the following counterfactual proposition: Would the United States (or any democratic government) have reacted any differently to the subprime-mortgage crisis had its government been authoritarian? My answer to this counterfactual is unequivocally positive: I believe that this government could have engineered an even more expensive and generous bailout under a different regime form.[5] As a simple thought experiment, consider whether the rather cavalier 3-page bailout plan presented by Secretary of the Treasury Henry M. Paulson on September 19, 2008, would have elicited so many demands—through congressional hearings, media attention, and citizen outrage channeled through representative institutions—to limit the extent of government involvement in a non-democratic regime.

Needless to say, arguments about causal effects regarding a single observation are inherently undecidable; after all, we only get to observe the United States government as a democracy. The very counterfactual proposition of an authoritarian United States taxes the imagination because the world we live in is one where we seldom see authoritarian regimes among countries with high levels of development. The most we can strive for is to understand whether democracies have, *on average*, a lower or higher propensity to engage in bailouts. I posit that several factors aside from democratic accountability have a bearing on government responses to banking crises. For example, the very level of economic development of a society and its income distribution have an indirect effect on government choices because they affect the policy preferences of voters. These factors confound attempts to tease out political regime effects on policy choice, and consequently any strategy of empirical validation must take them into account. To compound the difficulty of arriving at sound causal inferences about regime effects, verification of hypotheses in the social sciences depends mostly on observational, rather than experimental, data. In fact, the problem of empirical verification of regime effects based on observational data is one to which I devote ample attention throughout the book.

---

[5]Not that current plans point to an extraordinarily efficient form of bailout. Indeed, at the moment of writing the jury is still out on the main features that the US bailout plan will take. The US government is set to spend up to 700 bn. dollars to purchase bad loans, inject capital into private banks, and perhaps even to help mortgage-holders remain current in their payments to banks. This fund, if spent in its entirety and sunk in irrecoverable losses, will amount to about 5% of the United States' GDP, which is on the low end of expenditures during recent banking crises.

1.1 The Puzzle of Bailouts

I define bank bailouts as *government-sponsored delays* in the exit of insolvent banks that are explicitly or implicitly funded by public resources. In other words, a bank, group of banks, or entire banking system benefits from a bailout whenever it continues to operate even after its solvency status is called into question. This definition is more or less in line with the colloquial use of the term. The colloquial use, however, suggests that all policies that seek to prop up banks are essentially identical. Press accounts abound in descriptions of policies that are meant to alleviate different aspects of bank insolvency but are ultimately bundled together under this rather vague term. In contrast to this view, I seek to convey that bank bailouts are not discrete "either/or" events. Rather, when thinking about government management of banking crises it is more helpful from an analytical standpoint to think of a policy continuum that ranges in the abstract from *no government help to banks* to *complete government absorption of all losses.*

The first pole of this continuum would correspond to a radical strategy in which governments refrain from intervening to stabilize banking systems under financial duress and simply let banks fail. Because bank balance sheets are tightly integrated and bank capital is highly leveraged, the failure of a single insolvent bank may threaten to upset the entire banking system and have effects on the real economy; this "systemic risk" scenario is blandished frequently during banking crises, and indeed I know of no government in recent times that has chosen to wait by the sidelines while banks collapse left and right. In consequence, what could be called the Market pole of this dimension is not approximated in practice.

The other pole of this continuum corresponds to a situation where governments support banks liberally and with no strings attached. In this situation, even banks that are manifestly insolvent receive government support to continue operating and their losses are entirely subsidized by taxpayers' money. The distinguishing feature of this kind of response, which I label Bailout, is that it lifts the burden of insolvency away from banks and beyond the level of support actually needed to avoid the immediate meltdown of the banking system. In between the Market and Bailout endpoints, the responses of many governments approximate a model that I refer to as Bagehot. I use this label to recognize Sir Walter Bagehot's contribution to a doctrine of containment of banking crises that continues to guide government action today (Bagehot 1873). In order to contain a banking crisis, Bagehot's proposal was to set up a lender of last resort with capacity to loan freely on good collateral. This proposal sets Bagehot away from the Market pole of the policy continuum in that it calls for policy intervention to avoid collapse of the banking system. At the same time, the requirement not to provide liquidity to banks that cannot post "good collateral" underlines Bagehot's reluctance to artificially extend the life of insolvent banks. Hence, in practice, the Bagehot (rather than Market) and Bailout ideal-types of government response are the relevant endpoints of the policy continuum, with actual solutions to banking crises falling within these two extremes. I argue throughout the book that we can interpret the banking policy of governments, i.e., the choices they make in several policy arenas, as being driven by their positions along a latent Bagehot-Bailout continuum. In consequence, though we cannot directly observe the position that different governments take along the Bagehot-Bailout dimension, we can infer their bailout propensities from analysis of their banking policies during crises.[6]

What makes governments choose Bagehot over Bailout? To provide some intuition about the main dilemma, and thus to motivate the importance of political regimes as potential explanatory factors, consider the decision problem that governments face as they learn that insolvency threatens large portions of a country's banking sector. Governments can choose to enforce bank regulations strictly, forcing bankers to come up with fresh capital and write off insolvent loans or else face bank liquidation. In principle, this solution minimizes immediate public expenses, but has the potential downside of affecting other banks and non-financial actors, perhaps aggravating an existing economic crisis. Moreover, bank liquidation is itself costly: aside from the immediate administrative costs of taking banks over, paying off insured depositors, and losing a bank's pool of knowledge about creditors, banks support a nation's payments system, a service with some public good characteristics that may suffer damage if several banks are allowed to fail.

Alternatively, governments can choose to engage in regulatory forbearance, keeping insolvent banks alive in the hope that they can slowly redress their financial problems. In principle, this policy option diminishes the possibility and severity of a credit crunch and immediate disruption to the payments system, but entails the risk that insolvency may deepen, especially if banks and entrepreneurs "gamble for resurrection," i.e., if they take ever-increasing risks in the search to secure solvency once and for all. In the end, governments may still be called upon to liquidate insolvent banks at higher cost to taxpayers. Furthermore, regulatory forbearance requires a series of policies that subsidize the activity of banks and bank debtors at a hefty cost to taxpayers. Governments walk a fine line between discipline imposed by a

---

[6]In their analysis of the International Monetary Fund (IMF), Roubini and Setser (2004) also observe how everyday use of the loaded term "bailout" may be obfuscating. Their distinction between "bailout" and "bail-in" likewise captures the notion of a continuum going from IMF support to help countries meet debt payments, on the one hand, to semi-coercive postponement of payments to a country's creditors, on the other. As Roubini and Setser point out, a crucial difference between IMF "bailouts" of sovereign borrowers and taxpayer "bailouts" of banks is that the latter face true financial losses, whereas the IMF expects to be repaid in full.

Bagehot enforcer and moral hazard created by an imprudent and profligate spendthrift.

I purport to fulfill two goals in the following paragraphs: First, I sketch the main argument about the salutary effects of democracy on banking policy, an argument that I develop from explicit foundations and in a more rigorous framework in Chapter 3. Second, I place this argument within the literature on political institutions and financial crises. In this regard, I do not seek to provide an exhaustive record of the voluminous literature on finance and its many meanders in economics, industrial organization, political science, history, and anthropology, but rather to bring attention to aspects of the scholarly debate on the effects of political regimes that are more closely related to my research.

As a start, consider what we learn even from casual observation of banking crises: During a banking crisis, bank managers and shareholders, borrowers, and depositors face the prospect of concentrated losses; being a relatively small and powerful group, shareholders in particular are in a good position to lobby for protection. That "losers" organize to push for advantageous policies is no secret; that the characteristics of these groups would make it easier to organize successful collective action is also obvious (Olson 1965). As Honohan and Laeven point out:

Governments come under tremendous pressure to buy all the nonperforming or problematic loans in a distressed banking system, to subsidize the borrowers and to put the banks back on to a profitable basis with a comfortable capital margin. The goal of lobbyists is that there should be "no losers," yet someone has to bear the losses that have been incurred and are reflected in the need for recapitalization. As a result of these pressures, governments often assume obligations greater than they should, given other priorities for the use of public funds. (Honohan and Laeven 2005, 109)

In contrast, the taxpayers that are called upon to shoulder costs derived from public support of banks are not a ready-made interest group capable of pushing for lower amounts of burden-sharing. Within a strict logic of collective action, democratic regimes would seem ill-equipped to withstand pressure from organized interests to bail out insolvent banks. Thus, bank shareholders and major depositors may successfully organize collectively and push to dump losses on disorganized taxpayers, a logic that has been suggested, among others, by Rochet (2003). In democratic regimes, however, taxpayers actually have recourse to elections to make politicians accountable for their actions. Imperfect as elections may be in furthering accountability, this basic difference across democratic and non-democratic regimes ought to have an impact on government responses to banking crises, a possibility suggested by Maxfield (2003) and substantiated, for example, in accounts of voters' pressure on US politicians to avoid the transfer, from commercial banks to the public sector, of default risk by less-developed countries during the debt crisis of 1982–1983 Oatley and Nabors (1998).

Against the view that the ability of concentrated groups to engage in collective action will drive governments to choose Bailout, one must recall that the costs of these policies are so large and conspicuous that they excite the curiosity of taxpayers and invite their involvement. Over time, only a few issues stand a chance of becoming salient in the minds of voters. The heightened attention that mass media tend to place on banking crises, and their direct economic effects on citizens, all but guarantee that the main features of government response, if not the exact details, will turn into a salient political issue. Though taxpayers may see merit in implementing policies aimed to prop up distressed banking systems, they should also be wary of seeing governments assuming "obligations greater than they should." Only in democratic regimes are politicians forced to consider the policy preferences of disorganized voters.

I build on this basic insight and assume that democratically-elected governments, by virtue of electoral accountability, seek to implement the policy preferences of their constituents as they manage banking crises. The formal argument presented in Chapter 3, which I summarize here, suggests a number of consequences that should follow logically from this basic assumption. I start by recognizing that the condition of *asymmetric information* that characterizes financial markets affects all actors, including politicians and bank regulators. Governments act in an environment in which information about the exact risks that banks take—and, therefore, the probability that they may face insolvency in the future—is not known to parties other than banks themselves. Under these circumstances, governments are called to subsidize the continuation of banks that face a liquidity shortage. This liquidity shortage is not necessarily related to the underlying financial status of banks, which remains uncertain.

Politicians face a stark choice in democratic regimes, where they are bound by the accountability link to serve the preferences of typical constituents. On the one hand, providing liquidity support and engaging in regulatory forbearance will prolongue the life of distressed banks. This decision allows taxpayers to continue to enjoy the services that banks provide, especially the possibility of keeping deposits that gain interest and are callable on demand. Yet, if the financial situation of distressed banks is seriously compromised by imprudent risk-taking, keeping the bank open may ultimately lead to extreme costs that will be shouldered by taxpayers themselves. Under conditions of uncertainty about the true net worth of banks, democratic accountability provides politicians with incentives to implement a more conservative *closure rule* for distressed banks, i.e., to support distressed banks only if they stand relatively good chances of prompt recovery. Because governments make these decisions in an environment of asymmetric information, they may err both on the side of generosity when no help should be forthcoming and on the side of conservatism when they should instead support banks.

I argue that the behavior of economic actors is affected by the *expectation* that politicians will respond to the preferences of taxpayers. To understand the full effect of this mechanism, consider the time inconsistency problem in banking policy noted by a variety of scholars (cf. Gale and Vives 2002; Mailath and Mester 1994; Mishkin 2006; Rochet 2003). Before a banking crisis occurs, governments have an incentive to declare that they will act as stern Bagehot enforcers. This declaration sends a signal to banks that they should be prudent and avoid unnecessary risks. After a banking crisis hits, however, the resolve to act as a Bagehot enforcer may flounder under the need to contain the spillover effects of a crisis (systemic risk) or under the desire to help out crucial political supporters. As in other public policy areas, the misalignment between *ex ante* and *ex post* preferences of actors is at the crux of credibility problems in public policy (Kydland and Prescott 1977). Presumably, the inability to commit to a no-bailout rule has economic consequences because it induces carelessness on the part of depositors, investors, and bankers—the well-known problem of moral hazard—and ultimately fosters bank crises and bank bailouts.[7] Since bankers and entrepreneurs anticipate that the careers of elected officials may come to an abrupt end if they act contrary to voter preferences, they see the commitment to a no-bailout rule in a democratic regime as gaining in credibility. In democratic regimes, we should expect this gain in credibility to translate into lower risk-taking on the part of entrepreneurs and banks.

The nexus of accountability that leads democratic governments to implement the preferences of typical constituents is attenuated, if it exists at all, in non-democratic regimes. In these regimes, politicians may prefer to support distressed banks in the expectation of personal gain. This is the essence of "crony capitalism," probably the most succored explanation of both the prevalence of banking crises and the occurrence of bailouts. Though definitions of this concept vary, crony capitalism basically refers to a situation in which bankers and private entrepreneurs accrue rents as a direct consequence of their connection to politicians and bureaucrats. This connection is considered to be close and non-transparent and to benefit politicians directly through side-payments or indirectly through contributions to campaign funds or loans channeled to politically desirable projects.[8] The mechanism through which

---

[7]Mishkin (2006, 991) reviews evidence that economic actors incorporate bailout expectations into their actions.

[8]"Looting" and "related lending," though distinct, share with crony capitalism the idea that

crony capitalism generates banking crises in this account is moral hazard—connected entrepreneurs and bankers engage in excessive risk-taking because they believe that government cronies will bail them out in case of trouble.[9] An alternative mechanism consists of the purposeful or inadvertent weakening of banking agencies. In this view, politics may corrupt and compromise the supervisory and regulatory functions of bank agencies beyond whatever technical deficiencies these institutions may suffer.[10] The ostensible rationale behind this view is that politicians stand to gain from governmental failure to discharge basic regulatory functions. Through both of these mechanisms, crony capitalism aggravates the problem of time inconsistency of government preferences. However, against the most pessimistic implications of this view, I propose that electoral accountability should also temper the willingness of politicians to provide implicit bailout guarantees to cronies.

Because of the electoral accountability mechanism, politicians in democratic regimes seek to avoid excessive public outlays over and above expenses needed to contain banking crises. Because economic actors understand this limitation, the commitment to a more conservative closure rule is more credible in a democratic than in an authoritarian regime. Thus, the policy preferences of taxpaying voters have traceable effects on the banking policy of democratic governments even prior to the occurrence of a bank crisis; that democracies are less prone *ex post* to bail out banks means also that democratic banking policy should have *ex ante* consequences on the behavior of economic actors, especially on the risk-taking propensities of entrepreneurs and bankers. These behavioral changes should lower the probability of observing banking crises in democratic regimes.

My emphasis on the existence of a democratic effect in banking crisis resolution places this book within a wider research program that investigates the economic consequences of political regimes. The notion that voters might exert a salutary influence on economic policy-making through electoral accountability adds to the appeal of liberal democracy above and beyond any normative defense that one can make of this regime form. Minimalist definitions already consider the possibility of accountability through elections as the most basic characteristic of democracy (Dahl 1971; Schumpeter 1942).

---

bankers and entrepreneurs can act with guile to sabotage the net worth of banks (Akerlof and Romer 1993; La Porta, López de Silanes and Zamarripa 2003; Soral, İşcan and Hebb 2003).

[9]Crony capitalism has been invoked for example to explain the East Asian financial crisis (Backman 1999; Bartholomew and Wentzler 1999; Corsetti, Pesenti and Roubini 1999; Haggard 2000; Haggard and MacIntyre 1998; Kang 2002; Krugman 1998), general aspects of finance and banking policy (Haslag and Pecchenino 2005; Kane 2000; Kang 2002), and firm bailouts (Bongini, Claessens and Ferri 2001; Faccio 2006; Faccio, Masulis and McConnell 2006).

[10]Though not a mechanism I emphasize, one could think of crony capitalism as allowing interest groups to capture the design and implementation of financial regulation (Feijen and Perotti 2005; Kane 2000).

Rational choice theory has traditionally understood elections as devices that provide voters with the capacity to punish politicians that have failed to act as good agents; because politicians anticipate the possibility of electoral punishment as a consequence of bad policy, they face at least some incentive to act responsibly (Barro 1973; Ferejohn 1986). This point is also emphasized in the new institutionalist literature in finance, which poses the existence of a long-run "democratic advantage" in securing a government's ability to contract public debt through the mechanisms of limited government and elections as sanctioning devices (North and Weingast 1989; Schultz and Weingast 2003).

Admittedly, several arguments counter the rather sanguine view of democratic accountability as a mechanism that can potentially align policy choice with voters' preferences. Some of these arguments recognize that though elections may foster accountability, they can do so only imperfectly, and thus the link tying politicians to the electorate may be fragile. For example, voters may lack information about the degree to which unexpected economic outcomes are attributable to government policy, which is one of the many dilemmas of delegation to elected officials (Miller 2005). Even then, elections allow voters, at a minimum, the possibility of signaling displeasure with economic outcomes. A potentially more damning counterargument obtains when the very links of accountability meant to contain government action prove to be pathological. In this regard, a respectable argument can be made that democratic regimes actually provide politicians with incentives to choose political expediency over economic efficiency and to weight short-term consequences more heavily than long-term results. Previous scholarship on the topic of politics and financial crises has often emphasized these negative effects of democratic accountability. Thus, incentives for short-term behavior in democratic regimes may lead politicians to hide problems in the banking sector until after elections. Brown and Dinç (2005) have documented that bank closures tend to cluster immediately *after* elections much more so than at any other time during the electoral cycle, a finding that is robust to the possibility of endogenously-timed elections. Beim (2001) offers a controversial interpretation of this finding, which follows from his contention that governments have incentives to hide problems in the banking sector. Given this incentive, only newly-installed governments can afford to acknowledge bank insolvency. Failure to publicize insolvency during a new government's honeymoon period would leave it "owning" a problem inherited from the previous administration.[11] The accountability-as-culprit mechanism identified

---

[11] Further afield, scholars of the US Congress lay responsibility for deepening the US "savings and loans" crisis squarely on this institution (Romer and Weingast 1991); members of Congress succumbed to lobbying from mutual banks to postpone tougher regulation for as long as apparent costs to their constituents remained relatively low (see also Bennett and Loucks 1994).

by these studies seems to imply that in the absence of democratic elections governments would not hesitate to strike down insolvent banks.

The literature that focuses on variations *within* democratic regimes has also explored the possibility that the electoral connection between unorganized voters and organized interests on the one hand, and politicians on the other, might be mediated by electoral institutions. Rosenbluth and Schaap (2003) suggest that centrifugal electoral systems— i.e., systems in which politicians and political parties can thrive representing the interests of very small segments of the population (Cox 1990)—give politicians incentives to supply "profit-padding regulation" that transfers income from consumers of financial services to producers through use of policy that aims to protect banks. In centripetal political systems, conversely, politicians have an incentive to incorporate the policy preferences of unorganized voters, and are therefore more likely to choose "prudential" regulation that avoids pampering banks. Rosenbluth and Schaap inspect a set of advanced industrialized countries and find results that accord with this view.

From these strands of the political economy literature that emphasize variation *within* democratic regimes, we know that a short electoral horizon may predispose politicians toward regulatory forbearance and that centrifugal electoral systems provide incentives for politicians to choose profit-padding financial regulation. But these analyses are based on examination of banking systems in democratic polities, not on bank exit policies followed by authorities in non-democratic regimes. It is not possible to infer from these designs whether, despite potential pathologies, democratic regimes might still enjoy an advantage in banking policy over regimes where electoral accountability is muted or simply absent.

Within the literature that focuses on comparing policy-making *across* political regimes, Satyanath (2006) proposes an innovative variation on the commitment argument that leads him to conclude that democracies suffer from a particular defect not present in authoritarian regimes. He observes that informational asymmetries that plague the relationship between chief executives and finance ministers in democratic regimes make it difficult to credibly signal commitment to stringent regulation. The mechanism that he highlights is a miscommunication problem between chief executives and finance ministers, which is more likely to occur in democratic regimes because chiefs-of-government are not always in a position to select their ministers of finance. One observable implication of this argument is that democracies should be more vulnerable to suffering banking crises than non-crony authoritarian regimes, and indeed Satyanath finds support for this view in a detailed analysis of policy-making in seven East Asian economies during the financial crisis of the late 1990s.

Contrary to the view that stresses the negative effects of democratic accountability on banking policy, Keefer (2007) suggests that elections may provide politicians with incentives to limit the costs of restoring financial solvency to banking systems. In his model, voters cannot know with certainty whether banking crises are the product of unfortunate economic circumstance or bad government policy. Politicians can decrease the likelihood of banking crises by implementing stringent bank regulation, but this policy reduces the margin for rent extraction from bankers. Accountability is understood as an implicit contract between voters and a reelection-seeking politician: If the politician delivers policy outcomes beyond a certain threshold, voters will vote for reelection. The politician sets policy output after learning a private signal about the state of the world, namely, whether circumstances are ripe for a banking crisis. In this delegation model, voters face an excruciating dilemma: If they set a very high threshold, the politician may simply renounce to implement stringent bank regulation knowing that he has no chance of avoiding a crisis and instead act venally, maximizing rents from bankers. But if they set a very low threshold, the politician will find it easy to avoid bad policy *outcomes* even after setting bad policy *output*. Electoral accountability may prevent extreme rent-seeking by the incumbent, but even this positive effect may be attenuated because voters cannot readily observe the effects of bad policy. Though Keefer shows that government measures to prop up banks during banking crises are less costly under democracy, he discounts the possibility that political regimes may have preventive effects. In this regard, he argues that the most dire consequences of bad policy—i.e., banking crises— are only realized after very long lags, so voters have difficulty gauging the degree to which incumbents carry out appropriate policy and politicians will have little incentive to invest in preventing the occurrence of banking crises.

Clearly, my own interpretation of the effects of political regimes is in line with a more optimistic view of democracy. Like Keefer (2007), I believe that electoral accountability can tie the hands of politicians, in this case strengthening their commitment to avoid outrageous bailouts. My main contribution to this debate lies in extending the implications of the electoral accountability argument to suggest that democratic regimes pattern the behavior of economic actors even *prior* to a financial crisis. It is by considering both the *ex ante* and *ex post* consequences of political regimes that we should judge the full policy benefits or disadvantages of democracy.

1.2 Organization of the Book

I provide in Chapter 2 a brief introduction to basic accounting terms used in banking and to the policies that governments can implement in order to address bank solvency and liquidity problems. Specifically, I group governments' choices in five policy issue-areas—exit policy, last resort lending, non-performing loans, bank recapitalization, and bank liabilities—and I underscore the connection between observed policy output and the theoretical Bagehot-Bailout construct that defines government responses. I lay out the main theoretical argument about the salutary effects of democratic regimes in Chapter 3. To develop this argument within a coherent framework, I build a formal analysis of the distributive politics of banking crises on an existing model of banking regulation (Repullo 2005*b*). I extend this model to analyze the strategic interaction between government and a set of entrepreneurs that seek bank loans to make investments with various risk-return profiles. After observing an exogenous liquidity shock, governments decide whether to support a bank whose financial status is suspected to be weak as a consequence of the risky investment decisions of entrepreneurs. I explore within the model how different assumptions about the political regime within which governments operate affect this decision.

Chapter 4 considers banking policy in a democratic regime (Argentina) and a semi-authoritarian regime (Mexico) during the mid-1990s. Though the banking systems of these two countries were not identical, I claim that the most consequential distinction between these two polities was the fact that Mexican policy-makers were not immediately beholden to the electorate, while Argentine politicians were constrained by the need to win elections. The main purpose of the narrative in Chapter 4 is to illustrate the difference between governments that approximate the model of a stern Bagehot enforcer and those that approach the Bailout ideal-type, and to analyze the closure rule that governments in these countries followed in response to the *Tequila* crises. In this regard, I consider two basic issues: the speed with which insolvent banks "exited" the banking system, and the importance of extraneous non-economic factors in determining the lifespan of insolvent banks.

Unfortunately, it is not possible to place much stock on inferences about the effects of political regimes based on only two cases. Though I selected these cases because they of their similarities across a bevy of relevant characteristics—size of the economy, levels of inequality, or size of their financial sectors—there are certainly important differences beyond the political regimes of these two countries that may affect government response. Consequently, in Chapters 5 and 6 I study a sample of forty-six documented instances of policy response to banking crises. I infer the unobserved tendency of politicians to prefer solutions close to Bagehot or Bailout based on dichotomous information about implementation of seven different crisis-management policies. In these chapters, I also consider the possibility that governments might make "disjoint" choices along two different policy dimensions, one corresponding to bank solvency considerations, the other to liquidity concerns. I conclude that the effect of political regimes on the choice

of Bagehot/Bailout occurs largely through the implementation of policies
to cope with solvency problems, and make an effort to substantiate a causal
interpretation of this effect. In Chapter 7, the final empirical chapter, I analyze
two large-*n* cross-country time-series datasets to explore the occurrence of
financial distress across political regimes. I conclude that aside from limiting
government propensities to carry out bailouts, democratic regimes are indeed
less likely to suffer financial distress and banking crises. Finally, I offer in
the Conclusion a summary of main findings, discuss other implications of
the main argument, and suggest potential avenues for further research on the
politics of banking.

I finish this introduction with a word about my choice of empirical methods. Throughout the book, empirical verification of the theoretical arguments
relies on multilevel data, and consequently on the estimation of hierarchical
models. Multilevel or hierarchical models generalize standard regression
techniques to scenarios in which observations are nested within groups, a
situation I repeatedly encounter in my research—banks nested within ownership structures (Chapter 4), different forms of policy output nested within
countries (Chapter 6), or banking crises nested within countries and years
(Chapter 7). One problem with these data structures is that the assumption
of independence across observations is not reasonable, i.e., one cannot sen-
sibly claim that units nested within a group constitute independent draws
from some data-generating process. Multilevel models provide a principled
approach to analyze such data structures and, as a consequence, outperform
more traditional approaches. Aside from providing more accurate forecasts,
multilevel models furnish more realistic and honest estimates of uncertainty
than models that assume independence across observations.

Multilevel models can be fitted through a variety of techniques, including
maximum likelihood estimation, but I have chosen to estimate these models within the framework of Bayesian inference.[12] Bayesian methods offer
a panoply of advantages over classical approaches to statistical inference.
In contrast with the contrived confidence intervals of frequentist inference,
Bayesian credible intervals provide intuitive estimates of uncertainty about
parameters. Computer-based sampling algorithms permit full inspection of
the probability densities of these parameters, allowing the researcher flexibility in computing relevant quantities of interest. Furthermore, the suitability
of Bayesian estimates is not premised on large-sample assumptions, which
can seldom be met in practice, and only very rarely in comparative political
economy. In multilevel models, in particular, the number of observations
available at higher levels of aggregation is typically not sufficiently large,

---

[12]See Gelman, Carlin, Stern and Rubin (2004); Gelman and Hill (2007); Gill (2002) for an
introduction to Bayesian inference in the social sciences.

which means that the large-sample properties of maximum likelihood fail to apply. Under these circumstances, Bayesian standard errors are more realistic than under maximum likelihood (Raudenbush and Bryk 2002; Shor, Bafumi, Keele and Park 2007).

These advantages are part and parcel of Bayesian inference, which formalizes the process of updating prior beliefs about unknown phenomena from known data. A priori beliefs, codified in suitable probability priors, are fundamental in the Bayesian worldview, but many shudder at the possibility that informative priors inject a dose of subjectivity into empirical results. To dispel this concern, throughout the book I rely on diffuse prior probability distributions that have little bearing on inferences, and resort to informative priors only when required by model identification.

2

Accidents Waiting to Happen

Banks are in business to lend money for the *promise* of future payment. Consequently, their solvency status at any point in time depends on the ability of bank debtors to honor payment of their loans. Though banks make loans with expected positive returns, even calculated risks may eventually lead to dire results. Despite the use of techniques to hedge risk, the possibility of widespread bank insolvency is difficult to dissipate entirely, which is why banking crises are often portrayed as accidents waiting to happen.[1] Though the chain of events that leads to bank insolvency has differed across bank crises in the past, a typical episode starts with the deterioration of the balance sheet of a bank, group of banks, or the entire banking system. This deterioration almost always seems sudden, following an exogenous shock that leads to the reappraisal of a bank's assets and liabilities (for example, an unexpected depreciation of the national currency or a sudden drop in the value of real estate underlying mortgage loans),[2] but is more commonly the result of a relatively slow process of accumulation of non-performing bank assets. Very often, slow decay accelerates and becomes conspicuous after an exogenous shock exposes the feeble structure of bank balance sheets. Thus, a nation's banking system may suffer a slow buildup of non-performing loans during a long period, possibly years, without suffering a full banking crisis.

In this chapter, I offer an overview of bank accounting to distinguish between *solvency* and *liquidity* problems, and to showcase the variety of government policies that can be implemented to redress them. To frame the discussion about government bailout propensities throughout the book, I

---

[1] For an introduction to the literature on the microeconomics of banking and regulation the reader should refer to Dewatripont and Tirole (1994); Freixas and Rochet (1997); Goodhart and Illing (2002).

[2] The first is an example of *foreign exchange risk*, the second of *credit risk*. See Singer (2007, Ch. 2) for an introduction to capital regulation as a response to asymmetric information in financial markets.

Table 2.1: Stylized balance sheet of a solvent bank

Assets		Liabilities	
Loans	$950.00	Deposits	$1,000.00
Loan-loss reserves	150.00	Capital (Equity)	100.00
Total	$1,100.00		$1,100.00
Cash inflows		*Cash outflows*	
Interest on loans (rate = 12%)	$114.00	Interest on deposits (rate = 10%)	$100.00
		Net profit	14.00

underscore the policy responses that pure Bagehot or Bailout governments would seek to implement. A discussion of the main goals of these different policies requires some working knowledge about the basic operation of fractional-reserve banking, which I present in the context of a stylized example.

To motivate the series of concerns that besiege policy-makers during a banking crisis, consider the simplified balance sheet of a solvent bank as it appears in Table 2.1. In this illustration, shareholders have contributed $100.00 in *capital* to charter the bank and have accumulated $1,000.00 in *deposits*. Deposits are liabilities over which the bank owes principal and interest; the contractual deposit rate determines the amount that depositors get back from lending their money to the bank. Profits constitute the return on capital to bank shareholders; needless to say, bank shareholders may not only fail to make profits, but also stand to lose capital in hard times. On the asset side of the bank's ledger, bank managers have used $950.00 to build a *loan portfolio*. At this point, the bank is solvent, as assets plus capital more than suffice to cover the bank's liabilities. Furthermore, the difference in interest rates nets the bank a profit of $14.00, which can be returned to shareholders as profit or reinvested as capital in the bank.

Now consider a scenario in which a proportion of bank debtors stop payments to the bank. Table 2.2 displays a stylized balance sheet of a bank on the brink of insolvency.[3] Though drastically simplified, this balance sheet underscores the most important characteristics of financial intermediaries in modern banking systems. Under the practically universal system of *fractional-reserve banking*, banks keep a fraction of the deposits they receive as reserves,

---

[3]The example is adapted from Keefer (2007).

but maintain the contractual obligation to redeem all deposits upon demand. As before, paid capital amounts to $100.00, deposits to $1,000.00, and bank managers have used $950.00 to make loans.

Assume now that part of this loan portfolio fails, that is, bank debtors stop making scheduled payments on these loans. Because of the nature of banking—i.e., the difficulty of verifying the uses to which bank loans are put plus sheer uncertainty about investment payoffs—banks are exposed to *credit risk*, which means that there is a non-negligible probability that some loans will fail and turn into non-performing assets. Non-performing loans ($175.00 in this example) build up as the consequence of bad entrepreneurial decisions, careless assessment of potential risk on the part of the bank, crony deals between entrepreneurs, bankers, and politicians, and sheer bad luck. The ratio of non-performing to total loans in this example is about 18%, certainly on the high end but not unheard of in actual banking crises. Because non-performing loans are an inherent risk of banking activity, banks set aside *loan-loss reserves* to meet potential losses derived from unpaid loans (in the example, loan-loss reserves amount to $150.00).

It is easy to see how the accumulation of bad assets might prove disastrous. Consider first the bank's cash-flow situation. I have assumed that the bank faces a short-term liquidity problem in that $100.00 are due as interest payment on deposits, but only $93.00 will be flowing into the bank from interest payments on *performing* loans. In this case, the bank does not have enough reserves to replenish the total value of lost non-performing assets ($175.00), but loan-loss reserves are certainly high enough to meet interest payments in the short run. Aside from the cash-flow situation, consider a second problem that follows from the maturity structure of bank assets and liabilities. Bank assets have long-term maturities: Banks cannot require full payment of investment loans or mortgages whenever they see fit. Certainly, more developed economies have secondary markets where bad assets can be traded, but even these markets may stop working efficiently during a crisis (consider the difficulty of pricing so-called "toxic mortgages" in the midst of the United States' subprime-mortgage crisis). In contrast, deposits have short-term maturities, and are meant to be redeemable on demand. This mismatch in the maturity structure of bank balance sheets raises the specter that even a fundamentally solvent bank may go bankrupt if it faces a depositor run (Diamond and Dybvig 1983).

Imagine now that the situation that afflicts this bank affected other financial institutions, perhaps because of a common shock that affects the value of bank assets. In fact, assume that Table 2.2 represented, as it were, the balance sheet of an entire banking system under financial distress. Left unattended, this situation of financial distress would promptly generate liquidity crises, as depositors would run on the banks to salvage their assets. In case

Table 2.2: Stylized balance sheet of a bank on the brink of insolvency

Assets		*Liabilities*	
Loans	$950.00	Deposits	$1,000.00
Performing	*775.00*		
Non-performing	*175.00*		
Loan-loss reserves	150.00	Capital (Equity)	100.00
Total	$1,100.00		$1,100.00

Cash inflows		*Cash outflows*	
Interest on loans (rate = 12%)	$93.00	Interest on deposits (rate = 10%)	$100.00
		Net loss	(7.00)

of a depositor run, bankers would have to liquidate performing loans (and recover $775.00 under the best scenario), drain their entire loan-loss reserves ($150.00), and even cut into shareholders' capital ($75.00) in order to meet their obligations. The bank is not strictly insolvent (capital plus assets still suffice to cover deposits), but its capital buffer is barely adequate given the size of the bank's portfolio of non-performing loans.[4]

Under these circumstances, a country's banking agencies have a mandate to prevent further deterioration of the banking system. These agencies may be politically autonomous or could be housed within the Ministry of Finance or the Central Bank. It is also common for a single banking agency to entwine supervisory and regulatory functions.[5] In their supervisory capacity, banking agencies are charged with detecting the accumulation of non-performing loans and even potential problems in the loan allocation of the banks they oversee. In their regulatory capacity, banking agencies act upon this information to force banks (i) to raise adequate capital and (ii) to set aside sufficient reserves to meet potential loan defaults from their clients. Going back to Table 2.2, banking agencies could force the bank to write-off non-performing loans (−$175.00) and to seek to recover collateral from morose debtors, use part

---

[4]In this example, the banking system is not "highly leveraged," so its situation of financial distress could be reversed relatively easily. It has a rather healthy debt-to-equity ratio of 10-to-1, and even after discounting all non-performing loans (and assuming remaining loans have little risk of falling in arrears) its capital-asset ratio is 10%.

[5]The institutional setup of banking agencies may in fact affect their ability to carry out their mandated tasks, a subject of ample debate within the literature on microeconomics of regulation.

of the $150.00 in loan-loss reserves to meet cash outflows, and raise fresh capital to maintain minimum solvency requirements. By forcing banks to raise capital, banking agencies would increase the banks' capital buffer and reduce the likelihood of a devastating run.

Banks that are unable to meet cash outflows would try to obtain liquid funds by borrowing from other banks in the system or by liquidating some assets. If these options proved insufficient, they could approach the central bank, which in most banking systems plays the role of lender of last resort. The function of lender of last resort to a banking system exists because even solvent banks may sometimes be short on liquidity. This function is a normal, well-established, and relatively non-controversial part of the way in which fractional-reserve banking systems work. Thus, a distressed bank could ask the last-resort lender for *liquidity support*, posting its performing assets as collateral, rather than liquidating its remaining performing loans at what would likely be fire-sale prices if financial distress affected large segments of the banking system. According to Bagehot's prescription, the lender of last resort should loan freely to banks as long as these remain sound.[6] By lending to illiquid but solvent banks, the lender of last resort signals its confidence in the financial health of the banking system and its reluctance to let a liquidity problem turn into a full-blown insolvency crisis. Thus, the purpose of the lender of last resort function *is not* to bail out insolvent banks, but to prevent solvent banks from failing on account of a liquidity crunch. In fact, Bagehot's prescription is premised on allowing the bankruptcy of insolvent banks.

Returning to the illustration, deposit withdrawals would eventually run the bank to the ground if bank shareholders were unable to raise more capital, bank managers to increase loan-loss reserves, and the central bank to provide liquidity assistance. In this case, some depositors would likely take losses in the unfortunate eventuality that they were late in claiming their money.[7] Bank shareholders would also lose capital. Market discipline would force the bank's closure, and banking agencies would simply manage the orderly liquidation of the bank. Through a process of "survival of the fittest," remaining solvent banks could manage the assets of failed institutions and continue to provide services to their depositors. The banking system would presumably emerge strengthened from the collapse of one or more of its component units.

---

[6]Sir Walter Bagehot is commonly credited for laying out the theoretical rationale for the central bank's last-resort lending function (Bagehot 1873), though antecedents can be found in Thornton (1802).

[7]Panic runs would be less likely to close an insolvent bank in the presence of depositor insurance. With a safety net in place, banks need not fear having to liquidate assets in order to meet sudden cash demands from panicked depositors. However, deposit insurance schemes seldom cover high-end deposits, so they do not eliminate entirely the possibility of panic runs. Furthermore, investments in non-bank financial intermediaries, for example mutual funds, are not generally protected.

This brief account of how a small proportion of non-performing loans may grow to threaten the solvency of a banking system is premised on a rather heroic implicit assumption, namely, that banking agencies and central banks have perfect information about balance sheets. However, the ability to monitor banks is fundamentally impaired by sheer uncertainty and informational asymmetries in financial markets. Uncertainty cannot be eradicated from financial markets due to the extemporaneous nature of the goods that banks, bank depositors, and bank debtors exchange: Banks and other financial intermediaries are in business to exchange loans today for the *promise* of a future return, rather than for immediate gain. Even if bankers and supervisors build expectations about the likelihood of loan defaults that are informed by careful analysis of portfolio risk, it is difficult to assess with great precision the potential for bank insolvency at any given time. Asymmetric information complicates the supervisory, regulatory, and last-resort lending functions that governments perform in modern banking systems. In particular, it makes separating solvent from insolvent banks during banking crises a difficult task.

For example, referring to the potential effect on European banks of the recent subprime-mortgage global financial crisis, one member of the executive committee of the European Central Bank (ECB) declared that "[t]here is no central bank in the world that knows exactly the real situation of financial intermediaries, not even the Federal Reserve. One cannot expect the ECB to appraise potential losses when financial intermediaries have not themselves had the chance to make these assessments."[8] Even competently-managed and transparent banks may have trouble gauging the size of their non-performing portfolios, a problem that has been aggravated in recent times by the proliferation of derivative instruments in financial markets. It is certainly true that the ability of banking agencies to monitor the solvency status of banks improves with the amount of resources committed to carry out on-site inspections and to process accounting information passed on by banks, by improvements in technologies to price risk, and as regulators catch up to innovations in the development of financial instruments. However, banking agencies are not in general in a better position than banks to monitor balance sheets in a timely fashion.[9]

More importantly, allowing an insolvent bank to go bankrupt may threaten damage to solvent banks. Contrary to non-financial firms, the balance sheets

---

[8] José Manuel González-Páramo, *El País*, December 8, 2007, p. 20 (my translation).

[9] The literature on microeconomics of prudential supervision and regulation suggests that the risk of bank insolvency may not be fully dissipated even by proficient banking agencies staffed by competent and honest bureaucrats (cf. Chan, Greenbaum and Thakor 1992; Dewatripont and Tirole 1994; Freixas, Giannini, Hoggarth and Soussa 2000; Freixas and Parigi 2007; Freixas, Parigi and Rochet 2000; Freixas and Rochet 1997; Hall 2001). For views on the difficulty of distinguishing insolvency from illiquidity, see De Juan (1999); Lindgren (2005); and essays in Honohan and Laeven (2005) and Goodhart and Illing (2002).

of banks are highly leveraged and deeply intertwined; thus, even limited financial losses have the potential to produce cascading payments suspensions. In other words, bank insolvency may threaten to spill over to other financial intermediaries or even the real economy. Under these circumstances, even market-upholding governments may choose to prop up the banking system, providing liquidity support to what may well turn out to be insolvent banks and phasing the liquidation of bankrupt institutions to avoid panics and ripple effects throughout the economy. As a result of this uncertainty, even a conservative lender of last resort imbued in Bagehot's doctrine may end up providing liquidity support to an insolvent bank.

Be this as it may, some governments have succeeded in staying relatively close to Bagehot's prescription. On the opposite extreme, some governments have trespassed even the more liberal bounds of Bagehot's doctrine to avoid *closure* of insolvent banks. This latter type of government behavior approximates the Bailout model described in Chapter 1. To describe the Bailout ideal-type, consider that upon detection of non-performing loans bank regulators can always choose to do nothing—that is, as opposed to pushing for further bank capitalization—hoping that bankers can continue to attract new deposits in order to meet interest payments on old deposits. In other words, banking agencies and the governments that oversee them can engage first and foremost in *regulatory forbearance*. Regulatory forbearance lengthens the life of a troubled bank without forcing corrective action. Needless to say, non-performing loans could continue to build up and loan-loss reserves to dwindle under regulatory forbearance. In fact, this policy often has the unintended consequence of giving bankers a chance to "gamble for resurrection." Rather than taking advantage of regulatory forbearance to capitalize the bank and prune non-performing assets from their loan portfolio, bankers may be tempted to underwrite riskier projects, i.e., to provide loans with a low probability of a very high return in the hope of regaining solvency. In most cases, this behavior will further weaken the bank and at some point government action will be required anyway.

In the Bailout ideal-type, closing down insolvent banks is an option of last resort. Instead, governments implement policies that artificially prolong the life of insolvent banks and diminish losses to depositors and/or bank shareholders. On the asset side of a bank's ledger, governments can choose for example to transfer non-performing loans away from banks in exchange for government-backed assets or to support payments of bank debtors in arrears. On the side of liabilities, governments can also prevent or slow down cash outflows through different means. For example, they can extend blanket guarantees to all depositors, promising to protect their bank holdings, or they can simply prevent depositors from cashing their accounts through extended bank holidays or deposit freezes. Finally, governments can choose to inject fresh public resources to shore up the bank's capital buffer. These options are a burden to taxpayers, who will ultimately be called upon to absorb financial losses in one way or another. Consequently, the defining characteristic of the Bailout model is that it enacts a loss-sharing arrangement among bank debtors, depositors, and shareholders on the one hand, and taxpayers on the other, to the detriment of the latter. Needless to say, the socialization of bank losses that follows a Bailout response has no corresponding profit-sharing in good times. This is what scholars and pundits have in mind when they describe banking activity as a game of "heads I win, tails the taxpayer loses" (Krugman 1998).

I use the terms *crisis management* or *crisis resolution* interchangeably to refer to the set of actions that governments undertake in response to banking crises. As suggested in the previous paragraph, governments make decisions that affect the asset and liability structure of bank balance sheets when they confront liquidity and solvency problems in the banking sector. I identify *five* crucial arenas where we would expect to see policy changes during a banking crisis: *liquidity support, liability resolution, asset resolution, bank capitalization,* and *bank exit.* This categorization serves an expository purpose; these policies are so tightly interwoven that alternative classificatory schemes are possible. In the following paraghaphs I describe these policies very briefly, insisting especially on the kind of response that a coherent Bagehot or Bailout policymaker would implement in each of these five arenas. Table 2.3 highlights the main differences between these two types of policy response:

Liquidity support. As argued above, the established lender of last resort (LOLR) doctrine recommends generous liquidity support to banks as long as this is limited to solvent institutions, and money is lent against good collateral and at a premium. In principle, acting according to this doctrine would be the hallmark of a Bagehot response; even large cash-flows from the central bank to *solvent* banks would not be defined as bailouts, since this money would be eventually recovered by the central bank.[10] However, because the line between solvency and insolvency is blurred during crises, it is common to see liquidity support going to banks that ultimately fail. In general, the responsibilities of a central bank regarding the LOLR function may be codified in its charter and can be severely limited, as in the case of currency boards, so it is not uncommon to engage in legislative changes to grant added flexibility to central banks during banking crises. Again, I do not construe these changes as indicating necessarily a propensity to bail out banks, simply because this flexibility may be intended to support distressed

---

[10]This point is often lost in political commentary, as central bank loans to illiquid but *solvent* banks are construed as regressive transfers to support rich bankers. I insist that these policies are consistent with Bagehot's prescriptions.

Table 2.3: Alternative responses to banking crises in five policy arenas. Entries show the policy responses that a coherent Bagehot or Bailout policy-maker would implement.

Policy arena	Bagehot	Bailout
Liquidity support	Last-resort loans on good collateral, for a limited time, subject to precise rules	Last-resort loans for an indeterminate time, as requested by banks
Liability resolution	Only explicitly protected depositors, if any, receive compensation	Blanket protection of all depositors and/or deposit freezes
Asset resolution	Banks forced to write non-performing loans off their books	Non-performing loans transferred away from banks Support for bank borrowers to keep payment flows into banks
Bank capitalization	Private recapitalization of banks Banks that fail to comply with capital requirements are deemed insolvent.	Public recapitalization of banks Regulatory forbearance
Bank exit	Banks closed immediately after detecting insolvency	Insolvent banks allowed to continue operations

but solvent banks. Instead, what characterizes a bailout response in this arena is indiscriminate lending to insolvent banks or liquidity support during a protracted period.

Liability resolution. This arena includes policies that alter the liability structure of bank balance sheets, particularly payment schedules to depositors. Recall that in response to perceived or actual insolvency, bank depositors are prone to run on banks and thus accelerate their demise. In the Bailout model, governments implement policies that seek to prevent depositor runs or to stop them if they have already occurred. Governments can extend blanket guarantees to *all* depositors to prevent runs, thus insuring that all deposit claims will be met even if this requires use of public money. Alternatively, freezing accounts so that depositors cannot reclaim their money would also be consistent with the Bailout ideal-type. This is so because deposit freezes obviate the need for liquidity, and therefore lengthen the life of distressed banks. Naturally, the distributive implications of these two policies with regards to depositors may be different: Blanket guarantees accord depositors the capacity to claim their money and shift the cost of the guarantee to taxpayers, whereas deposit freezes prevent depositors from accessing their accounts, at least in the short run, and in principle require no support from taxpayers.[11]

In the Bagehot ideal-type, governments would not extend guarantees to bank depositors beyond those that may already exist in explicit deposit insurance. The cross-country variation in deposit insurance mechanisms, both in their coverage and funding, is staggering, and indeed some limited form of deposit insurance is generally perceived as a factor that mitigates the possibility of insolvency in situations of extreme uncertainty about the financial status of banks.[12] Thus, I consider that a government that complies with pre-existing deposit insurance arrangements is close to the Bagehot model; instead, extending insurance above and beyond pre-crisis legislation is consistent with the Bailout ideal-type.

Asset resolution. On the asset side of a bank's ledger, governments facing a banking crisis need to resolve the issue of non-performing loans (NPL). As explained above, NPLs are assets that have lost value, most commonly because holders of these loans have ceased to make interest payments. As suggested in Table 2.3, there are two basic mechanisms to restructure bank assets in the Bailout ideal-type. The first mechanism supports bank debtors so that they can continue to meet interest payments, a policy that subsidizes borrowers at the expense of taxpayers. By supporting bank borrowers, this

---

[11] I build on this distinction in the empirical analysis of Section 6.4.
[12] Cf. Diamond and Dybvig (1983). See Demirgüç-Kunt, Kane and Laeven (2008) for an analysis of the expansion of deposit insurance.

policy indirectly keeps a steady stream of cash-flows into distressed banks. The second mechanism affects balance sheets directly by removing NPLs from distressed banks. This may be the most expensive of all Bailout policies, as governments end up acquiring large volumes of loans of uncertain (but generally low) value in exchange for government bonds. There is also great variation in the details of these policies. For example, government bonds may or may not be negotiable; if they are not negotiable, banks are required to hold these bonds to maturity and receive periodic cash-flows from interest payments. The destiny of NPLs may also vary, as banks may be required to actively participate in recovering collateral from these loans as a condition for receiving support. Alternatively, governments may set up asset management agencies in charge of recovering collateral and closing off loans. In contrast to the Bailout model, requiring banks to write NPLs off their books would be the main characteristic of a Bagehot government. If NPL write-offs reveal widespread insolvency, a Bagehot government would then proceed to close the bank.

Bank capitalization. The best indicator of a bank's robustness or ability to withstand exogenous shocks is its degree of capitalization. Well capitalized banks have deeper pockets with which to confront unexpected losses from non-performing loans. Because of the vagaries of fractional-reserve banking, governments generally mandate a minimum level of capitalization to face unexpected losses. Indeed, the capital requirement—i.e., a bank's obligation to comply with a minimum capital-asset ratio (CAR)—is the main regulatory mechanism through which governments limit the possibility of bank failures.[13]

As mentioned before, a bank that fails to comply with mandatory capital ratios faces regulatory insolvency, even if the market value of its assets exceeds the market value of its liabilities, and should exit the banking system. In the Bailout model, governments can prevent the exit of an insolvent bank through different means. First, they can engage in regulatory forbearance, choosing to ignore low bank capitalization thresholds temporarily or to change the regulatory definition of insolvency. Needless to say, dropping capitalization requirements during a bank crisis should be properly considered a bailout, for banks considered insolvent under the old rules are now allowed to continue operating within the banking system. Second, governments may subsidize capitalization efforts through fund-matching arrangements that give bankers incentives to come up with fresh capital. Finally, governments can

---

[13]CAR is a solvency ratio that obtains from dividing capital by a weighted sum of assets. Despite standardization efforts following the 1988 Basel Accord, banking regulators have some discretion in defining the types of financial instruments to be counted as capital. As Singer (2007, 16–17) observes, cash reserves and other funding sources can be counted as capital along with bank shareholders' equity in some systems.

take over the bank (nationalization), which means *de facto* that public money will be used to provide bank capital. As was the case with liability resolution policies, the distributive implications of these policies vary; in some of these cases, bank shareholders do not lose control of their bank (regulatory forbearance), in others they lose partial control (fund-matching) or total control (nationalization). In all of these cases, however, the bank itself continues to operate after insolvency, and the immediate cost of this decision is borne by the taxpayer. In the Bagehot ideal-type, governments would not engage in regulatory forbearance; instead, failed efforts by bankers to come up with fresh capital would initiate a process of bank exit.

Exit policy. I define *exit policy* as the decision rule that politicians follow as they decide which banks to support and which banks to close during a banking crisis. In a sense, all other policy arenas are inextricably linked to decisions regarding exit policy. I follow Lindgren (2005) in understanding closure as a potentially long process that ends in one of several possible states: absorption, liquidation, or continuation under different ownership. Under the Bagehot ideal-type, bank exit would follow immediately from the realization that a bank cannot comply with capital requirements. Governments relax market discipline when they fail to enforce exit. Under the Bailout ideal-type, instead, insolvent banks continue to operate untrammeled by regulators, therefore increasing the risk of heftier financial losses down the line.

I argue that patterns of policy implementation in these five issue-areas provide information about the unobserved bailout propensities of different governments. In Chapter 4, I relate the experience of policy implementation of two governments that approximated the Bagehot (Argentina) and Bailout (Mexico) ends of the policy continuum; in Chapters 5 and 6 I analyze indicators of policy implementation during forty-six banking crises to understand the effect of political regimes on crisis management. Before doing so, I present in detail my argument about the effects of electoral accountability on banking policy in the next chapter.

3

Political Regimes, Bank Insolvency, and Closure Rules

The commitment to enforce the exit of insolvent banks is an important conduit through which the political process affects an economy's banking system. Under ideal conditions, politicians would act as responsible Bagehot overseers by pressuring bank agencies to improve their supervisory capacity and stepping up prudential regulation during hard times. While not entirely eliminated, the risk of bank insolvency could be detected early on; timely intervention would then prevent further deterioration of bank balance sheets by dissuading excessive bank risk-taking ("gambling for resurrection"), suspension of payments and therefore possible contagion to other economic actors and financial intermediaries, and deposit runs on solvent banks fueled by panic. Be this as it may, politicians do not always face incentives that lead them to act as strict Bagehot enforcers. I submit that democratic links of representation and accountability provide politicians with the wherewithal to temper the commitment problem in banking.

The main basis for my optimism about the ability of democracies to limit bailouts is the extremely high cost of sharing financial losses with taxpayers. In the presence of democratic accountability, the politician's calculus ought to be affected by taxpayers' preferences for a lower financial burden. One would need to assume an extremely heavy rate of discount of the future to admit that politicians can disregard this factor entirely. At the same time, accounts of crony capitalism suggest that political intervention in the realm of banking might go beyond policy choice in the face of bank insolvency. Politicians, entrepreneurs, and bankers may be tied together in cozy arrangements that generate rents from which a few profit at the expense of many. My contention is that the very links of representation and accountability that dissuade politicians in democratic regimes to engage in

30

costly bailouts also play a role in limiting their willingness to engage in crony deals.

To analyze these conjectures within a consistent framework, I develop a formal model of distributive politics with emphasis on the strategic interaction of entrepreneurs and politicians. The government can extend a lifeline to banks that face a liquidity shortfall upon receiving an imperfect signal about the potential success of entrepreneurial activity in the future. If entrepreneurial activity is successful, depositors and entrepreneurs benefit from government support to the bank. If entrepreneurial investments fail to pan out, the bank will be insolvent and the government will need to tax depositors in order to redistribute bank losses. The basic assumption is that costs derived from government policy are spread thinly among *all* taxpayers, even though the benefits of bank and entrepreneurial activity accrue disproportionately to some. The model thus explores how the interaction between government and entrepreneurs changes under different assumptions about the policy preferences of the median taxpayer/voter, which I hold to be decisive in a democratic regime. I also consider the possibility that the government may be venal, i.e., that it might choose to obtain rents from entrepreneurs in exchange for the *promise* of a bailout. By doing so, the model seeks to illustrate some of the consequences of electoral accountability on crony capitalism, and of electoral accountability and crony capitalism on bank solvency. The purpose is to derive theoretically-guided implications of the argument that can be tested empirically.

3.1 Setup of the Theoretical Model

I develop a model of the political decision to engage in regulatory forbearance based on a framework elaborated by Repullo (2005*b*).[1] This is a flexible framework that has been used in the literature on central banking and bank organization to study effects of alternative regulatory structures, moral hazard produced by emergency liquidity provision, and optimal bailout rules (Kahn and Santos 2005; Repullo 2005*a*). In its original formulation, the model considers the interaction between a bank that makes risky investment decisions funded by deposits and a government agency that considers whether to support a bank that may turn out to be insolvent. One attractive feature of this model is that it allows us to analyze how bankers or entrepreneurs change the *risk profile* of their investments under alternative circumstances, including changes in political regimes. Aside from preserving this feature, I extend Repullo's model to analyze whether the political decision to deal

---

[1] Other important insights come from work by Haslag and Pecchenino (2005), Feijen and Perotti (2005), Kane (2001) and Mailath and Mester (1994).

with distressed banks depends on different assumptions about the political and economic structure of society.

I consider a society divided among risk-neutral entrepreneurs of identical type and a large population of N citizens with individual incomes y_i. Entrepreneurs have the know-how to invest bank loans in projects that generate wealth. These projects are risky, in the sense that they return a potentially large positive payoff with probability strictly less than 1 but may also fail to return a profit. In this society, a bank exists exclusively as an entity that gathers funds from depositors and loans them to entrepreneurs.[2] For the sake of simplicity, I eschew consideration of bank capital or loan loss reserves in this model. At the beginning of the game (i.e., at time t_0), consumers deposit their income in the bank. The total amount of deposits in this economy is $D \equiv \bar{y}N$, where $\bar{y}$ is the income of the average citizen.

I assume that deposits captured by banks are loaned in their entirety to entrepreneurs. In order to carry out its lending activity, the bank secures illiquid collateral equal to w from each entrepreneur, which it returns upon successful repayment at t_2 ($w \in (0, 1)$). If entrepreneurs fail to repay the loan, the bank simply yields collateral to depositors.[3] Entrepreneurs obtain a bank loan at t_0 in exchange for the *promise* of returning it with interest r at the end of the game. The parameter r is exogenous in the model, and the bank simply passes on interest rate r to depositors that keep their money in the bank until t_2. Depositors in this economy derive utility from their gains/losses at date t_1 if the government decides to liquidate the bank or at date t_2 if the government decides to allow continuation of the bank. I assume as well that each entrepreneur receives a loan of value 1, and that the sum of all loans to all entrepreneurs totals D. Consequently, each entrepreneur is expected to return $1 + r$ to the bank at the end of the game, which leaves the bank with $(1 + r)D$ in total assets. If entrepreneurs fail to pay back their loans, the bank has wD in assets and D in liabilities, and is therefore insolvent ($wD < D$). Table 3.1 captures the balance sheet of this model bank in a format identical to that of Table 2.1. The balance sheet corresponds to a situation in which all entrepreneurs pay back their loans and all depositors see their deposits to maturity at date t_2.

Since all entrepreneurs are of identical type, I study decisions made by a representative entrepreneur. The feature of the model that I want to emphasize is that entrepreneurs exert control over the level of risk of their investments. Suppose then that entrepreneurs can choose from a continuum

---

[2] In fractional-reserve banking systems, banks use a large fraction of deposits from clients to make loans. They keep unspent deposits and capital from shareholders in hand to confront unexpected losses.

[3] In other words, I make the simplifying assumption that entrepreneurs have no assets beyond collateral that they can use to repay the bank.

Table 3.1: Bank balance sheet at the end of the game (t_2), assuming no deposit withdrawals at t_1

Assets		*Liabilities*	
Loans	D	Deposits	D
Loan-loss reserves	0	Capital (Equity)	0
Cash inflows		*Cash outflows*	
Interest on loans	rD	Interest on deposits	rD
		Net profit	0

D: Outstanding bank loans; r: Interest rate

of projects, which differ in their levels of risk and expected returns. In fact, the main assumption I borrow from Repullo's model is that entrepreneurs can determine the likelihood of success of their projects by directly choosing the risk profile $\pi \in [0, 1]$ of their investment. In a sense, "risk profile" is a misnomer for this parameter, since π actually captures the *probability of success* of the chosen project rather than the probability of failure, which is simply the complement $1 - \pi$. Projects return $R(\pi)$ at t_2 with probability π and 0 otherwise. Entrepreneurs face a dilemma in that projects with high potential returns are also less likely to pay off, but projects that are more likely to succeed have low potential returns. In other words, entrepreneurs undertake riskier projects (i.e., those with $\pi \rightarrow 0$) only if the potential return is high. To capture this dilemma, Repullo (2005*b*) assumes that $R(\pi)$ decreases as π increases (i.e., $R'(\pi) < 0$) and that there is no excess return when entrepreneurs choose to invest in a riskless technology (i.e., $R(1) = 1$).[4]

At t_1 depositors withdraw fraction $d \in (0, 1)$ of their bank deposits. The size of withdrawn deposits has known density function $f(d)$.[5] For simplicity, I assume that all depositors withdraw the same fraction d, even though their deposits differ in size. Furthermore, I assume that d is not correlated with π, as depositors are not informed about the risk profile chosen by entrepreneurs

---

[4]Furthermore, $R(\pi)$ is assumed continuous and twice-differentiable on the unit range, with $R''(\pi) < 0$. Conditions $R'(\pi) < 0$ and $R(1) = 1$ imply that the "good state" return of a totally risky asset ($\pi = 0$) is strictly larger than 1, i.e., $R(0) > 1$. Finally, a technical assumption about the functional form of R is that $R'(1) < -1$. This assumption about the slope of R when $\pi = 1$ makes it possible that an interior value of π might arise as the solution to the entrepreneur's investment-maximization problem (see also Repullo 2005*a*,*b*). This approach to risk-taking borrows from Allen and Gale (2000).

[5]I assume $f'(d) < 0$; this assumption suggests that small liquidity shocks are more likely to occur than large liquidity shocks.

(Repullo 2005*b*). When the withdrawn fraction *d* is relatively large, I refer to the bank as distressed. Given that fraction *d* is random, I consider this parameter to be "chosen" by Nature.

Since bank loans mature at t_2, withdrawals at t_1 imply that the bank faces a *liquidity shortfall* of magnitude *dD*. To meet this shortfall, the bank approaches the government as *lender of last resort*. The government can choose to loan *dD* to the bank against the bank's return in the good state of nature. All claims on the bank's assets—i.e., those of depositors *and* government—enjoy equal seniority status; in other words, if the bank becomes insolvent at t_2, each claimant receives fraction *w* of their claim. I build limited liability into the model by assuming that the insolvent bank does not bear the full consequences of unsuccessful entrepreneurial activity; the bank is thus not required to surrender more than *wD*. By choosing to support the bank, government bets that continued operations will lead to benefits down the road—interest payments for depositors and profits for entrepreneurs. The downside risk is that entrepreneurial projects may in fact fail, in which case financial losses will multiply. As I elaborate below, it is the potential multiplication of these financial losses that makes "resolution" of an insolvent bank at t_2 so costly.

The government can thus decide at t_1 to close down the bank rather than lend money to meet the liquidity shortfall. Closure implies liquidating all extant loans; I assume that loans can be liquidated at face value ($L = 1$), so the bank recovers *D* upon closure. Furthermore, I assume the following rank-order for exogenous parameters in the model: $r \ll w < L$. This means that bankers prefer to liquidate a loan rather than claim collateral, and entrepreneurs prefer to pay interest rather than surrender collateral.[6] Upon liquidation of the bank, the government returns *D* to depositors and *w* to each entrepreneur. Table 3.2 shows the different entries in the bank's balance sheet as they would appear if the government had supported the bank at t_1 and successful projects had allowed repayment of loans at t_2. Under these circumstances, the bank realizes a profit on withdrawn deposits equivalent to *rdD*.

The government's dilemma is compounded by the fact that it needs to act at t_1 without knowledge of the level of risk π chosen by the representative entrepreneur. Be this as it may, the government observes a signal *s* (*s* ∈ $\{s_0, s_1\}$) and, naturally, the size of deposit withdrawals *d* before making its choice. Signal *s* relays whether the return on investments $R(\pi)$ is likely to be positive (R_1) or 0 (R_0). Note that the government does not know the entrepreneurs' choice of π nor does it know, as a consequence, the actual

---

[6]The assumption that loans can be liquidated at face value is consistent with this preference ordering. Clearly, it would be more realistic to assume a value $L < 1$, but $L = 1$ simplifies the analysis and, because $w < 1$, is consistent with the assumed rank-order $r \ll w < L$.

Table 3.2: Bank balance sheet after a sequence of depositor run, government support, and success of entrepreneurs' projects

Assets		*Liabilities*	
Loans	D	Deposits held to maturity	$(1 - d)D$
		Government loan	dD

Cash inflows		*Cash outflows*	
Interest on loans	rD	Interest on deposits	$r(1 - d)D$
		Net profit	rdD

D: Outstanding bank loans; d: Proportion of withdrawn deposits; r: Interest rate

value of R_1. I assume that $\Pr(s_1|R_1) = 1$ and $\Pr(s_0|R_0) = q$, with $q \in [\frac{1}{2}, 1]$.[7] One can interpret the value of signal s loosely as the quality of economic information that the government can obtain. As $q \to 1$, the quality of the signal improves; in the limit, the government can infer with precision whether returns will be positive or 0.[8]

The extensive form of the game is depicted in Figure 3.1. At t_0, the representative entrepreneur makes a choice of π at its single-node information set E; at t_1 the government makes a decision at one of two information sets G after seeing liquidity shock d and signal s. The government cannot condition its choice at t_2 on the entrepreneur's choice of risk at t_1, but it can condition strategies on signal s. Incidentally, the extensive form of the game represents the outcome of investments R as a move *prior* to choice by the government; though this is not strictly the case, this representation corresponds to the information environment within which the government decides. In each information set, the government must decide whether to allow continuation of the bank (*open*) or arrange for its liquidation (*close*). A strategy G for the government thus consists of a choice of action {Open, Close} upon receiving signals {s_0, s_1} and observing deposit withdrawal d. Despite the representation of the game as one with a non-singleton information set for the government, the game is still solvable by backwards induction.

Payoffs Π to the representative entrepreneur and depositor i under end-states Success, Failure, and Closure appear in Table 3.3; all payoffs are

---

[7]This simplifies Repullo's framework, which assumes that $\Pr(s_0|R_0) = \Pr(s_1|R_1) = q$. In my analysis, as shown below, the government always closes the bank upon receiving a bad signal, as in this case there is no possibility of making mistakes about the present net worth of the bank.

[8]I interpret this signal broadly as the ability of a government to infer the likely status of entrepreneurial investments and, consequently, of the bank's present net worth.

Table 3.3: Payoffs for entrepreneurs and bank depositors under different endstates

	Entrepreneurs	Depositors
Π(Success)	$R(\pi) - (1 + r)$	$r(1 - d)y_i$
Π(Failure)	$-w$	$-(1 - w)(y_i - dy_i + d\bar{y})$
Π(Closure)	0	0

expressed as net gains or losses. The order of preferences for entrepreneurs and depositors is similar, in that they both prefer Success to early Closure to late Failure. To understand depositor i's payoff under failure at t_2 recall that government and depositors are claimants with equal seniority. If this endstage is reached, the bank will have assets amounting to wD, i.e., it will have a financial shortfall amounting to $-(1 - w)D$. *This shortfall constitutes the burden of bank insolvency.* Based on the assumptions of the model, this burden is assigned to individuals based on their relative position in the economy. Depositors reclaim $w(1 - d)D$ from the bank, which adds to the dD they had withdrawn at stage t_1. Collectively, depositors have lost $-D(1 - d)(1 + w)$ compared to their t_1 deposit D. Therefore, depositors bear part of the burden of insolvency directly from lost assets. Depositors bear a second part of the burden indirectly through their role in supporting government finances. Because government's expenses are exclusively funded through taxation in this economy, taxpayer money is needed to plug the deficit caused by government loans to the bank at t_1. Recall that the government disbursed dD at t_1 to support the bank, so it claims wdD of the bank's remaining assets. Upon receiving wdD from the bank at t_2, the government still faces a shortfall of $-(1 - w)dD$.

At this point, note that the setup of the game runs parallel to the discussion about government policy options in Chapter 2. The government is called upon to decide whether or not to support a bank with uncertain financial status. Early closure limits costs—in fact, depositors recover their period-1 deposits and entrepreneurs can reclaim collateral, so in the model economic actors incur no costs from closure. It is reasonable to interpret closure at stage t_1 as a commitment to "wind down" the bank early on by forcing it to stop all operations, call in all loans, and pay outstanding deposits. In practice, these operations are not costless, and require a commitment to spend taxpayers' money to close down the bank. The assumption of costless closure is a simplification meant to underscore the potentially large gap in taxpayer support that exists between the policy option of early closure and the policy option of keeping the bank open and facing potential insolvency. In other words, by intervening early and closing a bank that may be on its way to becoming insolvent the government is in fact preventing even larger potential losses. However, intervention at t_1 does not mean that the bank is permanently "saved." The bank can still crash at t_2 as its financial status is finally revealed. In those circumstances, the insolvent bank will be closed down, depositors will take their losses, and taxpayers will be called upon to finance the government's deficit of $-(1 - w)dD$.

I simplify by assuming that governments socialize bank losses through a lump-sum tax on all citizens. I conceive of this tax in very broad terms; it can be interpreted literally as an increase in taxes, or as the value of foregone government transfers to citizens, or as the opportunity cost of lost investments in infrastructure, or the debt that the government undertakes to finance the transfer at t_1.[9] The simplifying assumption that taxes are shared equally among all depositors, albeit a bit drastic, accords with the basic intuition that the benefits of banking activity accrue to some but eventual losses are distributed more vastly (i.e., they are "socialized"). In any case, the relevant intuition is that the cost of insolvency is spread more thinly than the benefits of banking activity. Based on this assumption, the per capita tax is $-(1 - w)d\bar{y}$. Each taxpayer therefore ends the game with payoff $dy_i + (1 - d)wy_i - (1 - w)d\bar{y}$. The net loss to depositor i in relation to initial income y_i is thus $-(1 - w)(y_i - dy_i + d\bar{y})$. This burden combines *deposit losses* and *taxation*, and corresponds to the entry on the "Depositors" column in the second row in Table 3.3.

In the next section, I build the main argument one step at a time by analyzing the choices that players make under two "non-political" scenarios. The first scenario describes the decision process of an entrepreneur in a situation in which no deposit withdrawals are possible and there is consequently no need for banking policy. By analyzing this simple scenario, I convey the basic dilemma that entrepreneurs face. The second scenario considers the possibility of deposit withdrawals along with a simple rule for banking policy, namely, one followed by a strict lender of last resort. I follow up with consideration of a third scenario. None of these scenarios include the political mechanisms—accountability and cronyism—at the heart of government responses to banking crises; these are considered in Section 3.2. Be this as it may, a careful consideration of the non-political scenarios provides a useful yardstick against which to compare further results and conveys the importance of entrepreneurial choices in determining levels of bank robustness.

---

[9]The latter interpretation is more appropriate, since in case of failure the poorest individuals will end up the game with negative income at t_2.

Figure 3.1: Extensive form of the banking crisis game between a representative entrepreneur (E) and government (G) (moves by nature are represented by N)

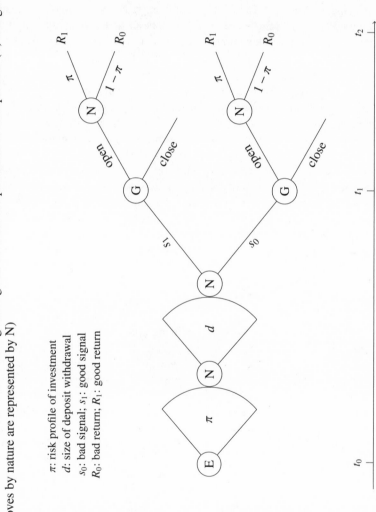

π: risk profile of investment
d: size of deposit withdrawal
s_0: bad signal; s_1: good signal
R_0: bad return; R_1: good return

3.1.1 Equilibrium without Government Intervention

I start by finding the equilibrium choice of π^* in a situation in which it is not possible to withdraw deposits at t_1 and there is in consequence no need for government intervention. In this situation, all payoffs are resolved at t_2 and the only possible endstates are project success or failure. The probability of reaching the good state of nature is π, and therefore the representative entrepreneur's expected utility is

$$\mathsf{E}(U_E) = \pi\underbrace{(R(\pi) - 1 - r)}_{\Pi_E(S)} - (1 - \pi)\underbrace{w}_{\Pi_E(F)}.$$

The optimal choice for entrepreneurs is $\pi^* \equiv \operatorname{argmax} \mathsf{E}(U_E)$, subject to the individual participation constraint $R(\pi) > 1 + r$. This choice of π^* obtains when Condition 3.1 holds:

$$R(\pi^*) + \pi^* R'(\pi^*) = 1 + r - w \qquad (3.1)$$

moreover, π^* is an interior solution, so the entrepreneur would not choose $\pi^* = 0$ or $\pi^* = 1$. (All proofs are provided in Appendix A.1.)

Note that the entrepreneur's chosen risk profile π^* is increasing in w and decreasing in r (this occurs because $R(\pi^*) + \pi^* R'(\pi^*)$ decreases monotonically on π, while $1 + r - w$ is constant with respect to π). This suggests that higher values of collateral at risk increase the choice of π^* and, consequently, lower the entrepreneur's risk-taking incentives. In contrast, larger interest rates decrease π^*, corresponding to more risky investments.[10] In other words, entrepreneurs are *more* willing to make riskier investments—i.e., they choose *lower* π^*—if they have higher interest payments to meet.

The bank does not make decisions in this game. Were the bank able to set π^* directly, it would seek to maximize $\mathsf{E}(U_B) = \pi \cdot rdD$, a function that is clearly increasing in π^*. In other words, the bank would never choose to make risky investments.[11]

3.1.2 Equilibrium with a Bagehot Enforcer

Because of the absence of liquidity shocks, there is no rationale for government intervention in the simple version of the game analyzed in the previous section. In this section, I consider government intervention but still omit complications from the inclusion of political mechanisms; thus, I simply assume

---

[10]By the envelope theorem, expected utility can be seen to be decreasing in r and w.

[11]This counterintuitive result follows from the assumption that the bank makes no profits from its lending activity. In this setup, the bank can only incur disutility from choosing $\pi^* < 1$. In a more realistic setup, one could divide interest payment r between bank and depositors, which would lead to a bank's choice of $\pi^* < 1$.

that the government has a mandate to close banks at t_1 upon observation of s_0 and to leave the bank open upon observation of s_1. Under these circumstances, the government would simply loan dD to the bank at t_1 upon observation of s_1 and recover this same amount at t_2 provided that the good state of nature obtains. In other words, the government acts as a "no-nonsense" Bagehot enforcer that closes banks to prevent further deterioration of balance sheets if "things look dire," but always leaves banks open if it receives a good signal *regardless of the size of the liquidity shock.*

Knowing that she faces a Bagehot government, the entrepreneur calculates her payoff based on the *ex ante* probabilities of observing s and R. Hence, the expected payoff to the representative entrepreneur is

$$\underbrace{\pi^*}_{\Pr(R_1,s_1)} \Pi_E(S) + \underbrace{(1-q)(1-\pi^*)}_{\Pr(R_0,s_1)} \Pi_E(F),$$

which reaches a maximum when the first-order condition captured in Equation 3.2 is satisfied:[12]

$$R(\pi^*) + \pi^* R'(\pi^*) = 1 + r - (1-q)w \tag{3.2}$$

The entrepreneur's expected utility is now weighted by the quality q of signal s. Compare this equilibrium choice of π^* to the one that obtains in the absence of government intervention (Equation 3.1). Because $1 + r - w \leq 1 + r - (1-q)w$, entrepreneurs are willing to take more risk when interacting with a Bagehot government. By being forced to forego projects upon observation of signal s_0, entrepreneurs diminish the probability of losing collateral in hard times. In fact, the incentive to take on more risk (lower π) increases as $q \to 1$, i.e., as the signal about endstates becomes more reliable. Paradoxically, a Bagehot government with recourse to a perfect signal about future losses would provide entrepreneurs with an incentive to choose riskier projects. In this extreme case, the government would be acting as a *de facto* agent of entrepreneurs, tying their hands and forcing them to cut potential losses early on.

Furthermore, depositors are similarly protected. They might bear some costs in case of bank liquidation (recall that we have assumed $L = 1$ for the sake of simplicity, but admit that liquidation might produce inconveniences

---

[12]Based on assumptions about signal s, we can calculate the *ex ante* probabilities of observing different endstates:

$\Pr(C)$	$=$	$\Pr(s_0\|R_0)\Pr(R_0) + \Pr(s_0\|R_1)\Pr(R_1)$	$=$	$q(1-\pi)$
$\Pr(F)$	$=$	$\Pr(s_1\|R_0)\Pr(R_0)$	$=$	$(1-q)(1-\pi)$
$\Pr(S)$	$=$	$\Pr(s_1\|R_1)\Pr(R_1)$	$=$	π

to depositors), but these would be minimal compared to the potential loss $-(1 - w)(y_i - dy_i + d\bar{y})$ endured by depositor i if a bank that may be insolvent were allowed to continue. Under a Bagehot enforcer with recourse to a clear signal one would observe higher risk-taking and more forceful liquidation of banks, but not too many costly banking crises obtaining from government forbearance that results in eventual failure. In the extreme, as $q \rightarrow 1$, a Bagehot enforcer would be able to separate solvent from insolvent banks perfectly. Thus, the scenario depicted in this section has close affinity to Bagehot's recommendation to lend freely to solvent banks and to close down insolvent banks, with the proviso that insolvency can be detected without error only if the signal about future endstates is perfect ($q = 1$).

3.2 Democratic Accountability, Crony Capitalism, and Systemic Risk

So far, I have considered neither the role of government as representative of taxpayers nor the pernicious effect of venal politicians that extract rents from project owners in exchange for government provision of insurance in bad times. As mentioned before, these are candidate mechanisms to explain the role of politics in responding, and possibly contributing, to banking crises. In short, I have not made government choices endogenous to political mechanisms. I expand the basic model of Section 3.1 to consider a government that by virtue of democratic accountability enacts the policy preferences of the median voter (Section 3.2.1) and the possibility of crony links between government and entrepreneurs that might further imperil banks (Section 3.2.2). These extensions complete the description of the political setup. I develop comparative statics results in Section 3.3.

3.2.1 Closure Rule under Democracy

Democratic governments carry out banking policy with an eye on the electoral arena, where they need to be mindful of the preferences of their constituents. I argue that electoral accountability limits bailouts because it makes credible a government's commitment not to pump taxpayers' money indiscriminately into bad banks. To elaborate this argument, I assume the policy preferences of the median voter to be most relevant under democracy. This view, which is broadly consistent with the economic analysis of majoritarian institutions pioneered by Downs (1957), abstracts from institutional variation within democracies but is extremely useful to highlight differences across political regimes.[13] As I argue in this section, implementing the policy preferences of

---

[13] An influential literature studies how institutional variation determines the size of a government's winning coalition even across political regimes. For example, some institutions may facilitate political survival in requiring politicians to form less-than-majoritarian coalitions in

the median voter makes democratic governments less likely to finance heavy deposit withdrawals that might eventually lead to large financial losses.

If one assumes the primacy of the median voter's preferences in public policy, and if these preferences reflect the economic positions of voters, then the economic structure of society becomes paramount in understanding banking policy. An essential component of bank bailouts is that taxpayers are called to extend the life of banks from which they obtain *unequal* benefit in ordinary times. To see this, consider that citizens place different demands on banking services. For example, the World Bank's database on bank outreach reports that the median number of deposits per one thousand people was 528.9 in a sample of fifty-four countries around 2001–2003, but this distribution is strongly bimodal, with extremely low values in some countries (the minimum is 14.5 for Madagascar). As one would suspect, the number of bank deposits is strongly correlated with a country's per capita GDP ($r = 0.68$). These statistics do not reflect the probability that any one individual will own a bank deposit, let alone the level of variation in the size of deposits, but they convey the basic idea that the costs of banking policy are spread among all even when the benefits of banking activity are more concentrated.[14]

To capture differences in inequality I assume that individual incomes y_i follow a Pareto distribution. This distribution is commonly employed in the analysis of inequality because it reflects a situation in which there are many poor individuals with low income/assets, a smaller number of individuals with middle income, and a very small fraction of wealthy individuals.[15] The Pareto distribution is characterized by location ($\mu > 0$) and spread ($\sigma \geq 1$) parameters. The location parameter μ is simply the value of the lowest income in society. The spread parameter σ—also referred to as the Pareto index—determines relative levels of wealth between poor and rich; thus, as σ increases, the proportion of very wealthy individuals drops, and therefore inequality decreases. Thus, different patterns of inequality obtain as these two parameters vary. For each pattern of inequality, there are three characteristics that we need to consider. First, I capture the level of inequality through the Gini index $g \equiv 1/(2\sigma - 1)$; higher values of the Gini index (lower values of σ) correspond to more inegalitarian societies. Second, the income of the average voter is the expected value of the Pareto distribution, $\bar{y} = \sigma\mu/(\sigma - 1)$. Finally,

---

order to retain power (Bueno de Mesquita, Smith, Siverson and Morrow 2004).

[14]For these figures, we can look at Mexico, where only 16% of the population had deposits in a national bank on the eve of the banking crisis of 1995. As in many other economies, deposits in Mexico are highly concentrated. In 1999, a minimum of 63,116 accounts (0.2%) made up 64.3% of the value of total deposits, whereas 13,520,453 accounts (43.7%) account for only 0.24% of the value of total deposits. In 1979, 68% of bank loans and credit were given to 5% of borrowers (Maxfield 1990, 103–106). See Beck, Demirgüç-Kunt and Martinez Peria (2008) for an analysis of banking outreach around the world.

[15]See for example Clementi and Gallegati (2005); Mitzenmacher (2003); Rodríguez (2004).

the income of the median voter is simply the median of the Pareto distribution, $y_m = 2^{1/\sigma}\mu$. Parameters g, $\bar{y}$, and y_m capture the relevant distributive structure of the economy.[16]

With these assumptions in place, we can now consider government's options at t_1. Contrary to the scenario of Section 3.1.2, we now consider whether it makes sense to allow bank continuation at t_1 upon observation of signal s_1. This decision should be conditional on the size of deposit withdrawals d, which is the second piece of information available to the government. Under these circumstances, the government does not rely on *ex ante* probabilities, but computes the probability of success and failure—$\Pr(R_1|s)$ and $\Pr(R_0|s)$—premised upon observation of signal s and knowledge of $\Pr(s|R)$. Upon observing s_1, the government should leave the bank open if and only if

$$\Pr(R_1|s_1)S + \Pr(R_0|s_1)F \geq C.$$

For the sake of argument, let us consider a government that perfectly represents the preferences of the median voter, which has income y_m. The government engages in forbearance if the condition in Equation 3.3 holds:

$$\underbrace{\frac{\pi^*}{1 - q + \pi^* q}}_{\Pr(R_1, s_1)} \underbrace{r(1 - d)y_m}_{S} \geq \underbrace{\frac{(1 - \pi^*)(1 - q)}{1 - q + \pi^* q}}_{\Pr(R_0, s_1)} \underbrace{(1 - w)(y_m - dy_m + d\bar{y})}_{F} \quad (3.3)$$

I characterize the propensity of a government to choose forbearance by defining a *closure rule*. The closure rule depends on the size of the deposit withdrawal that will impel the government to push for bank exit. Solving for d in Equation 3.3, we find that a democratic government will choose to keep a bank open after observing s_1 if and only if $d \leq c_d^*$, with c_d^* defined in Equation 3.4:

$$c_d^* \equiv \frac{\pi^* r - (1 - \pi^*)(1 - q)(1 - w)}{\pi^* r + (1 - \pi^*)(1 - q)(1 - w)\left(\dfrac{\bar{y}}{y_m} - 1\right)} \quad (3.4)$$

Since the probability that the good state will obtain upon observing the bad signal is nil (i.e., $\Pr(R_1|s_0) = 0$, see Appendix A.1), the government would never allow the bank to continue upon seeing s_0. Upon observation of s_1, the government's optimal choice is to leave the bank open for values of the liquidity shock smaller than c_d and to close it for values larger than this cutpoint. Figure 3.2 shows the condition implied by Equation 3.4. The

---

[16]As in Meltzer and Richard (1981) and Acemoglu and Robinson (2005), the distance between the voter with average income ($\bar{y}$) and the voter with median income (y_m) will be crucial in building auxiliary assumptions about the effects of inequality on public policy.

Figure 3.2: Conditions under which a liquidity shortfall at t_1 will trigger immediate bank closure

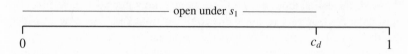

optimal strategy G_d^* is {Open if $s = s_1$ and $d \leq c_b$, Close otherwise}. As cutpoint c_d shifts rightwards, the government is willing to leave the bank in operation for a wider range of observed liquidity shortfalls.

We can read comparative statics off Equation 3.4. Note that $c_d \to 1$ as $q \to 1$, i.e., the government is more likely to support banks under wider ranges of liquidity shocks as its information about the likelihood of project success at t_2 becomes more precise, which is only to be expected. We also observe that cutpoint c_d shifts rightwards as entrepreneurs choose lower levels of risk—i.e., as $\pi^* \to 1$.[17] This result has an intuitive explanation in that higher values of π^* make it more likely that R_1 will obtain. In turn, this changes the distribution of signals, making it more likely that the government will see s_1—i.e., $\Pr(s_1|R_1)\Pr(R_1)$ increases with π^* (see footnote 12). Note also that the cutpoint increases on values of w and r.

As mentioned before, we should also see variation in government responses to banking crises premised upon varying levels of wealth distribution in society. We can see from the definition of c_d^* that the liquidation cut-off point—the closure rule—moves leftwards as the ratio $\bar{y}/y_m$ increases. Formally, this result follows from signing $\partial c_d^*/\partial \sigma > 0$ (see Appendix A.1). Since the distance between median and average income-holders is much greater under unequal than in egalitarian societies, a government's closure rule should be more liberal in relatively egalitarian societies. The rationale behind this result is that as the distance between the incomes of the average and median depositors increases, the ensuing redistribution of losses affects the median voter more heavily.

After solving for the government's optimal strategy at t_1, we can now restate the entrepreneur's decision problem at t_0. Her situation is now different in that the good state of nature needs to obtain *and* the government must allow the bank to continue if she is to get the high payoff $\Pi_E(S)$. In other words, the entrepreneur claims the high payoff if investments pan out ($R = R_1$), government sees s_1, and the liquidity shock is smaller than the government's closure rule, i.e., $d \leq c_b$. Because entrepreneurs know the prob-

---

[17]This result follows from signing $\partial c_d/\partial \pi^* \equiv (1 - w)(1 - q)/\pi^{*2}r > 0$.

ability distribution of R (after all, they choose π) and s ($\Pr(s|R)$ is common knowledge), they can estimate the *ex ante* probability of success at $t = 0$, which is $\Pr(R_1, s_1, d \leq c_d)$. Based on the assumption of independence of d and R (i.e., liquidity shocks are uncorrelated with future states because depositors do not monitor entrepreneurial investment choices) and the definition of marginal and conditional distributions, the full joint probability $\Pr(R, s, d \leq c)$ can be expressed as $\Pr(s|R)\Pr(R)F(c_d^*)$, where $F(c_d^*) \equiv \Pr(d \leq c_d^*)$. By the same token, the *ex ante* probability of failure is $\Pr(R_0, s_1, d \leq c_d)$.

After taking into account these probabilities, the entrepreneur's *ex ante* utility can be expressed as in Equation 3.5:

$$\mathsf{E}_d(U_E) = \underbrace{\pi^*\left[F(c_d)\right]}_{\Pr(R_1, s_1, d \leq c_d)} \Pi_E(S) + \underbrace{(1 - \pi^*)\left[(1 - q)F(c_d)\right]}_{\Pr(R_0, s_1, d \leq c_d)} \Pi_E(F) \qquad (3.5)$$

The entrepreneur's *ex ante* utility is now weighted by two additional factors, the quality q of signal s and the probability distribution $F(\cdot)$ of liquidity shocks d. These weights complicate the characterization of an equilibrium choice of π^*. Recall that the government cannot directly observe the entrepreneur's action (i.e., his choice of π^*), but it can observe a *consequence* of this action (i.e., the distribution of s is driven by $R(\pi^*)$). In the environment of imperfect information that I consider, π^* changes the distribution of signals s, and the entrepreneur must take this effect into account when choosing her optimal action.

As Repullo notes, it is difficult to find an analytical solution of a form similar to that of Equations 3.1 or 3.2, let alone an explicit solution, because the terms $F(\cdot)$ are a non-linear function of π^*.[18] In Section 3.3, I resort to computational methods that allow characterization of equilibrium choices of π^* and G^* under different combinations of exogenous parameters.

---

[18]To see this, consider the expression for the partial derivative of $\mathsf{E}_d(U_E)$ with respect to π in Equation 3.6:

$$\frac{\partial \mathsf{E}_d(U_E)}{\partial \pi} \equiv F(c_d)\left[R(\pi) + \pi R'(\pi) - 1 - r + (1 - q)w\right]$$

$$+ f(c_d)\frac{\partial c_d}{\partial \pi}\left[\pi(R(\pi) - 1 - r) - (1 - q)(1 - \pi)w\right] \qquad (3.6)$$

This expression is a complicated function of π^*. An analytical solution to the game is easy to find when one factors out the terms inside the square brackets of Equation 3.5. Repullo (2005*a*) proposes this simplification, reasoning that the entrepreneur cannot manipulate the location of cutpoint c_d through his choice of π^*, since π^* remains unknown to the government (see Repullo 2005*a*, p. 56). This line of reasoning is not entirely satisfactory because π^* affects the probability of observing signal s_1.

3.2.2 Closure Rule under Crony Capitalism

Up to this point, I have developed the closure rule of a government that merely reflects the policy preferences of the median voter. I now consider a more realistic scenario where governments are willing to directly distort the structure of entrepreneurial incentives by accepting a crony contract from entrepreneurs. I model crony capitalism as an implicit contract in which entrepreneurs pay per capita rent z in exchange for government support to pay fraction κ of collateral w in case of project failure.[19] The sum of all entrepreneurial rents is Z.

As I show below, the upside of the crony contract is that it provides entrepreneurs with an incentive to take on riskier investments, and therefore allows the possibility of potentially higher economic growth and larger returns to depositors. The downside of the crony contract is that, in case of failure, the government needs to increase taxes above and beyond those needed to finance loans at t_1. This occurs because the government also needs to finance $\kappa w D$ to cover the collateral of crony capitalists. A cynical view of crony governments is that they do not care about the burden imposed on society, and therefore are happy to pass whatever costs ensue from the crony contract on to depositors. *Under this extreme view, crony governments would never close banks at t_1, even upon observation of very large deposit withdrawals.*[20] In a democratic regime, however, governments internalize at least partially the cost of failure. How then would democracy change the propensity of a crony government to engage in forbearance?

To answer this question, we reconsider the payoffs to the median voter in different endstates. Under S, the median voter still obtains $r(1 - d)y_m$, but under F she will not only lose $-(1 - w)(y_m - dy_m + d\bar{y})$, but will be called upon to pay $\kappa w \bar{y}$ as a tax to cover the entrepreneur's collateral. Under these circumstances, the median voter's expected utility appears in Equation 3.7:

$$E(U_{mv}) \equiv \frac{\pi^*}{1 - q + \pi^* q} r(1 - d)y_m$$
$$- \frac{(1 - \pi^*)(1 - q)}{1 - q + \pi^* q}\Big((1 - w)(y_m - dy_m + d\bar{y}) + \kappa w \bar{y}\Big) \quad (3.7)$$

Even in democratic regimes, we often find close partnerships between government officials and private entrepreneurs and bankers.[21] In line with this

---

[19]At the heart of theories of crony capitalism we find the exchange of rents for policy favors. For example, Haslag and Pecchenino (2005) model cronyism as a government guarantee to pay interest on loans. See also Vaugirard (2007).

[20]This interpretation is popular in journalistic accounts and in politicized narratives of banking crises. A good exemplar is López Obrador (1999), a diatribe against the bank bailout in Mexico that catapulted its author to political prominence.

[21]See for example Faccio (2006).

view, I assume that politicians also include rents as part of their utility function. I stipulate that the crony contract generates rents Z that are an increasing function of κ. I assume further that rents increase at a decreasing rate.[22] These rents can be interpreted broadly: As economic support from entrepreneurs that politicians can enjoy privately or spend in electoral campaigns, as ego rents derived from close contacts with friends with money, or as future profit opportunities made possible by building extensive networks of business contacts while in government. In the model, the government enjoys rents whenever the bank remains open at t_1 and investments pan out at t_2, and obtains 0 otherwise.

Under this broad interpretation of crony rents, governments may devise a banking policy that provides entrepreneurs with incentives to pursue riskier investments. A government's banking policy now comprises two interrelated aspects, namely, a decision about the closure rule and a decision about the extent of opportunities for cronyism. To analyze the effect of alternative political regimes over a government's banking policy, we consider the expected payoff of a government that has separable utility over crony rents and the discounted policy preference of the median voter (Equation 3.7). The discount weight α captures gradations in the government's incentive to represent the median voter. As $\alpha \rightarrow 1$, which corresponds to a fully democratic regime, government ponders the preferences of the median voter fully. The government's expected utility from accepting a crony deal of size κ appears in Equation 3.8:

$$
\begin{aligned}
\mathsf{E}_{cd}(U_G) \equiv\ & \frac{\pi^*}{1 - q + \pi^* q}\Big(\alpha r(1 - d)y_m + Z(\kappa)\Big) \\
& - \frac{(1 - \pi^*)(1 - q)}{1 - q + \pi^* q}\Big(\alpha(1 - w)(y_m - dy_m + d\bar{y}) + \alpha\kappa w\bar{y}\Big) \quad (3.8)
\end{aligned}
$$

There is no reason to consider the crony contract κ to be an exogenous parameter in the model. Instead, I consider κ to be endogenously determined by the government. Rather than adding a bargaining game over the choice of κ to the model, let us simply assume that the government has the chance to reject crony deals that fail to maximize its expected utility and that there are no commitment problems between government and entrepreneurs. Under these circumstances, an authoritarian regime that is absolutely unresponsive to the median voter would have no qualms admitting a crony contract setting $\kappa^* = 1$ in return for $Z(1)$. But as soon as consideration of the median voter's preferences weighs in on the government's utility function, a contract stipulating $\kappa^* = 1$ would no longer be desirable. Based on Equation 3.8, the

---

[22] $Z(\kappa)$ is assumed continuous and twice-differentiable, with $Z'(\kappa) > 0$, $Z''(\kappa) < 0$, $Z(0) = 0$, and $Z'(0) = \infty$.

entrepreneur's decision problem reasoning backwards from the last stage of the game is to offer government the value of κ that maximizes $E(U_G)$. This value obtains when the following condition is met (see Appendix A.1):

$$Z'(\kappa) = \alpha \frac{1 - \pi^*}{\pi^*}(1 - q)w\bar{y} \qquad (3.9)$$

We would like to understand how the crony contract changes under gradations in the representativeness of the political regime and in levels of inequality and wealth in society. Consider first how κ changes as α approaches 1. Because $Z'(\kappa)$ is decreasing over the range of κ (see fn. 22), increases in the right hand side of Equation 3.9 correspond to lower values of κ^*. It follows that as α increases, the entrepreneur offers lower values of κ^*, i.e., a crony contract that is less onerous to society. Now consider parameters σ and μ. By an identical argument, it follows that as the average income in society increases, the size of the crony deal that entrepreneurs offer to government decreases. Since $\bar{y}$ increases with both μ and σ, I conclude that higher overall income levels and more egalitarian distributions of income reduce the propensity to engage in crony capitalism (see Appendix A.1).

The constraining effect of democracy on banking policy extends then to the decision to limit or expand crony networks in the banking system. Because democracy compels politicians to consider the policy preferences of the median voter, and because cronyism increases the potential cost of restoring bank solvency, it follows that in democratic regimes politicians will choose *not* to engage in onerous forms of crony capitalism. This may sound altogether as an extremely rosy interpretation of the links between democracy and cronyism. This conclusion, however, is in line with common interpretations of the prevalence of cronyism. For example, Haber (2002*b*) suggests that cronyism is a second-best solution to the fundamental dilemma of political economy, namely, the inability of authority to commit credibly not to expropriate wealth. Democracy is presumably a first-best solution to this problem, as under this political regime governments are constrained by assemblies that represent the interests of propertied individuals and cannot expropriate at will. In the absence of democracy, governments can credibly commit not to expropriate the wealth of at most a few cronies only by sharing rents with them.[23]

To present a full picture of the changes in banking policy across political regimes and economic situations, we finally need to consider the effects of cronyism, democracy, and inequality on the government's closure rule upon

---

[23]More generally, several studies have documented a negative association between democracy (and economic development), on the one hand, and corruption, on the other (Gerring and Thacker 2004; Montinola and Jackman 2002; Treisman 2000).

observation of signal s_1:

$$d \leq c_{cd}^* \equiv \frac{\pi^*\left(r + \dfrac{Z(\kappa^*)}{y_m \alpha}\right) - (1 - \pi^*)(1 - q)\left(1 - w + \kappa^* w \dfrac{\bar{y}}{y_m}\right)}{\pi^* r + (1 - \pi^*)(1 - q)(1 - w)\left(\dfrac{\bar{y}}{y_m} - 1\right)} \tag{3.10}$$

We can say that democracy has a partial *direct* containment effect on the government's closure rule: For constant levels of κ, an increase in α shifts the cutpoint c_{cd} leftwards, which translates into a tougher closure rule. The *total* effect of democracy on the government's closure rule is more convoluted, as c_{cd} is a function of the equilibrium choices of π^* and κ^*, *which are themselves affected by changes in political regime*. In fact, it is not possible to sign the net effect of democracy on the government's closure rule through analytical means. To anticipate some of the results in Section 3.3, I find that higher values of α lead to lower values of c_{cd}. In other words, the propensity to forbear is lower in more democratic regimes, all else equal.

Finally, I solve for the entrepreneur's equilibrium choice of π^*, taking into account the equilibrium choice of κ^*. The representative crony entrepreneur's expected utility appears in Equation 3.11:

$$\mathbb{E}_{cd}(U_E) \equiv \pi\left[F(c_{cd}^*)\right]\left(R(\pi) - 1 - r - Z(\kappa^*)\right)$$
$$- (1 - \pi)\left[(1 - q)F(c_{cd}^*)\right](1 - \kappa^*)w \tag{3.11}$$

The entrepreneur thus sets π^* to satisfy the first order condition in Equation 3.12, subject to $R(\pi^*) \geq 1 + r + Z(\kappa^*)$:[24]

$$F(c_{cd})\left[R(\pi) + \pi R'(\pi) - 1 - r - Z(\kappa^*) + (1 - \kappa^*)(1 - q)w\right]$$
$$= f(c_{cd})\frac{\partial c}{\partial \pi}\left[(1 - \kappa^*)(1 - q)(1 - \pi)w - \pi(R(\pi) - 1 - r - Z(\kappa^*))\right] \tag{3.12}$$

The equilibrium in this game is a choice of a strategy profile (π^*, G^*) from which neither player has an incentive to deviate. Equilibria are guaranteed to exist in this game, because the choice-sets of players are finite in the case of government, and closed and bounded in the case of the entrepreneur. Because of the difficulty of signing the effect of α on choice parameters, I propose a computational approach in Section 3.3 to analyze comparative statics in this game.

---

[24]I assume that the restriction $R(\pi^*) \geq 1 + r + Z(\kappa)$ is not binding at π^*.

Table 3.4: Assumptions about functional forms and values of exogenous variables used in the computational analysis

Function	Specific form	Param.	Values
$Z(\kappa)$	$\sqrt{\kappa}$	g	0.25, 0.35, 0.45, 0.55
$R(\pi)$	$5 - (\pi + 1)^2$	q	0.5, 0.6, 0.8, 0.9
$F(c)$	$\begin{cases} 2c - c^2 & \text{if } c \in [0, 1] \\ 0 & \text{otherwise} \end{cases}$	w r	0.6, 0.7, 0.8, 0.9 0.04, 0.06, 0.08, 0.10

3.3 Solving for Equilibria of the Bagehot-Bailout Model

Because of the sheer difficulty of finding analytical solutions to the model, the purpose of this section is to use computational tools to analyze the behavior of entrepreneurs and government under alternative scenarios. The first step to proceed with this analysis is to choose appropriate forms for the functions that have so far remained unspecified, namely, $R(\cdot)$, $F(\cdot)$, and $Z(\cdot)$. The second step is to consider equilibrium strategies under combinations of a manageable set of reasonable values of exogenous parameters, in this case σ, q, r, and w. Recall that I characterize democratic regimes as those where $\alpha \rightarrow 1$, and authoritarian regimes as those where $\alpha \rightarrow 0$. Ultimately, I seek to derive the impact of α on the choice of endogenous parameters in the model—risk profile π^*, closure rule c^*, crony contract k^*, and the *ex ante* probability $\Pr(F)$ of observing failure. The behavior of these four endogenous parameters is the object of interest in this section.

Table 3.4 summarizes the values of exogenous parameters and functional forms for $R(\cdot)$, $F(\cdot)$, and $Z(\cdot)$ that I consider in this exercise. Since the results of the analysis are dependent on the chosen functional forms and values of exogenous parameters, it is important to consider these with care. Regarding functional forms, I choose as simple a function as possible while still complying with the assumptions of the model. Regarding exogenous parameters, I sought reasonable values that corresponded to historical experience. For example, the range of Gini indices spans the experience of countries such as Denmark or Finland, with Gini scores in the neighborhood of 0.2, to Brazil or Mexico, with Gini indices hovering around 0.55.[25] The chosen values for r reflect the historical minima and maxima of the US prime rate over the past ten years; different choices, for example 1 or 2 points over LIBOR,

---

[25]The values in Table 3.4 correspond to values of σ of 2.5, 1.9, 1.6, and 1.4.

would have yielded scores in the same ballpark. The more difficult choice corresponds to values of w because the market value of loan collateral shifts during financial crises, a complication not considered here; for this parameter, I consider a broader range from 0.6 to 0.9. The model becomes uninteresting as q approaches 1, in which case the government is assumed to have perfect foresight about bank net worth and acts as a flawless Bagehot enforcer, so I choose values for this parameter that are bounded away from 1. Finally, I allow α to take on values from 0.01 to 1, which correspond to the full range of this parameter while avoiding undefined results when $\alpha = 0$.[26]

As I discuss the major implications of the analysis, it is inconvenient to present graphically or numerically the equilibria that obtain under all combinations of exogenous parameters.[27] Instead, I present some illustrations in Figures 3.3 and 3.4; these figures provide a rather complete summary of how endogenous parameters change in response to changes in political regime, i.e., they offer an accurate representation of the comparative statics that obtain under other combinations of parameters. With one exception, I find that the relations between democracy, on the one hand, and π, κ, and c, on the other, are easy to characterize, as most of these are monotonically increasing or decreasing. Where appropriate, I indicate some of the exceptions that I have found and discuss what impact these may have on predictions.

Figure 3.3 shows the profiles of closure rule (c_d) and risk choice (π), the main endogenous parameters in this analysis, under different combinations of parameters r, w, and q, and for different values of the democracy weight α. Consider the leftmost panel first, which comprises a 4×3 matrix of plots. In each column within this matrix, the clarity of signal q is held constant at values of 0.6, 0.75, and 0.9, respectively. Within each of the twelve plots, the values of interest rate r and collateral w are held constant at levels that appear in a corner of the plot; these levels result from combinations of both high and low values of these exogenous parameters. Also within each plot, Gini indices are held constant at high and low levels of inequality (the thicker line corresponds to a Gini of 0.55, the lighter line to a Gini of 0.25). Thus, for example, the northwest plot in the left panel of Figure 3.3 corresponds to the choice of closure rule c_d as a function of democracy when exogenous parameters are held constant at the following values: $q = 0.6$, $r = 0.06$, and $w = 0.7$.

The easiest result to characterize is the government's choice of closure rule, which is monotonically decreasing on α at all inspected combinations of exogenous parameters (see the right panel in Figure 3.3). Note that for

---

[26]One last exogenous parameter, μ, remains fixed at 10. This parameter simply shifts the scale of results through its effect on factor $Z(\kappa)/y_m$ in Equation 3.10.

[27]The number of combinations of exogenous parameters is $4^4 \times 10$, a relatively small but still cumbersome set of combinations.

Figure 3.3: Choice of *closure rule* (c_d) and *risk profile* (π^*) under alternative values of democracy (α) and inequality (g). Thicker lines correspond to a higher level of inequality ($g = 0.55$), thinner lines to a lower level of inequality (0.25). The numbers within the plots correspond to values of r and w, and columns correspond to values of q equal to 0.6, 0.75, and 0.9, respectively.

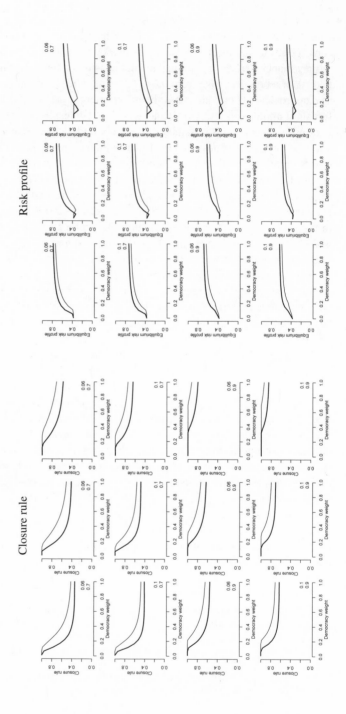

Closure rule

Risk profile

very low values of α, the optimal closure rule is 1, which means that the government would always leave banks in operation regardless of the size of the deposit withdrawal at t_1. In contrast, lower values of c_d, corresponding to tougher closure rules, appear as α approaches 1. As the plot reveals, closure rules are more liberal for higher values of w and lower values of r, though the latter effect is minuscule. Also as expected, closure rules become more liberal as the clarity of signal s improves (i.e., the curves representing choice of c_d shift upwards from column 1 to column 2 to column 3). Note finally that closure rules are more liberal in more egalitarian societies. This is a direct consequence of the mechanism assumed here, which leads governments to weight heavily the distance between median and average taxpayers when setting the closure rule. This effect is less powerful as parameter α approaches 0, as under these circumstances diminished electoral accountability leads the government to place less weight on the preferences of the median voter. At high levels of α, government has an incentive to internalize the policy preferences of the median voter, which are for lower redistribution of the burden of financial loss. This incentive should lead democratic governments to adopt more cautious banking policies, i.e., to avoid "kicking the can down the road" and wind down distressed banks sooner rather than later. On the basis of this result, I posit Proposition 1:

Proposition 1 *Democracies are more likely to adopt harsher closure rules, all else constant.*

Proposition 1 flows more or less directly from assumptions about the costs of different banking policies to taxpayers. After all, if taxpayers dislike footing the bill of bank insolvency, and if governments are faithful agents of taxpayers, they will be less likely to "wait and see" for the happy eventuality that distressed banks will deliver good results. However, this proposition is far from trivial. First, the strength of this result does not follow from a government's reaction to a banking crisis, but from government anticipation about the potential burden of insolvency. Second, the comparative statics portrayed in the left panel of Figure 3.3 provide an auxiliary implication, namely, that more egalitarian societies will have more liberal closure rules when holding levels of democracy constant. Third, Proposition 1 holds even when we factor in the possibility that governments may want to prevent systemic risk derived from bank failures, as I show in Section 3.3.1. Finally, the explanatory power of the theory rests not only on this proposition, but on two other testable implications.

The second implication follows from analysis of the risk profile chosen by entrepreneurs. The ease with which one can characterize equilibrium choices of c^* is almost replicated in the analysis of π^* in the right plot of Figure 3.3. Here we find that, in general, π increases as societies become more democratic ($\alpha \to 1$), which means that entrepreneurs would choose investments with lower risk. A logic of anticipation is also at play, as entrepreneurs have incentives to rein in their propensity to take on higher risks once they understand that democratic regimes enact tougher closure rules.[28] Based on these results, I submit Proposition 2:

Proposition 2 *Democracies provide lower incentives to engage in excessive risk taking, all else constant.*

The constraining effect of democracy is also at play in the choice of crony contract, itself a function, among others, of risk profile π^*. Across the board, the size of the crony contract diminishes monotonically on α, as can be gleaned from the left plot in Figure 3.4. For low values of this parameter, lack of democratic accountability means that the government will find it attractive to accept the highest possible crony contract, i.e., $\kappa = 1$. Furthermore, the government's closure rule is increasing in the size of the crony contract (results not shown). In my theory, democracy has a direct effect on the choice of the closure rule through minimization of the burden of financial insolvency, but democracy also has an indirect effect on the choice of closure rule through minimization of crony contracts. In fact, the willingness of democratic governments to accept large crony deals increases with the clarity of signals about future states. Were this signal perfect ($q = 1$), the government would have no qualms accepting the high crony contract because it would be able to avoid the downside risk of a bad payoff (this effect is clearly seen in Equation 3.9). However, the incentive to take on a crony contract decreases very fast once a certain threshold of representation is achieved. After reaching values of $\alpha \approx 0.5$, the choice of crony contract as a function of α continues to decrease, though at a much lower pace. Incidentally, the choice of crony contract is lower in more unequal societies across political regimes. This effect is consistent with assumptions about the preferences of the median voter. When inequality is high, the burden of insolvency will be relatively more onerous to the median voter. To reduce this burden, governments in more unequal societies will choose tougher closure rules, as explained above, but they also choose lower crony contracts (lower κ^*), which in turn increases the equilibrium choice of π^*.

Aside from these metrics, which are of direct interest and are more or less easy to characterize, I briefly consider the predictions of the model concerning

---

[28]The "kinks" in the equilibrium risk profile that appear in the rightmost column are the result of two effects. As $\alpha \to 0$, the equilibrium choice of $\kappa^* = 1$, which eliminates the negative term in the entrepreneur's expected utility in Equation 3.11. A similar result obtains as $q \to 1$; this also results in minimizing the size of the entrepreneur's loss in the bad state of nature, as discussed in Section 3.1.2.

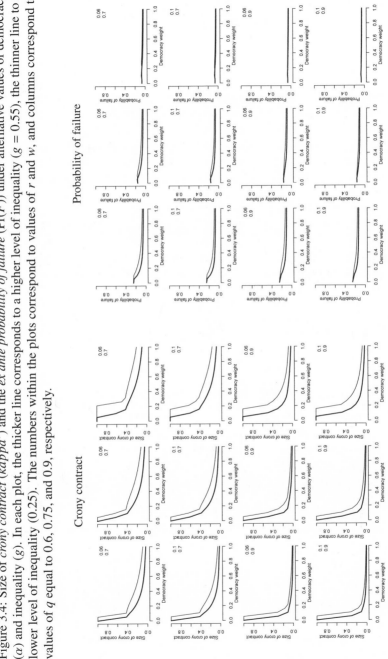

Figure 3.4: *Size of crony contract* (*kappa**) *and the ex ante probability of failure* (Pr(*F*)) under alternative values of democracy (α) and inequality (*g*). In each plot, the thicker line corresponds to a higher level of inequality (*g* = 0.55), the thinner line to a lower level of inequality (0.25). The numbers within the plots correspond to values of *r* and *w*, and columns correspond to values of *q* equal to 0.6, 0.75, and 0.9, respectively.

expected financial losses. For high values of signal q and exogenous parameters w and r, the potential financial loss under Failure is flat for all values of α (plots not shown). But as the signal loses clarity and exogenous parameters take on lower values, the higher risk-taking propensity of entrepreneurs combines with a more liberal government's closure rule to produce higher losses under Failure. The tendency of authoritarian regimes to yield higher losses under Failure is consistent with evidence in Keefer (2007), who finds that democratic regimes tend to produce lower fiscal costs than non-democracies as they seek to contain banking crises.

Finally, I underscore the fact that democratic regimes limit not only the costs of potential failure, but also the probability of failure itself. This is shown in the right plot of Figure 3.4 where, in parallel with the discussion about potential financial losses, inequality seems to have no strong effect on the probability of failure. Note also that the effect of democracy on the probability of failure diminishes as the signal about future endstates becomes clearer. In the limit, as $q \rightarrow 1$, political regimes stop having an impact on the probability of failure. To the extent that political regimes matter, my account suggests that their effect occurs through representation of taxpayers' preferences in an environment of uncertainty about future payoffs. This leads to Proposition 3:

Proposition 3 *Democracies are less likely to suffer banking crises, all else constant.*

The diminished propensity of democracies to meet an endstate of Failure is not necessarily accompanied by a larger propensity to reach Success. Admittedly, the probability of Success is higher for democracies than for authoritarian regimes for high values of q. For lower values of q, however, authoritarian regimes are more likely to achieve higher rates of Success than democracy. It is clear that democratic regimes manage to minimize the probability of Failure by adopting tougher closure rules; these tougher rules do not necessarily guarantee Success, but by more credibly threatening bank closures under high realizations of deposit withdrawals they do manage to avoid very costly instances of bank failure.

3.3.1 Preventing Systemic Risk

Even casual observation of recent banking crises suggests that governments occasionally adopt expensive policies to restore banks to solvency, rather than to merely see them wane. Politicians commonly appeal to the specter of devastating financial meltdowns as a justification for aggressive bailouts. To see why this rationale is important, consider that banks operate as payments clearing-houses that allow economic agents the chance to carry out transactions with minimum effort and that modern economies rely on banks to manage the maturity mismatch in their income and payment streams. Thus, businesses depend on keeping lines of credit open with banks in order to carry out their day-to-day operations. Allowing the failure of large financial intermediaries entails accepting disruptions in the payments system (systemic risk) and decreasing the amount of credit lines available to economic actors (credit crunch). The possibility of a prolonged credit crunch and major disruption in the system of financial intermediation is not one that governments are willing to entertain. As a consequence, some banks and other financial intermediaries can be considered as simply "too big to fail."[29]

As pointed out by Singer (2007), defusing systemic risk is an important rationale behind bank regulation at the domestic level. Here, I consider the possibility of systemic risk as a rationale for avoiding failure at t_2. Within the formal setup, I model this possibility as a requirement that the bank recover full solvency at t_2. This means levying taxes to cover the bank's full financial loss of $-(1 - w)D$ rather than simply the loss of the government loan at t_1. By restoring bank solvency, depositors are assured of recovering their remaining deposits at t_2. This means that their final payoff under failure would be $y_i - (1 - w)\bar{y}$, for a total *taxation* loss to depositor i of $-(1 - w)\bar{y}$ (i.e., there is no direct *deposit* loss).[30] This policy choice corresponds to a bailout in the sense that the full burden of financial insolvency is passed on to taxpayers. As I explain in Chapter 4, the bank itself may merge into a larger entity or be nationalized, but the characteristic feature of "too big to fail" interventions is that a huge portion of the financial burden of bank insolvency becomes a government liability that is ultimately backed by the taxpayer.

Within the logic developed in this chapter, a bank that is big enough to threaten systemic risk would invite a different type of reaction. In particular, the government's decision problem is to leave the bank open upon observation of the "good" signal s_1 if Inequality 3.13 holds:

$$\frac{\pi^*}{1 - q + \pi^* q}\Big(\alpha r(1 - d)y_m + Z(\kappa)\Big)$$
$$\geq \frac{(1 - \pi^*)(1 - q)}{1 - q + \pi^* q}\Big(\alpha(1 - w)\bar{y} + \alpha\kappa w\bar{y}\Big) \quad (3.13)$$

Again, we can solve Inequality 3.13 in terms of d to find the government's

---

[29]On the hazards posed by the failure of large banks, see Stern and Feldman (2004). A variety of "optimal bailout" arguments rationalize support of distressed banks that are not necessarily too big to fail; see for example Aghion, Bolton and Fries (1999); Cordella and Levy-Yeyati (1999); Gorton and Huang (2004).

[30]Because $y_m - dy_m + d\bar{y} < \bar{y}$, the median voter suffers lower loss when the bank *is not* entirely bailed out. The implicit assumption is that the failure of a bank that threatens systemic risk would be so costly that the median voter still prefers a bailout.

closure rule c_s under the threat of systemic risk:

$$d \leq c_s^* \equiv \frac{\pi^* \left(r + \frac{Z(\kappa^*)}{y_m \alpha} \right) - (1 - \pi^*)(1 - q)(1 - w + \kappa^* w) \frac{\bar{y}}{y_m}}{\pi^* r} \qquad (3.14)$$

These changes in the government closure rule under systemic risk also have an impact on the entrepreneur's utility and therefore on her choice of π^*.[31] Consequently, analytical comparison of rules c_d and c_s is rendered difficult because of the indirect effects of α on c_d and c_s through κ and π. I thus resort to the same kind of computational analysis performed in Section 3.3. Figure 3.5 provides a summary comparison of c_d^* and c_s^* (Equations 3.10 and 3.14) under the same set of circumstances explored in Figures 3.3 and 3.4. Rather than directly displaying the behavior of different endogenous parameters under alternative combinations of exogenous variables, the plots in Figure 3.5 display the values of closure rule, risk profile, crony contract, and probability of failure conditional on varying democracy weights but averaged across *all* combinations of exogenous variables. We can read these plots as expectations about the values that endogenous parameters take conditional on political regime.

The most relevant feature revealed by these plots is that the effect of democracy is not altered substantially; compared to non-democratic regimes, democracies still exhibit tougher closure rules, lower risk-taking, and lower probability of failure. In other words, Propositions 1 to 3 hold whether one considers the possibility of systemic risk—banks that are too big to fail—or the more limited intervention in which only the fraction of financial loss that corresponds to government support at t_1 is socialized. Within a given political regime, banks that threaten to irreparably affect the system of financial intermediation benefit from more generous closure rules (Figure 3.5, Plot a) and are likely to offer higher crony contracts to the government (Plot c). Be this as it may, this kind of bank is slightly less prone to take on risk, as suggested by the higher value of π in Plot b. In the end, the combination of these factors leaves banks with and without systemic risk potential about equally likely to fail on average. This is especially true in countries with middling to high democracy weights (Plot d).

3.4 Toward a Strategy of Empirical Validation

I submit that democracies have an advantage over authoritarian regimes in the realm of banking policy, an advantage that stems from the nexus of electoral

---

[31]In contrast with Equation 3.5, the entrepreneur's utility is $\pi [F(c_s^*)] \Pi_E(S) - (1 - \pi)[(1 - q)F(c_{s^*})] \Pi_E(F)$.

Figure 3.5: Average values of *closure rule* (c_d), *risk profile* (π), *crony contract* (κ), and *probability of failure* ($\Pr(F)$) conditional on democracy (α) and *systemic risk* (thicker lines correspond to a bank that threatens systemic risk)

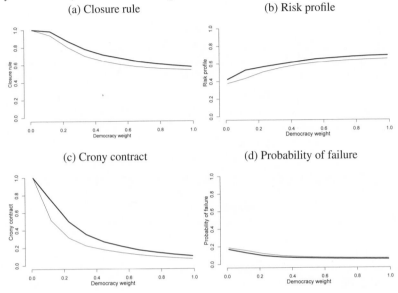

accountability. The fear of electoral retribution in democratic regimes means that politicians are not able to downplay entirely the policy preferences of citizens for avoiding extreme costs in the face of breakdown of the system of financial intermediation. In my argument, electoral accountability keeps politicians on their toes, forcing them not only to minimize public outlays in responding to banking crises, but also intervening forcefully and early on to avoid the multiplication of costs from keeping heavily distressed banks alive. The effects of electoral accountability filter through a government's banking policy to the investment decisions of entrepreneurs. Entrepreneurs anticipate that aggressive risks increase the chances of early and forceful government intervention, which might deprive them of the possibility of seeing their investments to fruition. These alleged effects of democracy on various banking policy aspects are summarized in Propositions 1, 2, and 3. In general, democratic regimes should be associated with smaller crony contracts, tougher closure rules, and lower incentives for risk-taking. Furthermore, democratic regimes should also be associated with lower probabilities of observing costly failures.

My argument does not imply that democratic regimes will *never* engage in bank bailouts, let alone suffer from crippling banking crises. Aside from the most recent spate of bank failures and bank bailouts associated with the US subprime mortgage crisis, politicians in democratic regimes have been called upon multiple times to contain the damage caused by insolvency of financial intermediaries. In the model analyzed in this chapter, banking crises and the choice to prevent financial meltdown by forcing taxpayers to carry the full burden of insolvency occur because of uncertainty about the future state of the economy. In the absence of uncertainty about future entrepreneurial payoffs, governments would be perfectly able to discern a bank's financial status down the line and would intervene early on to minimize the costs of closure. However, governments make decisions that may prove wrong in an environment of uncertainty about future payoffs. The most costly decision is to leave open a bank that eventually proves to be insolvent. In this situation, governments will be stuck with the burden of financial loss, a burden that will in one way or another be carried by taxpayers.

Be this as it may, I do expect the banking policies of democratic regimes to be different on average than those of non-democratic regimes. In the remainder of the book, I will present the case for empirical estimation of this *democratic effect*. Because I rely on observational data, presenting the case for a causal interpretation of a democratic effect on banking policy requires care in setting up empirical models. In fact, I will return in future chapters to some of the auxiliary implications of the argument developed here to guard against potential pitfalls in a strategy of empirical verification. For example, the analysis presented in this chapter suggests that levels of economic inequality exert important effects on banking policy. At the same time, we know from a well-established literature in political economy that economic inequality is an important determinant of democratic consolidation.[32] Consequently, economic inequality is theoretically related to both banking policy and political regimes, and shoud be controlled for in any attempt to estimate the effect of democracy on banking policy. This is not necessarily the case of cronyism. Though I expect an important degree of association between political regime and cronyism, on the one hand, and cronyism and bailout propensities, on the other, I also expect crony contracts to be endogenous to political regime. In this sense, cronyism should be seen as a post-treatment variable that should not be controlled for in models of political regime effects. In Chapters 5 and 6, I look at government bailout propensities under democratic and authoritarian political regimes. These propensities are the empirical correlate of closure rules in this chapter. In Chapter 7, I consider indicators of the risk of failure and aggregate net worth of banking systems, which I construe as empirical proxies of probability of failure and risk-taking profiles. Before embarking

---

[32]See for example Acemoglu and Robinson (2005); Boix (2003); Moore (1966).

on empirical tests of the validity of Propositions 1 through 3, I consider the policy responses of Argentina (a democratic regime) and Mexico (a semi-authoritarian regime) to the *Tequila* crisis and associated bank failures of the mid-1990s. Chapter 4 bridges the gap between the abstract representation of policy actions as parameters in a model and the nitty-gritty details of actual policy-making, and shows that patterns of bank survival in these countries are broadly consistent with expectations derived from my account of the banking policy consequences of political regimes.

4

Argentina and Mexico:
A Closer Look at Bank Bailouts

Models are caricatures of reality that isolate a small number of factors presumed relevant in understanding complex phenomena. Contrary to the simplified portrait of crisis resolution developed in Chapter 3, the day-to-day management of banking crises involves a variety of decisions regarding which banks to close, how to promote recapitalization of the banking system, how to empower banking agencies to deal with problem banks, and how much autonomy to grant to these agencies, among others. I claim that we can look at these policy actions as indicators of the underlying bailout propensities of governments. As suggested in previous chapters, I see these propensities as falling between Bagehot and Bailout ideal-types and consider that policies close to Bailout shift a larger share of the burden of financial insolvency to taxpayers.

In this chapter, I review government responses to the *Tequila* banking crises in Argentina and Mexico. The selection of cases is driven by the fact that these countries were similar in respects presumed relevant by the theory in Chapter 3—both were middle-income economies with unequal patterns of economic opportunity—but differed in one crucial respect: Mexico was still in 1994–1995 a semi-authoritarian regime (admittedly, one in the process of transiting towards open electoral contestation), whereas Argentina was a democratic regime (though one with a chequered political history punctuated by gruesome dictatorial interludes and with remaining authoritarian enclaves). As suggested by the theoretical argument, the set of policies carried out by Argentine decision-makers to address banking sector problems during the *Tequila* crisis exemplify a Bagehot response, whereas the Mexican government response approximates the Bailout model. Ideally, one would trace differences in electoral accountability through the thought processes and political calculations of incumbent politicians all the way to variations in policy implementation. However, few politicians in non-democratic regimes are prone to admit publicly that they remain unmoved by the plight of taxpayers; to the contrary, like their counterparts in democratic regimes, these politicians are quick to argue that their policies safeguard the interests of all.

Thus, I do not provide in this chapter the "smoking gun" of politicians in Argentina that tremble thinking about the wrath of the Argentine voter and thus make haste in striking down distressed financial intermediaries, nor politicians in Mexico laughing off the ineffectual threat of electoral accountability before extending a helping hand to insolvent banks. This chapter offers instead a closer look at how specific policies relate to the Bagehot-Bailout construct of Chapter 1. The chapter shows that though these governments lacked tools that were needed to confront a systemic banking crisis, they both succeeded in altering the rules and framework of supervision and regulation in order to counter liquidity and solvency problems in the banking sector. As a result of these changes, Argentine policy-makers were able to minimize taxpayer expenses, whereas the Mexican response was overtly generous to banks and therefore onerous to taxpayers.

Finally, the chapter inspects the process of resolution of individual banks in these countries for important clues about political motivation. I focus on bank-level information as I seek to understand the determinants of the length of bank survival. A government closer to the Bagehot ideal-type would seek to arrange for the exit of highly distressed banks and would do so in as short a time as possible, whereas a Bailout government would lengthen the survival times of distressed banks and would not necessarily base its decisions about bank exit on the financial status of banks. Rather than indulging in an excessively detailed account of bank restructuring policies, my purpose is to provide a broad outline of how the Argentine and Mexican governments faced problems of liquidity and insolvency in the banking sector.

The chapter is organized as follows. Section 4.1 considers actual policy-implementation in Argentina and Mexico along the five issue-areas identified in Chapter 2. The main evidence regarding the different bailout proclivities of these governments comes from empirical analysis of the Argentine and Mexican processes of bank exit. Section 4.2 shows not only that the exit process of Argentine banks was more rapid, but also that it remained close to the Bagehot ideal-type by eliminating weaker banks. In Mexico, in contrast, financial indicators are not particularly good predictors of bank survival. Finally, I discuss in Section 4.3 some of the reasons why a paired comparison of these two countries is still insufficient to arrive at inferences about the effects of political regimes on banking policy. This discussion paves the way for a broader analysis in the rest of the book.

4.1 Argentina and Mexico in Comparative Perspective

In this section, I summarize the policy actions of the Argentine and Mexican governments with regard to the first four arenas described in Chapter 2: liquidity support, liability resolution, asset resolution, and bank capitalization. These cases differ in their political regimes but are otherwise similar in factors such as economic inequality and level of development. Be this as it may, I do not want to overplay the similarities, as it is difficult to see these cases as "perfect matches" in all but one dimension. To wit, other differences limit my ability to extract conclusions about the effect of political regimes on bank bailouts from this paired comparison. Most importantly, the Argentine and Mexican banking sectors were different in some respects in the run-up to the *Tequila* crisis.

Historically, bank ownership in Latin America has been highly concentrated, and incentives for safe banking practices have not always been in place.[1] In the 1990s, after the first efforts to liberalize the banking sector, the market share of the five biggest banks amounted to 71% in Mexico and 40% in Argentina, compared to 10–30% in developed economies.[2] The Mexican system included 23 private banks (17 banks were reprivatized in 1991–1992 and six more were chartered afterwards), eight public development banks traditionally laden with bad portfolios, and a couple of foreign banks that carried out "second floor" operations (foreign banks were not allowed in retail banking). Mexican commercial banks had been nationalized in 1982 and remained public until 1991, at which time they were auctioned to private investors. The rapid sequence of bank auctions in 1991–1992 replenished government coffers, but left the new private banks severely undercapitalized. Indeed, the average bid-to-book-value ratio for seventeen reprivatized banks was a rather high 3.08 (Solís 1999, 46).[3] Furthermore, prudential bank regulation after privatization remained inadequate.[4]

The Argentine banking system was certainly more competitive, with 73 domestic private banks (which held about 38% of all assets in the banking system), 31 foreign banks, 30 provincial banks, and 34 mutual or co-operative

---

[1] De Krivoy (1996, 23).

[2] *The Economist*, April 12, 1997, p. 36.

[3] On the nationalization see Maxfield (1990) and Elizondo (2001). The process of privatization is told by its main architect in Ortiz Martínez (1994). Changes to the *Ley de Grupos Financieros* in 1990 and 1991 allowed a system of universal banking in which banks could participate in all financial markets (insurance, factoring, retail banking, investment banking, etc.). Passive interest rates and mandatory credit channeling were also eliminated, as were all reserve requirements for commercial banks.

[4] For example, banks presented their balances based on different accounting principles. Indeed, one condition for the US-IMF sponsored bailout of the Mexican treasury was that banks adopted Generally-Accepted Accounting Practices (Rubio 1998, 64).

banks with small market share (about 6% of all assets). Despite the vagaries of Argentine financial history, the set of regulatory reforms that accompanied the Convertibility law of 1991 had created a small but relatively efficient banking system. As I explain below, the Convertibility law turned the *Banco Central de la República Argentina* (BCRA) into little more than a currency board, with limited ability to play the role of lender of last resort to the banking system. Perhaps because of this constraint, Argentine banks were much better capitalized than Mexican banks on the eve of the crisis; in 1994, the average capital-asset ratio was 14.66%, much higher than the 8% recommended by the 1988 Basel Accord, while deposits amounted to 18% of GDP. Throughout the 1990s, the Argentine authorities invested in building a state-of-the-art system of prudential supervision of bank activity (Calomiris 1997).

The Mexican banking crisis started in earnest in December 1994, when the government announced that it would no longer sustain the official peso-dollar exchange rate. The hike in interest rates that followed currency devaluation forced bank debtors into arrears: In the first quarter of 1995, the inter-bank interest rate rose from 34.4% to 109.7%. Currency depreciation also increased the value of dollar-denominated liabilities in bank balance sheets. In short, economic agents were caught overtly exposed to *interest* and *foreign exchange* risks (see Mishkin 1996). However, the deterioration of loan portfolios that led to generalized bank solvency had started well before December 1994. Indeed, the Mexican bank crisis had been brewing for at least two years as non-performing loans accumulated in bank ledgers. After privatization, Mexican banks had aggressively expanded credit to the private sector. This credit expansion was not pernicious *per se*; to the contrary, increased credit availability was one of the purposes behind bank privatization and financial deregulation. Nor was credit expansion surprising, given that in the era of nationalization banks were constrained to serve first the financial needs of the government. Two unforeseen circumstances, however, made credit expansion suspect. First, credit continued to be expensive and spreads between lending and borrowing interest rates remained rather high following privatization. Second, credit increased at the expense of asset quality, which plunged when a speculative bubble in real estate and stock markets burst; when asset prices dropped, strategic defaults became more common.[5] As a result, the official— probably underestimated—proportion of non-performing loans to total loan portfolio in Mexico expanded from 0.99% in 1988 to 9.02% in the months prior to the *peso* devaluation to 18.65% after the crash in 1995.

According to an official account of the crisis, the government entertained three possible strategies to deal with bank insolvency (Secretaría de Hacienda

---

[5] Strategic default occurs when a debtor with paying capacity is better off foregoing collateral than continuing interest payments—i.e., when the unpaid portion of a loan is worth more than collateral.

y Crédito Público 1998). First, do nothing, which would have meant the *de facto* bankruptcy of the banking system, with generalized bank runs and a scramble by banks to cash assets and obtain expensive financing, if any, in international capital markets. The consequences of this choice would have been even higher interest rates and a more pronounced depreciation of the *peso*, both leading to a harsher economic recession. This would have corresponded to the Market extreme of Chapter 1. Second, (re)nationalize the banking system, an extremely costly option as the government would have had to recapitalize banks on its own, would have been subject to political pressures impairing asset recovery, and would have had to compensate expropriated bankers. In short, the second strategy would have implied larger involvement of taxpayers in sharing the losses derived from bank insolvency. The third possibility, which was eventually adopted, was to design a variety of programs to address liquidity and solvency concerns piecemeal. Over the following year, as the extent of bank distress became widely recognized, the Mexican government launched a number of programs that aimed to capitalize banks, reschedule payments for bank debtors, and restructure banks' bad loan portfolios. These actions required the coordinated effort of the *Secretaría de Hacienda y Crédito Público* (SHCP), *Banco de México* (Banxico), and the *Comisión Nacional Bancaria y de Valores* (CNBV), Mexico's bank supervisory agency. Transfers to banks were channeled through the depositor insurance fund, the *Fondo Bancario de Protección al Ahorro* (Fobaproa).

The Argentine bank crisis can also be precisely dated: The crisis started with a deposit run on December 20, 1994, following the devaluation of the Mexican *peso*, and was finally halted in May 1995, after presidential elections returned Carlos S. Menem to a second term in office.[6] Government action to stop the crisis was not immediately forthcoming, and from several accounts it seems to have been insufficient when it finally arrived a couple of weeks into the crisis. As a matter of fact, the banking system improvised a liquidity safety net to stall the deposit run, which was coordinated by the *Banco de la Nación Argentina* (BNA), the largest public bank in the country (Fernández 1995). When the deposit run did not immediately abate, the government reacted by reducing bank reserve requirements, i.e., by allowing banks to cash nonremunerated bank reserves (*encajes*) at the BCRA.[7] Further reductions were granted throughout January, as *encajes* fell from 43%, 3%, and 1% before

---

[6]For accounts of day-to-day aspects of the crisis, see Arnaudo (1996); Banco Central de la República Argentina (1995); D'Amato, Grubisic and Powell (1997); Di Bella and Ciocchini (1995); Fernández (1995); Rozenwurcel and Bleger (1997).

[7]*Encajes* constitute the fraction of every dollar in a deposit account that banks are forced to immobilize, unremunerated, at the Central Bank. In Argentina, these reserves served no monetary purpose—i.e., they were not meant to reduce the effect of the money multiplier mechanism—but worked as implicit *liquidity* insurance.

the crisis—for sight deposits, short-term certificates of deposit (CDs), and medium-term—to 30%, 1%, and 0% by the end of January 1995 (Fernández 1995, 1). Though this action at once freed over 3 billion dollars that were used to pay depositors that fled the system, the amount was not enough to ease the bank run. The December run re-started on February 28 after the Ministry of the Economy announced a "light" fiscal program to alleviate solvency problems in the banking sector. The limited nature of this package suggests that financial authorities miscalculated the extent of bank insolvency, and considered that minimal intervention would suffice at least until the end of the presidential electoral campaign.[8] It was only after this limited package failed to stem the deposit run that Argentine authorities decided to combat insolvency in earnest. By the time the deposit run was finally stopped five months into the crisis, deposits in the Argentine financial system had dropped by $8.8 billion, approximately 19% of total deposits.

After this brief account of the genesis of the *Tequila* crises, I now turn to the different measures that the Argentine and Mexican governments enacted to contain them. I start with a description of how central banks and executive agencies tackled the functions of lender of last resort, asset management, and bank recapitalization.

4.1.1 Liquidity Support

One basic difference between these two countries was the institutional setup within which they conducted monetary policy. Reforms to the charter of the Mexican central bank in 1993 had provided Banxico with relative political autonomy with respect to the executive.[9] Monetary policy was therefore in the hands of a relatively autonomous board with a primary mandate to preserve low inflation in a semi-fixed exchange rate regime, as well as the subsidiary expectation of acting as lender of last resort.

Argentina, instead, had renounced to sovereign monetary policy in an effort to preserve a fixed exchange rate regime. The Organic Charter of the BCRA, approved in 1992, had reaffirmed BCRA's responsibility for oversight and guidance of the financial system—the banking regulatory agency, the *Superintendencia de Entidades Financieras* (SEF), was formally part of the BCRA—but the BCRA was under obligation at all times to keep

---

[8] According to Sturzenegger, "Cavallo [Minister of Economy] never thought that there was a risk of a systemic run, and calculated that he could keep going until May 14, election day, with only very light measures" (Fernández 1996, 79, my translation). This interpretation is endorsed by the *Asociación de Bancos de Argentina* (AdeBA) (see Ribas 1998).

[9] Among the institutional innovations that made political autonomy possible, the new charter established non-overlapping tenure of board members and the executive and provided fixed terms for Banxico board members.

enough reserves to support the technical convertibility ratio.[10] Thus, the 1991 Convertibility Law in essence required Argentina's central bank to turn into a currency board forced to back *pesos* in the domestic economy with an equivalent amount of US dollars in its reserves. In principle, BCRA could perform only very limited last-resort lending functions, whereas Banxico had more latitude in carrying out these functions. The law of Convertibility made policy-makers think that the BCRA could safely eschew instruments to combat systemic bank crises, for these would never occur within a framework of monetary stability. The *Tequila* crisis proved these expectations wrong, and the government had to retool the central bank hastily to confront the crisis (Rozenwurcel and Bleger 1997). As I try to make clear in the following paragraphs, the Argentine government managed to partially free the BCRA from the fetters of Convertibility so that it could participate in managing the banking crisis.

Upon announcement of the *peso* devaluation in December 1994, Banxico joined negotiations with the International Monetary Fund, the United States, Canada, and the Bank of International Settlements for a set of emergency loans amounting to $53 billion.[11] These resources allowed Banxico to increase its lending tenfold to commercial banks in an effort to assuage liquidity concerns. Indeed, Mexican banks faced short-term dollar payments that had become more difficult to fulfill after the devaluation. Over the first quarter of 1995, the Central Bank injected $3.9 billion into sixteen domestic banks, which were able to repay these loans within six months. Prior to privatization of Mexican banks, Banxico had mandated that all banks deposited *encajes* in its vaults—a proportion of each deposit that could be employed to relieve liquidity shocks—but this practice had been eliminated in 1991. Consequently, aside from direct help from Banxico's discount window, the Mexican government's first regulatory measure after the crisis was to force banks to set aside loan loss provisions equal to 60% of past-due loans or 4% of total bank credits. These regulatory measures strengthened the ability of banks to face the immediate deterioration of their loan portfolios, but left banks severely undercapitalized.[12]

Banxico's charter had equipped the central bank with tools to act as lender of last resort, and the emergency rescue package negotiated with international lenders provided it with enough liquidity to help banks confront the currency shock. Furthermore, Mexico had at the time a universal system of depositor insurance that in principle limited the potential for deposit runs. Eventually,

---

[10]The main legal dispositions are included in Law 24.144, passed by Congress on September 23, 1992. This framework was slightly modified by decrees 1860/92 and 1887/92.

[11]Unless otherwise noted, all amounts are in current US dollars.

[12]This section is based on Gavito and Silva (1996); Murillo (2001); Navarrete (2000); Solís (1999).

the Zedillo administration sought to secure even greater autonomy for the central bank, along with a stake in supervising the banking sector. These reforms, however, were passed in 1998; they were informed by the experience of the banking crisis, but were not meant to re-tool Banxico to face the crisis.

In contrast, the Argentine executive decreed measures to broaden the BCRA's margin of action to combat the banking crisis in what became known as the Easter package (Law 24.485, promulgated by decree 538/95 on April 5, 1995). Prior to these measures, the BCRA's Organic Charter included provisions for limited last resort lending subject to the external convertibility constraint. Thus, BCRA loans could not exceed 30 days and could not be larger than the requesting bank's capital. Additionally, banks were mandated to keep reserves (*encajes*) at the central bank (3% for certificates of deposit, 43% for sight deposits), which they could access to confront localized deposit runs. Also in contrast with Mexico, the fixed exchange rate in Argentina was not immediately threatened thanks to the Convertibility law, but the ability of banks to cash sight deposits was imperiled by the extent and speed of the deposit run and by legal limits placed on last-resort lending by the central bank. To counter liquidity problems, the Easter reforms extended repayment schedules for banks accessing the central bank's discount window (from 30 to 90 days) and increased the maximum amounts that the central bank could lend (in any case, the requirement that discount loans should be guaranteed with good collateral remained). Concurrently, the government announced resumption of Argentina's access to the IMF's extended fund facility (2.4 billion dollars), which had expired the previous year, and reduced the reserve requirement that forced banks to keep money in the central bank (Fernández 1995; Rozenwurcel and Bleger 1997).[13]

4.1.2 Liability Resolution

As was the case with the institutional configuration of the monetary authority, Argentina and Mexico differed with regard to the extent of their safety nets for depositors. Undoubtedly, their different arrangements regarding depositor insurance reflected historical experience with previous banking crises. Argentina, to a greater extent than Mexico, had experienced previous banking crises in which the agency in charge of deposit insurance had extended coverage to all depositors, producing heavy losses that were publicly funded (Baliño 1990; Piekarz 1981). In consequence, the architects of the post-Convertibility financial system abolished deposit insurance (Braes-

---

[13]Rozenwurcel and Bleger (1997) provide the following breakdown of resources to stop the deposit run: \$4.1 bn. were freed from reduction in central bank reserve requirements (*reservas*), \$2.2 bn. from direct BCRA assistance (*pases* and *redescuentos*), and \$2.5 bn. from commercial banks' reluctance to extend new loans.

sas and Naughton 1997). The Argentine financial system went practically overnight from enjoying a generous safety net to having none, and indeed some commentators claim that the absence of a safety net for depositors contributed to the propagation of the *Tequila* crisis in Argentina (Ribas 1998). Mexican depositors, in contrast, enjoyed the explicit backing of Fobaproa; the generous protection it afforded depositors was eventually seen as one of the factors producing moral hazard in the Mexican banking system. Against this institutional difference, it is notable that both governments restructured deposit insurance protection radically as they sought to contain solvency and liquidity problems.

In Argentina, the central bank charter explicitly stipulated that the BCRA could not grant guarantees "that directly or indirectly, implicitly or explicitly, covered liabilities of financial entities, including those originating from deposit-taking" (Article 19, Paragraph K, my translation). Small depositors were given seniority status in the event of bank closure, and there was legal basis to use *encajes* (bank reserves in the central bank) to liquidate their deposits.[14] In consequence, one would think that instances of bank closure during the *Tequila* crisis should have produced large losses to depositors, but in fact only a handful of individuals lost money.[15] The reason why depositors failed to take large losses was the creation of system of *asset* resolution that Argentine regulators perfected during the *Tequila* crisis. As mentioned before, it is difficult in practice to separate asset and liability resolution. In the case at hand, the asset resolution mechanism that prevented depositor losses was managed by *Seguro de Depósitos, S.A.* (Sedesa), a deposit insurance agency created in April to manage the *Fondo de Garantía de Depósitos* (Fogade).[16] Stakeholders of Sedesa included the Central Bank and all commercial banks in proportion to the size of their deposits. In calculating each bank's participation in the Fogade, Argentine regulators embraced best practice by requiring payments that were a function of the bank's risk level. Thus, payments to the fund were between 0.015 and 0.06% of all peso- and dollar-denominated deposits. Participation in the fund became mandatory for all banks, domestic or foreign, operating in Argentina.[17]

During the crisis, Sedesa was steered by an Executive Committee that included a BCRA representative alongside four to seven Board members that

---

[14]Law 24.144, modifying the *Ley de Entidades Financieras*, as quoted in Fernández (1994).

[15]To my knowledge, there were only two banks that produced widespread depositor losses: *BCP*, a fraudulent case where it was impossible to make all depositors whole, and *Banco Platense*.

[16]Sedesa's legal framework appeared in Law 24.485/95 and presidential decrees 538/95 and 540/95.

[17]Decree #540/95, Art. 10 bis. According to Hernán del Villar, vice president of Sedesa, only a few banks are Sedesa stockholders. This is so because buying shares was strictly voluntary, while contributing to the fund is strictly obligatory (Buenos Aires, July 11, 2000).

represented bankers. The BCRA representative had veto power, but could not vote. Sedesa's mandate included the obligation to make depositors whole for up to $30,000 in case of bank closure. To do so, Sedesa was awarded the ability to provide fresh capital to banks in the process of regularization and restructuring, banks that had absorbed deposits of closed banks, and banks in the process of acquiring bad banks and undergoing regularization.[18] In other words, Sedesa was an active partner in overseeing Purchase and Assumption (P&A) operations, i.e., partial sales in which "part of the assets of a failing institution are purchased together with part or all of its liabilities" (Lindgren 2005, 79).[19] Upon learning of the decision to close a bank, Sedesa's board could decide to pay off small depositors. However, since revoking a bank's charter entailed undergoing a costly litigation process and risked loss of value of assets, Sedesa could petition the BCRA for a P&A operation as a least costly resolution method. In these cases, liabilities would be transferred to a healthy bank, who would also receive Sedesa funds as compensation. Sedesa could thus guarantee coverage of *all* depositors while minimizing expenses derived from deposit insurance.

Much as a depositor insurance agency was a fundamental piece in carrying out asset resolution policies in Argentina, Mexico's Fobaproa became the agency in charge of the administration of banks' non-performing assets. However, the degree to which Fobaproa's liabilities grew as a consequence of its *asset resolution* operations merits discussing it in the next section.

4.1.3 Asset Resolution

Through legal changes in its ability to act as lender of last resort, the BCRA obtained tools to confront liquidity shortfalls in Argentina's banking system. Along with these changes, the Easter package reformed Article 35-Bis of the *Ley de entidades financieras*, which established the legal framework that allowed the central bank to transfer assets and liabilities from insolvent to solvent banks. The BCRA board obtained the power to hand-pick assets to be transferred to healthier banks, thus precluding insolvent banks from dropping non-performing loans off their balance sheets at will. This was a crucial difference when compared to the Mexican experience in restructuring banks.

The Easter reform package also ensured that the executive and the BCRA would not face judicial action for acts related to the suspension and revocation of bank charters, except where the existence of purposeful malfeasance could

---

[18] As I explain below, a different fund was set up to aid recapitalization efforts.

[19] In these operations, an insolvent bank gets stripped of its good assets, which are transferred to a receiving bank along with matching liabilities. Solvent banks have an incentive to receive these packages because they neither add to nor subtract from their balance, and they improve their market share.

be substantiated (Fernández 1996, 8). Thus, Article 35-Bis delivered a powerful tool to the BCRA. In practice, Article 35-Bis allowed complete cession of controlling rights over private property from commercial banks to the central bank, without congressional or judicial oversight. A check to arbitrary action was provided in that Article 35-Bis could only be invoked with the *explicit consent* of a bank approaching the BCRA for liquidity assistance. In other words, an illiquid bank would accept the possibility of dismemberment in exchange for liquidity support. Thus, the provisions of Article 35-Bis also served as a screening device: Fear of dismemberment guaranteed that banks would self-select into this facility when they were basically solvent despite liquidity problems. Moreover, since provisions included strict upper bounds on the amount of money (and length of time) that banks were allowed to borrow, Article 35-Bis prevented the BCRA from throwing taxpayers' money into a financial black hole.

The BCRA's power to alienate balance sheet items came, at least in theory, with no strings attached, i.e., there was no need to compensate a good bank for absorbing a bad bank. However, as I explained before, the creation of Sedesa allowed the possibility of supporting receiving banks. More importantly, Sedesa's participation in P&A operations was instrumental in establishing good incentives for resolution of bad assets. After transferring a balanced portfolio of loans and deposits from an insolvent to a solvent bank, Sedesa established fiduciary trusts managed by private corporations to administer the non-performing assets of the closed bank. The receiving bank had seniority over any assets recovered by the trust; Sedesa, instead, was only a subordinate claimant.

This virtuous incentive structure was not replicated in Mexico. On the asset side of bank ledgers, the Mexican government allowed the survival of insolvent banks *sine die* through (i) direct support to bank borrowers and (ii) subsidized purchases of bad loans. The first policy was organized mostly around the creation of *Unidades de Inversión* (UDIs), a new unit of account that preserved the real value of loans. Because of the inflationary spiral set in motion by the *peso* devaluation, bank debtors were facing a tilted loan payment schedule. Debtors that chose to restructure their peso-denominated loans into UDI-denominated loans became protected from interest rate risk (i.e., the risk that their interest payments would increase explosively) in exchange for lengthier payment schedules. Banks benefited because UDI-denominated loans guaranteed a constant flow of income on interest payments and prevented further defaults. However, banks continued to pay nominal interest rates on deposits, and therefore continued to bear interest-rate risks. This mismatch between bank incomes and expenses would obviously have aggravated their capitalization problems had the Mexican government not assumed potential losses from hikes in nominal interest rates. To do so, banks received UDI-denominated loans from the government for each credit they managed to restructure. In addition, as we shall see below, banks also exchanged their non-performing loans for government bonds that paid *nominal* interest rates. From the point of view of the government, UDI loans were assets on which the government received *real* interest rates, whereas government bonds were liabilities on which it paid *nominal* interest rates. Consequently, neither bankers nor debtors bore the total brunt of interest rate risk, but this risk was *de facto* socialized. Three years into the crisis, the market value of loans restructured under the UDI program was $17.3 billion.

Unfortunately, the first UDI programs, which targeted small- and medium-sized enterprises as well as mortgage-owners, did not completely abate loan defaults. The main problem was that the market value of collateral was still lower than the value of the restructured debt, so many debtors still faced incentives for strategic default. Consequently, the government started a second debtor program—the *Programa Emergente de Apoyo a Deudores de la Banca* (ADE)—on August 23, 1995. ADE's purpose was to support heavy discounts in interest rates during a year to help debtors stay current in their payments. The program immediately benefited holders of performing loans; debtors in arrears could participate in the program upon rescheduling loan payments to banks. Generous discounts in interest rates were eventually absorbed by the taxpayer: Interest rates were discounted from 65 to 38.5% on credit cards, from 52 to 34% on consumer loans, from 52 to 24% on commercial loans, and from 50 to 6.5% on mortgage loans. About two million loans were restructured under ADE by the end of 1996. Both ADE and *Punto Final*, a fourth debtor program whose description I omit (see Calomiris, Klingebiel and Laeven 2005, 37-40), managed to stop further deterioration of bank loan portfolios. More than four years into the crisis, the share of non-performing loans tied to housing, industry, and agriculture finally started to abate during the last quarter of 1999 (Murillo 2001).

The second asset resolution policy pursued by the Mexican government aimed to swap non-performing loans from commercial banks for government bonds. This policy, the Loan Purchase and Recapitalization Program, was implemented through Fobaproa. Fobaproa had been created in 1990 to substitute for Fonapre, the previous depositor insurance agency.[20] Like Fonapre, Fobaproa rested on charging flat insurance—as opposed to risk-based—premia to participating banks.[21] Fobaproa's coverage was almost universal, as it only excluded subordinate obligations, liabilities derived from irregular, illegal, or fraudulent contracts, and credit derivatives; all bank

---

[20] The *Ley de Instituciones de Crédito* was reformed on July 18, 1990, to create Fobaproa.

[21] Banks were required to pay as much as $5 to $7 for every $1,000 under Fobaproa, a much higher premium than under Fonapre.

deposits were covered regardless of size. Banks were expected to participate actively in guaranteeing deposits and were required to extend guarantees of repayment upon accessing Fobaproa's facilities.

By September 1994, three months before the *peso* devaluation, Fobaproa held assets valued at $1.8 billion, which were drastically insufficient to face obligations derived from the banking crisis. Indeed, by the first quarter of 1995, Fobaproa had already extended guarantees for $15 billion (Solís 1999, 76). If we consider that bank privatization in 1991–1992 netted the government $12.4 billion, the extent of governmental intervention to stop the banking crisis becomes painfully clear. Fobaproa became an ever more important agency within the government's bailout strategy as the bank crisis extended. As a percentage of total outlays to restore bank solvency, Fobaproa's expenses grew from 47% in 1995 to 76% in 1998. As a percentage of GDP, Fobaproa's liabilities increased from 2.4% to 10.9% from 1995 to 1998 (Solís 1999, 81). Fobaproa's liabilities ballooned because its use as an asset purchasing device exceeded its more limited expected role as guarantor of deposits. The swap mechanism that the Mexican authorities designed worked as follows: Banks sold past-due loans to Fobaproa, which bought them with 10-year non-negotiable interest-bearing bonds backed by the government.[22] These bonds paid Cetes interest rates quarterly.[23] Upon maturity in 2005, Fobaproa bonds have been swapped for other interest-bearing notes. Thus, the bulk of Fobaproa's liabilities continues to burden public finances even thirteen years after the beginning of the banking crisis.[24]

By swapping non-performing assets for bonds the government managed to prevent continued deterioration of banks' loan portfolios, but the related goal of recovering collateral on non-performing assets was not achieved. In the government's calculus, recovered assets would be used to liquidate outstanding Fobaproa bonds. Contrary to what happened in Argentina, however, banks were free to choose which loans to exchange for Fobaproa bonds and to propose an asking price for these loans. Needless to say, bank managers transferred their worst portfolio to Fobaproa, which ended up paying hefty amounts for worthless assets, including crony loans.[25] The share of bank loan

---

[22]Simultaneously, the government tied a new recapitalization program—the Programa de Capitalización Permanente (Procapte)—to Fobaproa. I describe Procapte in Section 4.1.4.

[23]Cetes are *Certificados de Tesorería*, the Mexican government's *peso*-denominated short-term paper.

[24]As of December 31, 2007, the balance sheet of the *Instituto para la Protección al Ahorro Bancario*, the successor to Fobaproa, reported total assets amounting to 39.2 billion pesos and total liabilities of 752.9 billion pesos, for a deficit of around 713.7 billion pesos (about $67.7 billion dollars). Data from www.ipab.org.mx, last accessed on April 11, 2008. In 1998, the reform of banking laws allowed conversion of 63% of Fobaproa assets into public debt, while the other non-performing loans were returned to the originating banks.

[25]After the July 1997 midterm elections returned a divided Congress, opposition parties

portfolios that were transferred to Fobaproa was staggering. For example, one of the largest banks—*Banca Serfín*—transferred about 47.9% of its loan portfolio to Fobaproa (Murillo 2001, 28). In time, it became obvious that asset resolution through traditional asset warehouse mechanisms would not be possible. In other national experiences of bank restructuring, governments had set up specialized agencies to manage and liquidate non-performing loans (Calomiris, Klingebiel and Laeven 2005; Dziobek 1998). These agencies seldom micro-manage loan portfolios or monitor the performance of individual lenders. Instead, they assemble non-performing loans in bundles of varying quality and auction them to interested bidders. Fobaproa sponsored two such auctions for asset packages.[26] The first auction netted a little over 10% of the face value of some of the best assets owned by Fobaproa, whereas the second failed to attract any bidders. Consequently, the government decided to reinstate recovery of non-performing loans to the banks that originally held them, with the understanding that whatever income they managed to obtain would go to Fobaproa. Bankers had weak incentives to recover bad assets, since they were only required to carry 25% of losses, while the rest would be absorbed by the government (Murillo 2001).

4.1.4 Bank Capitalization

The main instrument to aid bank recapitalization efforts in Argentina was the *Fondo Fiduciario de Capitalización Bancaria* (FFCB).[27] To set up the FFCB, the Argentine government issued a 10-year "patriotic bond" (*Bono Argentina*) for $2 billion, which was mainly subscribed by large Argentine corporations, and a complementary World Bank-Inter American Development Bank loan for $2.6 billion.[28] The directorate of FFCB included representatives from large domestic banks, foreign banks, and bondholding corporations. Since the FFCB was partially funded by the Argentine executive, it was staffed by the Ministry of the Economy, not by the central bank.

Loans from the FFCB would be doled out at market rates, would mature

---

carried out an independent audit of Fobaproa's assets (Mackey 1999). These audits revealed that Fobaproa bought assets derived from connected lending to bank insiders or from speculative behavior by stockbrokers. The Ministry of Finance was forced to recognize that only about 30% of all Fobaproa assets were recoverable (Navarrete 2000, 54–59).

[26]Rather, the agency in charge of these auctions was *Valuación y Venta de Activos*, an asset valuation and sale facility created in 1996, which became the *Dirección de Activos Corporativos* in 1997.

[27]The Fiduciary Fund for Bank Capitalization was created by decree 445/95, thus avoiding congressional debate over its organization or mandate.

[28]The patriotic bond and the World Bank loan actually financed two different funds: the FFCB, which purported to aid in the recapitalization of the private bank sector, and the *Fondo Fiduciario de Desarrollo Provincial*, which fostered the privatization of provincial banks (on provincial banks see Clarke and Cull 2002).

after seven years, and would be used to constitute fresh Tier II capital (this meant that the FFCB's claimant status was junior to that of depositors, but senior to bank shareholders' capital). Bank stockholders were expected to come up with matching funds to constitute fresh Tier I capital. Moreover, banks capitalized under this scheme were subject to close supervision by the *Superintendencia de Entidades Financieras*, which ensured compliance with a restructuring scheme agreed upon by bank and government. In addition, the FFCB controlled the lending rates of recipient banks with the stated purpose of avoiding gambling for resurrection practices.[29] The FFCB had some leeway in the use of its funds. Up to 5% of its resources, a meager amount by any standard, could be used to finance other types of operations.[30] The FFCB directorate decided that its limited funds could best be used to recapitalize ailing banks, than to acquire what would anyway be insubstantial amounts of non-performing assets.[31]

The framework and organization of FFCB were transparent and readily understandable. The demarcation criterion that the FFCB followed in deciding which banks to help is less clear. In principle, the FFCB directorate was solely in charge of deciding which banks to fund. But two selection mechanisms ensured that only banks with viable restructuring projects would arrive at the FFCB. First, ailing banks had to clear their restructuring project through SEF, which officiated as a first gatekeeper. Second, an FFCB refusal meant reputation losses for the ailing bank, so formal petitions were always preceded by informal consultations. Hence, there were strong incentives for self-selection that forced bad banks out of asking help from the FFCB.[32]

---

[29] The FFDC composed an operational credit rulebook, voted by its board members, which described the guidelines it would follow to aid banks. These guidelines established that loans should pay 1% over the World Bank's lending rate, provided that the loans funded mergers or acquisitions. The relevant rate would be LIBOR+4 for capitalization funds or for liquidity loans (Acta número 11, *Reglamento operativo de crédito*, August 1, 1995, Art. 10). In practice, the FFCB lent money at LIBOR+2, and afterwards even at lower rates. With regard to the upper bound on loans, the following rules applied: FFCB could lend up to 25% of the requesting bank's risk-adjusted assets to finance stock purchases, 15% to fund mergers, and 10% in case of restructuring.

[30] As a matter of fact, FFCB's first loans were granted for liquidity purposes or, rather, to allow banks to repay last-resort loans to the BCRA. Interview with Dr. Enrique Folcini, former President of the BCRA and former Director of the FFCB, July 27, 2000. By October 1996, the BCRA calculated that banks still needed to repay $453.5 million dollars for liquidity assistance. To this amount one should add $814.2 million that had already been paid, and $254.3 million dollars guaranteed with public bonds (Fernández 1996, 8).

[31] Hugo N.L. Bruzzone, Assistant to the Director, Banco Macro (July 23, 2000).

[32] Hard data on the number, let alone the identity, of petitioners is not available, but FFCB honored about half the number of requests it received and conducted about 20 to 25 transactions involving ca. sixty banks. Incidentally, Calomiris and Mason (2003) report that the Reconstruction Finance Corporation happened upon a triage mechanism that allowed it to deny support to banks that were deemed "hopelessly insolvent" in the aftermath of the Great Depression; the

Anecdotal evidence suggests that the FFCB was somewhat arbitrary in its lending decisions. Even FFCB officials accepted that there was no deep analysis of the merits of each case. Instead, the working knowledge that FFCB's directorate had of bank managers seemed to determine who would be supported. This need not mean that FFCB's decisions departed drastically from what would have obtained under a more serene case-by-case analysis. After all, the directorate internalized the knowledge and preferences of important market players, well acquainted with the moral qualities of bankers. FFCB was an integral part of the government's restructuring policies; its existence allowed a swifter and less controversial process of bank exit because bank closure was easier to carry through after a bank failed to obtain FFCB support. Without this support, the BCRA had a stronger case to close the bank without fearing judicial action on behalf of stockholders or depositors.[33] Thus, FFCB support provided access to fresh funds, but it was also a boost to a bank's credibility.

The Mexican government enacted the *Programa de Capitalización Temporal* (Procapte) with the avowed purpose of helping banks comply with minimum capital regulatory requirements (at least a 9% capital-asset ratio). Given the extant problem of non-performing loans, forcing banks to increase loan loss provisions at the beginning of the crisis had left many of them severely undercapitalized. Thus, to prevent banks from falling below mandated capital-asset ratios, Banxico doled out credit to troubled banks that desired to participate in the program. As was the case with Argentina's FFCB, Banxico participations were considered Tier II capital, with the added proviso that these would turn into ordinary bank shares if loans were not amortized within five years and that Fobaproa could demand conversion of Procapte loans into ordinary bank shares sooner if the bank's capital ratio fell below 9%. Bankers had the prerogative of buying these obligations back at any time during the five-year period in order to avoid losing ownership of their banks. Originally, Tier II capital was included in mandatory capital requirements (after reforms to banking laws in December 1998, Tier II capital no longer counted towards fulfillment of this requirement). Six banks had entered Procapte by April 1995; within eighteen months, most of them had settled their debt with Procapte ($6.5 billion pesos), with the exception of two banks that were thus "intervened" by Fobaproa (Murillo 2001). After Procapte was closed off, further recapitalization efforts were conducted through Fobaproa,

---

Corporation's independent status made this possible in their account.

[33]There were about five instances of judicial action against Central Bank officials that were started by members of Congress, which at the time were construed as proof of congressional involvement in the restructuring process. However, a great majority of judicial actions were started instead by disgruntled depositors that took losses (*Denuncias contra directores de B.C.R.A.*, private communication with Manuel Domper).

whose main characteristics I have already described. Fobaproa's capitalization program was meant to match shareholders' capital injections with bad asset purchases in a proportion of 2-to-1, i.e., for every peso that shareholders managed to raise, Fobaproa would buy 2 pesos in non-performing loans. However, it is well known that purchases of non-performing loans were not always matched by injection of fresh capital, but by *promises* that these injections would occur. Consequently, Fobaproa purchases were more generous than the official 2-to-1 ratio (Rubio 1998). By 1998 bankers had managed to raise up to $3.7 billion in fresh capital, and purchases of non-performing loans amounted to about $10 billion (see Murillo 2001, 27).

Eventually, the only way to rebuild the capital buffer of Mexican banks was by allowing an expanded role for foreign capital. Within the framework of NAFTA, Mexico had agreed to liberalize the domestic financial sector during a transition period that would start in 1994 and end in December 1999. During the transition period, caps on foreign investment in Mexican banks would be kept at 1.5% of capital share for a single bank and 15% globally.[34] After the banking crisis hit, these limits were almost immediately extended to 49% and 25%, respectively, and eventually were eliminated to allow outright foreign purchases of domestic banks. As we will see in Section 4.2, the modal way of bank exit in Mexico became purchase by a foreign bank. In fact, the main structural consequence of the Mexican banking crisis is that foreign capital became primordial in the banking sector. In 1994, 6.4% of capital share belonged to foreign shareholders, and only 1.3% was tied to banks over which foreigners had majority control. By 2001, total foreign participation had increased to 87.6% (Murillo 2001). These measures were unable to reactivate credit in Mexico: In 1994, bank credit to the private sector as a proportion of GDP was 0.43. It declined precipitously since then, reaching a low of 0.089 in 2001 (Murillo 2001).

4.2 Exit Policy in Argentina and Mexico

The set of regulatory changes that Argentina and Mexico undertook after 1994 allowed their governments the ability to dictate the pace of bank exit as they saw fit. Exit policy is the rule that politicians and bureaucrats follow in deciding which banks to support and which banks to close. I focus on exit policy because the degree to which governments extend the life of insolvent banks provides key insights into their bailout propensities. Exit policy is the centerpiece of crisis management, as all the other policies inspected in the previous section equip decision-makers with the tools to arbitrate between

---

[34] In this context, capital share is the ratio of a bank's shareholder capital to total capital in the industry.

bank insolvency and bank exit. A lax bank exit policy has both indirect and direct costs. By failing to enforce exit, a lax policy gives bankers a chance to gamble for resurrection and likely increases resolution costs down the road. Direct costs obtain because an insolvent bank stays in business through implicit or explicit public transfers that may not be recovered. The costs of bank crisis resolution—i.e., the burden passed on to the taxpayer—increase with the amount of time that passes between bank insolvency and bank exit.

I base my analysis of bank exit on balance-sheet information compiled from publications of the *Comisión Nacional Bancaria y de Valores* in Mexico and the *Superintendencia de Entidades Financieras* in Argentina.[35] The Argentine data comprise *monthly* balance sheets for the full population of 164 banks and mutual banks that operated in the country during at least part of the period from March 1991 to August 1998; in Mexico, I have bank balance sheets for the population of 59 banks observed *quarterly* from December 1991 to June 2000. Differences in the length of the observation period correspond to differences in the length of the process of bank exit, which was decidedly faster in Argentina. Because of differences in the total number of banks and the frequency of balance sheet reports, the Argentine dataset comprises 7,180 bank/month observations, against 1,104 bank/quarter observations in the Mexican dataset.

The analysis is organized as follows: Section 4.2.1 offers a stylized description of the decision problem that politicians face when dealing with insolvent banks on an individual basis, and details the coding rules that I followed in deciding when a bank had exited the system. This is a preamble to the main goal, which is to explore empirically how politicians solve this decision problem in actual bank crisis contexts. I achieve this by developing and estimating a duration model of bank exit in Section 4.2.2. This model takes into consideration the layout, limitations, and advantages of bank balance-sheet data as well as the peculiar pattern of bank lifespans in Argentina and Mexico. Section 4.3 concludes with a discussion of crisis-management policies in these countries.

4.2.1 Bank Exit in Theory and Practice

Policy-makers confront two problems in deciding which banks to close: First, the "true" solvency status of banks is not readily observable. In Chapter 3, I captured this basic uncertainty by assuming that governments observe an imperfect signal about the financial status of illiquid banks. Uncertainty is larger in financial systems without first-class accounting standards and without arrangements for accurate market valuation of banks, but even in de-

---

[35] I acquired the Argentine data through BCESWIN, a private financial consulting company.

Figure 4.1: Modes of bank continuation or exit observed in Argentina and Mexico

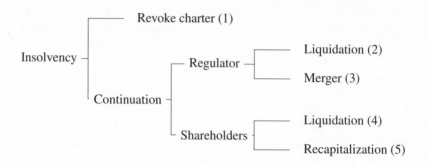

veloped economies it is difficult to assess the exact financial status of banks.[36] This makes it difficult to comply with the main dictum in Bagehot's doctrine—close insolvent banks, provide liquidity to good banks. It is therefore common to see banks surviving for long periods after the beginning of a banking crisis, even in situations that approximate the Bagehot ideal-type.

Second, the options that regulators have at their disposal to solve bank distress are certainly not as simple as close or leave open. Figure 4.1 offers a stylized description of a bank's exit process as a sequence of dilemmas. Following recognition of insolvency, the regulator chooses between mutually exclusive actions at each node in the decision tree: Should the insolvent bank's charter be immediately revoked or should it be allowed to continue? If so, should the government appoint a manager to oversee bank continuation or should the bank remain under the control of its shareholders? The decision tree ultimately leads to three distinct outcomes: *liquidation, recapitalization,* and *merger* with another bank.[37] Except for immediate suspension of a bank's charter, all other options in Figure 4.1 imply continuation of an insolvent bank in the short run. For example, politicians might sponsor takeovers of troubled

---

[36]Consider how difficult it has proven to price the "toxic assets" held by banks during the subprime-mortgage crisis.

[37]I emphasize that *bank insolvency* and *bank closure* are not necessarily related. The econometric literature on the US S&L crisis sometimes downplays this distinction. For example, Thomson (1992) codes a bank as *failed* when it is liquidated, merged, intervened, *or requires FDIC assistance to remain open* (Thomson 1992, 9, my emphasis). However, as Cole and Gunther (1995) argue, bank exit is ultimately a regulatory choice, not necessarily a market outcome.

banks under the administration of a banking agency through a subsidized P&A operation (merger) or by selling the bank after removing non-performing loans from its balance sheet (liquidation). Liquidation entails paying off insured depositors, writing off non-performing loans, collecting whatever residual loans are left, and then selling the bank's physical infrastructure. In contrast, an insolvent bank may be kept under its original ownership and management, taking advantage of governmental willingness to engage in regulatory forbearance. In some cases, the bank will only regain solvency status through new capital injections from the original shareholders or from new investors.[38]

Despite the manifold intricacies of the closure process, what really matters in defining bank exit is whether the government has wrestled control rights over managerial decisions from the original bank owners (cf. Lindgren 2005, 79). The Argentine and Mexican governments reformed existing regulation to provide banking agencies with the ability to manage the process of bank exit. In both cases, most insolvent banks were eventually sold to or merged into solvent institutions, after undergoing a period of administration by bank regulators. In the Argentine case, these periods of administration by a banking agency were brief and mostly ended up with merger operations subsidized by the FFCB and Sedesa, as explained before; the modal form of bank exit in Argentina could be characterized as falling in node 3 in Figure 4.1. In Mexico, node 3 was also the main way through which banks exited the system, though the process of intervention was in some instances lengthier than originally planned (Murillo 2001). Moreover, the process of exit of four Mexican banks is best characterized as liquidation after administration by original shareholders (node 4). In these four cases, the regulatory agency practiced an administrative, as opposed to managerial, intervention, which for all practical purposes left day-to-day decisions in the hands of the original bank managers. Given that the relevant benchmark to consider a bank as closed is to assess whether original stockholders have ceased to control their bank, I consider *government-induced mergers*, *managerial interventions*, and *liquidations* to be instances of bank exit.[39] In consequence, I code the occurrence of any of these events as a bank closure or exit; I do not consider administrative interventions as instances of bank exit.

---

[38] On the process of bank restructuring see Dziobek and Pazarbasioglu (1999); Enoch, Garcia and Sundararajan (1999); Hawkins and Turner (1998); Lindgren (2005).

[39] Private mergers—i.e., those not sponsored by the regulator—as well as voluntary exits from the banking system are not common in the data. In Mexico, only two banks (*Fuji* and *Nations*, both foreign) left the system voluntarily. Voluntary mergers and voluntary exits from Argentina's financial system were more common for foreign banks before the *Tequila* crisis (eight instances). For the sake of simplicity, I code these voluntary exits as forced closures, but also control for the foreign ownership status of banks, so in any case this coding decision does not affect inferences about the survival rates of other types of banks.

Table 4.1: Distribution of "bank durations" in Argentina, in months, from March 1991 to August 1998. Cell entries contain number of banks classified by type of ownership and endstate. "Censored" banks are those that survived through the end of the observation period.

| | Domestic banks | | | | Foreign banks | |
| | Mutual banks | | Private | | | |
Duration	Censored	Closed	Censored	Closed	Censored	Closed
0–10		3		3	3	2
11–20		2		1	1	
21–30		3	2	2		
31–40				2		
41–50		12	3	5	1	1
51–60		16	2	12		1
61–70			2	3		3
71–80		2	2	4		
81–90	5		32	8	24	2
Total	5	38	43	40	29	9
Share (%)	14	86	52	48	76	24

These yardsticks lead in most cases to uncontroversial coding decisions, but the exact timing of bank exit is not always obvious. In Mexico, CNBV stopped publishing the balance sheets of seven banks several quarters before finally intervening them.[40] The alleged purpose of these embargoes was to allow on-site inspectors to gather accurate information about the bank before deciding whether to intervene or not. During these quarters, banks still remained in the hands of their original managers. For this reason, I code bank exit as corresponding to the quarter at which the bank was finally intervened by the regulator, even if this means having missing values for the final quarters of some banks' lifespans.

Though lags between *last observation* and *actual bank exit* are more conspicuous in the Mexican database, the Argentine set is not without flaw. Some closed banks show the exact same information in the last two or three periods leading to their closure. Given that bank balance-sheet data in Argentina are reported *monthly*, this delay in closing banks after the last publication of their financial status is not excessive. Thus, I code the last month for which data are published as the exit time of Argentine banks, even if their last monthly report shows no variation from the next-to-last report. Exit times so defined coincide with public announcements of bank closures as they appear in secondary sources and internal memoranda of the Argentine central bank.

Tables 4.1 and 4.2 summarize information on bank survival spells in these two countries during the 1990s. The cross-tabulations sort banks by the duration of their lifespans (rows), by their endstate (columns distinguish *censored* from *closed*) and by ownership category (meta-columns distinguish *foreign* from *domestic* banks, and in the case of Argentina *domestic banks* from *domestic mutual banks*). These tables display variation in the life histories of Argentine and Mexican banks, though they eschew information on the different *entry* and *exit* points of banks. In fact, bank lifespans in Mexican and Argentine banks are not entirely overlapping; this means that there is not a single period (i.e., month or quarter) in these countries during which the entire population of banks were in operation.

4.2.2 Determinants of Bank Survival

I argued in Section 4 that many of the policies implemented by the Mexican government in the wake of the banking crisis can be best described as Bailout policies, whereas the Argentine government's crisis-management policies approach the Bagehot ideal-type. When it comes to exit policy, we would

---

[40]The following banks show lags (measured in quarters) between their last published balance and the date of regulatory intervention (Mackey 1999; Solís 1999): *Anáhuac* (5), *Capital* (3), *Confía* (3), *Industrial* (2), *Inverlat* (2), *Promotor del Norte* (8), and *Sureste* (3). Mackey (1999) finds these embargoes to be in line with experiences in other countries.

Table 4.2: Distribution of "bank durations" in Mexico, in quarters, from December 1991 to June 2000. Cell entries contain number of banks classified by type of ownership and endstate. "Censored" banks are those that survived through the end of the observation period.

	Domestic banks		Foreign banks	
Duration	Censored	Closed	Censored	Closed
0–5		2		
6–10		6		1
11–15	1	8	2	1
16–20			16	
21–25	7	6		
26–30	2			
31–35	5	1		
Total	15	23	19	2
Share (%)	40	60	90	10

expect a Bagehot government (i) to carry out the process of bank exit promptly and (ii) to base the decision to close banks exclusively on their solvency status. Certainly, even a Bagehot government might postpone the first bank closures after the beginning of a banking crisis if it lacks precise information about the extent of damage to a bank's loan portfolio. At a minimum, however, we would still expect financial solvency indicators to be the best predictors of the *length of survival* of banks in the aftermath of a banking crisis.

A first glance at bank exit in Argentina and Mexico supports the view that this process was relatively swift in the first country. Figure 4.2 shows non-parametric estimates of the survival of Argentine and Mexican banks *after* December 1994. These estimates are based exclusively on the lifespans of banks that were already in operation in these countries during the fourth quarter of 1994 as the banking crises started (134 in Argentina, 24 in Mexico); the observation window extends through the third quarter of 1998, at which point surviving banks become "censored."[41] To allow direct comparison, bank survival lengths in Mexico are expressed in months even though information is only available quarterly. The narrower interval estimates of the proportion of

---

[41]Censored banks are those that survived throughout the end of the observation window. That is, since they were not closed by the end of this observation window, the length of their actual survival is "censored."

Figure 4.2: Non-parametric (Kaplan-Meier) estimates of bank survival in Argentina and Mexico after the onset of the *Tequila* crisis. The solid line corresponds to the mean survival rate; broken lines are 95% confidence intervals.

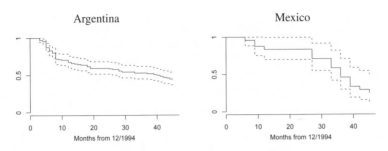

surviving banks in Argentina reflect a larger bank population as well as higher observation frequency (months rather than quarters). Based on the observed duration of banks, I estimate one-year survival rates to be 67.4% (with a 95% confidence band of 59.7–75.6) in Argentina, and 83.3% in Mexico (69.7–99.7%). These estimates suggest that a government like Mexico's would have intervened or closed down 17% of banks a full year into a banking crisis, whereas a government similar to Argentina's would have forced the exit of 32%.

This finding comports well with the view that Bagehot governments close insolvent banks promptly. However, one is still left to wonder whether indicators of bank insolvency are good predictors of bank exit in Argentina, as corresponds to a Bagehot government. The main indicator of financial insolvency is a bank's capital-asset ratio. In principle, a bank's CAR contains sufficient information about its ability to withstand distress, and is therefore the main indicator that regulators employ to decide whether a bank should remain under shareholders' control (Freixas and Rochet 1997, 275–279). If the Argentine government acted as a stern Bagehot enforcer of market outcomes, we would expect a bank's CAR to be a negative predictor of its *hazard rate* (alternatively, a positive predictor of *bank survival* or *duration*). In contrast, we would not expect CAR to be a good predictor of bank duration in Mexico if authorities in that country were indeed bailout-prone. I estimate the association between a bank's capital-asset ratio in December 1994 and the length of its lifespan up to August 1998 in Argentina, or June 2000 in the case of Mexico. Aside from CAR, I also include *bank size* (the value of bank assets) as an additional regressor. I do so because some banks may have been considered "too big to fail" (Stern and Feldman 2004); a Bagehot government should in principle resist the urge to postpone exit of an insolvent bank, regardless of size.

Table 4.3 summarizes the posterior distribution of effect parameters in a Bayesian exponential survival model.[42] Covariates *CAR* and *bank size* are standardized, so their coefficient estimates can be interpreted as the expected change in the linear predictor of a bank's hazard rate that would follow from shifting values of covariates one standard deviation away from the mean. Prima facie, it would seem that there is scant difference between Argentina and Mexico in terms of their propensity to bail out larger banks. In both cases, the coefficient on *bank size* is centered about -1, and the posterior distribution of this parameter is clearly bounded away from 0 (note that the credible intervals do not straddle 0). A bank with *CAR* and *bank size* fixed at Argentina's mean sample values would be expected to last about 38 months; a bank one standard deviation larger than Argentina's mean *bank size* would survive about 105 months. In Mexico, comparable expected durations are 40 and 73 months. Not only are larger banks expected to last longer in both countries, but capital-asset ratios are good predictors of bank survival in both countries. Admittedly, better capitalized banks have lower hazards in Argentina (-0.91) than in Mexico (-0.60), but even a Mexican bank with *CAR* one standard deviation above the sample mean would be expected to survive about 33 months longer than a bank with mean capitalization levels. Note, however, that the posterior distribution of the CAR coefficient in Mexico has some probability mass on the positive orthant (the upper bound of the 95% credible interval is 0.2). In practice, this means that, after controlling for bank size, there exists a non-negligible probability that better capitalized banks would survive less than ill-capitalized banks in Mexico. This is not the case in Argentina: Larger banks may have been expected to survive longer periods, but ill-capitalized banks faced a much larger chance of being forced out of the system.

These inferences are premised on a rigid model of bank duration that fails to take full advantage of information collected from balance-sheet data and from known characteristics of the Argentine and Mexican banking systems. In what follows, I account for three of these characteristics. First, the observed values of *CAR* and *bank size* indicators vary not only across banks, but they also change period-by-period and can vary drastically from one month or quarter to the next. It would be desirable to incorporate this "time-varying" information into an analysis of length of bank survival. Aside from *CAR* and

---

[42]I stipulate normally-distributed priors centered at 0 and with low precision for all parameters in the model (i.e., $N(0, 0.001)$—I stick to convention in expressing the spread of normal distributions as precisions rather than variances). This structure of priors has little effect on posterior distributions.

Table 4.3: Exponential models of bank survival in Argentina and Mexico. Covariates are measured at the beginning of the observation window (December 1994). Estimates are median and 95% credible intervals of the posterior distribution of effect parameters.

	Argentina		Mexico	
Parameter	Median	95% CI	Median	95% CI
CAR	−0.907	−1.29 −0.56	−0.597	−1.56 0.20
Bank size	−1.007	−1.32 −0.71	−0.927	−1.80 −0.08
Intercept	−4.016	−4.30 −3.77	−2.964	−3.44 −2.50

bank size, I include *loan concentration* as a time-varying covariate. A bank has more concentrated assets to the degree that it lends to similar firms and households; concentrated banks are more fragile because they cannot hedge against risks. My measure of *loan concentration* is a Herfindahl index of the degree to which loans to a small number of economic sectors dominate a bank's balance sheet. In the case of Mexico, I also include the ratio of non-performing to total loans (*NPL ratio*) as a further bank/period predictor of survival. Appendix A.2.1 reports all covariates used in the analysis.

Second, the process of bank exit was probably influenced by variables that changed period-by-period but remained constant *across* banks. Changes in the rate of economic growth at the national level (*GDP change*) or, more germanely, the level of liquidity support from the central bank to the banking system (*CB credit*) are variables that affected the chances of survival of *all* Argentine and *all* Mexican banks. In other words, bank/quarter (bank/month) observations in Mexico (Argentina) are nested within quarters (months) during which system-level variables changed; it is therefore necessary to account for this hierarchical structure in a more flexible model specification. Furthermore, the period-level covariates were markedly different *before* than *during* the banking crises; to compare the effect of period-level covariates before and during the crises, I extend the observation window backwards to 1991. In the Mexican database I observe actual bank starting points, i.e., the date at which banks were chartered as private enterprises. In Argentina, I have extended the observation period back to March 1991, which coincides with the end of the period of hyperinflation and, in essence, the start of a new era in Argentina's financial system following the approval of the Convertibility law and a new Central Bank charter later that year. Observing banks at an early stage mitigates the problem of "left truncation" that threatens biased inference in survival analysis.[43]

Third, banks themselves vary markedly depending on their ownership structure and the political prowess of bankers. This fact suggests that bank survival may vary across bank categories in Argentina and Mexico. In Argentina, the setup of the banking system around 1994 suggests considering three categories or bank types. Private banks with domestic majority participation, traditionally organized around Argentina's AdeBA, comprised the first group (80 banks). The second group was made up of large foreign banks (34), which had increased their market share in the country even before the *Tequila* crisis. The last group included *cooperativas bancarias*, or mutual banks (42). As is common elsewhere, these tended to be smaller and had less diversified assets. Because mutual thrift banks have no shareholders and are much smaller than regular banks, it is possible that their closure imposed lower political costs on regulators,[44] which would compromise their ability to survive the crisis unscathed. By August 1998, banks in the first group went from 80 to 41, whereas only five mutual banks survived out of 42 at the beginning of the observation window.

Legal impediments prevented foreign banks from entering the Mexican banking system in full force before 1995; only two foreign banks operated in Mexico at some point during the observation window, though naturally many more entered as they took over failing domestic banks (see fn. 39). The other banks in the system were owned by private investors, many of them from the ranks of stockbroking companies that had flourished during the boom years of the Salinas administration and bid for banks during the privatization process of 1991–1992. The larger banks, however, were controlled by active members of the *Consejo Mexicano de Hombres de Negocios* (CMHN), an informal lobbying organization that gathers some of the most influential businessmen in Mexico (Teichman 1995). In Mexico, banker membership into the CMHN may thus be associated with longer bank survival. In consequence, I distinguish three bank types in this country: foreign (two banks), domestic CMHN (5), and domestic non-CMHN (27).

To provide appropriate estimates of the association between financial status and bank duration, a model of bank survival must accommodate a nested data structure in which indicators of interest vary at the bank/period level (*CAR*, *bank size*, and *loan concentration*), the period level (*GDP change* and *CB credit*), and the bank level (*bank type*). In addition, the lifespans of banks are highly correlated because the observation window includes a period before the onset of the crisis during which only a handful of banks

---

[43] Bank histories are left-truncated if their lifespans precede the beginning of the observation window.

[44] This view is expressed by Cole (1993, 301) for closures during the US S&L crisis.

exited the system, and a post-crisis period during which banks failed at increasing rates. This correlation is an artifact of the way in which I set up the observation window, and it should be controlled for in the model by allowing the possibility of an increasing hazard rate. Thus, I consider the baseline *duration t* of banks to follow a Weibull distribution; this assumption allows me to accommodate hazard rates that increase throughout time.[45] To accommodate nested data levels, I model the scale parameter μ of the Weibull distribution as a function of bank/period characteristics and period-level covariates. Equations 4.1 and 4.2 display the basic structure of the model:

$$t_{ij} \sim Weibull(\nu, \mu_{ij}) \tag{4.1}$$

$$\mu_{ij} = \exp(\alpha_k + \gamma Z_{ij} + \beta X_j) \tag{4.2}$$

Because at the lowest level of aggregation data vary by bank/period, the dependent variable is the length of survival (in months or quarters) of bank *i* in period *j*. If bank *i* has not exited the banking system in the last period of observation (the 90th month in Argentina, the 35th quarter in Mexico), then the survival distribution is a truncated Weibull.[46] I include a vector of random effects α_k to allow for different frailties or heterogeneity in underlying hazard rates across bank categories ($k \in \{1, 2, 3\}$ corresponding to foreign, private, and mutual banks in Argentina and to foreign, private, and CMHN banks in Mexico). Coefficients γ and β are the effect parameters for covariates that vary at the bank/period and period levels, respectively. To complete the model setup, I stipulate proper but diffuse priors on model parameters; diffuse prior distributions have negligible impact on posterior distributions.[47]

I fit the hierarchical Weibull model of Equations 4.1 and 4.2 to Argentine and Mexican bank balance-sheet data.[48] Summaries of the posterior distribution of parameters appear in Table 4.4; recall that negative coefficients imply lower hazard rates and, consequently, longer bank durations (except for shape parameter ν, where the opposite relation holds). There are several noteworthy findings, which I discuss briefly before reconsidering the

---

[45]Because few exits appear at early periods but exits start bundling together at later dates, I expect the shape parameter ν of the Weibull distribution to be larger than 1. This would be consistent with a survival process in which failures are uncommon at the beginning, but occur with high probability toward the end of the observation window.

[46]This arrangement permits the piecewise estimation of the hazard function. As can be glimpsed from Figure 4.2, right censorship is more common in the Argentine bank population (72 banks that were already established in March 1991 survive throughout the entire observation window), but the rate of censorship is not identical across categories of banks.

[47]The prior distributions are $\alpha, \beta, \gamma \sim N(0, \tau = 0.001)$; $\nu \sim Gamma(1, 0.001)$.

[48]The Winbugs code appears in Appendix A.3.1. Inferences are based on 1,000 draws (thinned every 10th value) of two chains started at dispersed initial values, after dropping the first 1,000 draws. Convergence was monitored using the Gelman-Rubin R^2 statistic.

Table 4.4: Weibull models of bank survival in Argentina and Mexico, with time-varying covariates, period-specific covariates, and random effects for bank type. Estimates are median and 95% credible intervals of the posterior distribution of effect parameters.

Parameter	Argentina		Mexico	
	Median	95% CI	Median	95% CI
Bank/quarter time-varying covariates				
CAR	−1.27	−1.34 −1.20	−0.02	−0.15 0.12
Bank size	−0.31	−0.33 −0.29	−0.78	−0.91 −0.62
Loan conc.	0.05	0.02 0.07	0.14	0.06 0.21
NPL ratio			−0.029	−0.11 0.05
Quarter time-varying covariates				
GDP change	0.74	0.71 0.77	−0.49	−0.57 −0.41
CB loans	0.71	0.69 0.74	0.14	0.06 0.21
Bank type intercepts				
Private bank	−8.41	−8.55 −8.28	−5.06	−5.43 −4.72
Mutual	−8.42	−8.54 −8.27		
CMHN			−4.33	−4.67 −3.95
Foreign bank	−8.43	−8.56 −8.30	−5.47	−5.95 −5.04
Base hazard	2.34	2.30 2.37	1.96	1.85 2.08
Survival (+)	33.83	33.37 34.29	10.96	10.26 11.59
Survival (−)	26.70	26.36 27.12	10.94	10.37 11.55
N	10,389		702	
Banks	156		34	
Periods	90 months		35 quarters	

nexus between *financial status* and *bank survival*. First, despite employing a non-informative prior on the shape of the baseline hazard rate I find that the risk of exit increases with bank duration (the posterior distribution of v lies entirely above 1 in both countries). This is not surprising given that a majority of failed banks in both countries started their lifespans during the first observation period and exited the system within a relatively short time halfway through the observation window after the banking crisis started. Second, I observe noticeable differences in the survival of banks according to their type in the case of Mexico, but not in Argentina. Consider Argentina first: After controlling for bank size, there is practically no difference in the distribution of the coefficients that correspond to the three different bank types (private, mutual, and foreign). In particular, despite the fact that mutual banks failed at larger rates and their assets were often merged into private banks, it would be difficult to argue that there was a differential exit policy for banks based on their ownership structure or idiosyncratic lobbying capacity. Any variation in failure rates between private banks and mutual banks is accounted for by differences in bank size and capitalization levels, especially the latter.[49] In other words, it is hard to believe that high rates of failure among mutual banks were the result of an orchestrated effort to benefit private banks at the expense of *cooperativas bancarias.*

In contrast, different types of banks in Mexico show different frailties. These frailties defy expectations, as results suggest that banks owned by members of the *Consejo Mexicano de Hombres de Negocios* enjoyed shorter staying power than non-CMHN banks, after controlling for size and capitalization. The expected bank duration of a CMHN bank was 6.31 quarters when holding all variables constant at sample means; non-CMHN banks were expected to survive 9.13 quarters. Consider however that bank size and CMHN membership are very highly correlated (the mean log size of CMHN banks is 11.6, 8.9 for non-CMHN banks). In fact, we do not observe small CMHN banks, which would be an oxymoron. Results are therefore consistent with the view that CMHN banks survived longer than non-CMHN banks because of sheer size, and not necessarily on account of the lobbying power of CMHN bankers. An average-sized CMHN bank has expected duration equal to 10.35 quarters, whereas an average-sized non-CMHN bank was expected to live 8.20 quarters, all else constant. Aside from *bank size*, a larger index of *loan concentration* is associated with slightly lower bank duration, but the effect is substantively negligible (in Mexico, for example, a drop in a bank's *loan concentration* index of one standard deviation below the sample mean increases expected survival by less than three months).

I include short-term *GDP change* and central bank *liquidity support* as covariates that affect *all* banks within a period but vary across periods. My decision to include *GDP change* follows from the expectation that shifts in national economic fortunes ought to affect bank balance-sheet items, especially if a severe economic downturn limits the ability of bank debtors to pay their loans. Furthermore, changes in GDP may also affect the political decision to close insolvent banks, though the direction of this effect is not entirely clear. In fact, I find that the association between period-to-period changes in

---

[49] Admittedly, the capitalization levels of private banks may have been improved because of preferential access to government-sponsored capitalization programs. I cannot disavow this explanation with the data at hand. However, recall the various quandaries set up by the Argentine government to prevent access by *ex ante* insolvent banks to capitalization funds.

GDP and bank survival is different in Argentina and Mexico. In Argentina, positive GDP change is associated with an increase in the mean hazard rate across banks; the opposite association holds in Mexico. More interestingly, an increase in *CB credit* is associated with an increase in the mean hazard rate in both countries. Because the Argentine and Mexican models are based on different samples, the effect on bank duration of changes in central bank expenditures are not directly comparable. However, the positive association between *CB credit* and hazard rates is consistent with the lender of last resort role that central banks in both countries played during their banking crises— indeed, we would expect central bank liquidity injections *and* bank closures to be much more frequent during banking crises than during tranquil periods.

The main parameters of interest are the coefficients for *CAR* and, in the case of Mexico, *NPL ratio*. These coefficients reveal the extent to which the bank exit process in these countries reinforced or counteracted market outcomes. In Argentina, we see that a bank's capital-asset ratio is a substantively important predictor of expected survival, even after controlling for an array of bank- and period-level covariates. In short, better capitalized banks had lower hazard rates. In Table 4.4, the rows labeled "Survival" display the distribution of median survival times for banks with low capitalization levels (25th percentile of the sample distribution of CAR) and high capitalization levels (75th percentile). Median survival times correspond to the number of periods that one would need to wait to see the exit of 50% of banks in a population. The posterior distribution of these survival times suggests with very high probability (0.95) that the median Argentine bank in a set of well-capitalized institutions would survive between 33.4 and 34.3 months, holding all covariates constant at mean levels. In contrast, the median ill-capitalized Argentine bank would live between 26.4 and 27.1 months. Compare these predictions against those that obtain in the Mexican sample: there is in fact no difference in the expected length of median survival of well- versus ill-capitalized banks. Simply put, capitalization levels *are not* good predictors of bank exit in Mexico. Furthermore, non-performing loan ratios are also useless as predictors of bank survival in that country. In short, Mexican politicians seem to have considered *bank size* as the sole criterion to determine bank exit.[50]

4.3 Concluding Remarks

The analysis of bank survival in Section 4.2.2 resonates with the depiction of Argentina and Mexico as, respectively, Bagehot and Bailout governments. In

---

[50]This result is not an artifact of collinearity between NPL and capital-asset ratios. Though the correlation between these variables is negative, as one would expect, and relatively strong ($\rho = -0.32$), similar results obtain when excluding *NPL ratio* from the model.

Argentina, the Menem administration was relatively quick in enabling regulatory agencies to combat bank liquidity and insolvency problems. Though only three banks had been suspended two months into the banking crisis (*Basel, Finansur*, and *Trader*), the Easter legislative package granted financial authorities the power to close several other financial institutions right away. With the power to allocate assets, intervene banks, and subsidize mergers of bad banks into good banks, Argentine regulators forced the exit of a large number of insolvent financial institutions expeditiously. By election day on May 14, the bank run that had started with the December devaluation of the Mexican *peso* had abated, and bankers and regulators were starting to get a handle on remaining insolvency issues. Though my analysis suggests that the Argentine government was not immune to "too big to fail" considerations, capitalization levels are unarguably important predictors of bank exit, as corresponds to a Bagehot enforcer. In contrast, capitalization levels are irrelevant in understanding bank exit in Mexico. The Mexican authorities did not readily implement a comprehensive program to cope with the banking crisis, despite the fact that banking agencies (Fobaproa and CNBV) were not equipped to deal with the grievous insolvency problems that affected domestic banks. Instead, the Zedillo administration pushed through a pastiche of crisis-management programs that were not necessarily out of line with restructuring policies elsewhere, but did not seem to follow a coherent plan based on sober assessments of insolvency either.

Some preliminary lessons can be drawn from these two experiences of bank crisis response. First, banking crises are costly affairs, even when governments limit the size of financial losses transferred to taxpayers. In order to deal with financial insolvency, the Argentine taxpayer subsidized mergers of good and bad banks and the monetary authority was granted the ability to perform last-resort lending functions. Some would characterize these subsidized operations as "bank bailouts" because they amounted, in essence, to the continuation of bad banks under different names and/or to the continuation of illiquid banks. This indiscriminate use of the term "bailout" is essentially useless, as it throws in the same bag very different crisis-management styles. Instead, my interpretation of bailouts corresponds to an essentially continuous construct that measures the amount of financial losses that are passed on to the taxpayer. In this sense, policies to contain and redress banking crises run the gamut from taxpayer absorption of all financial losses derived from bank insolvency to more limited taxpayer help to restructure a distressed banking sector. Crisis-management policies reveal ample information about the bailout propensities of different governments. Analyzing bailout propensities is the first step towards verifying the existence of political regime effects on banking policies.

Second, the institutional setup of banking agencies may have an impact on the way in which banking crises are managed, but though it is common to argue that banking agencies matter it is less obvious which features are consequential. Furthermore, the structure of bank supervision and regulation seems to be endogenous to political decisions to cope with banking crises. It is clear that the governments of Argentina and Mexico scrambled to grant old and new banking agencies the ability to deal with insolvent banks. In this regard, it is noteworthy that Argentine policy-makers were able to tweak the currency board arrangement so that the BCRA could carry out LOLR functions. When it comes to reforming banking agencies, it is not uncommon to see governments patching the ship at sea. The Argentine authorities took advantage of the crisis to strengthen their bank supervisory institutions and to develop bank restructuring expertise while keeping down costs passed on to the taxpayer. Instead, Mexican officials designed a series of policies that varied in their ability to elicit optimal banker behavior. On one extreme, the temporary capitalization programs limited moral hazard incentives. On the other extreme, the set of policies coordinated through Fobaproa to purchase bad assets in exchange for fresh capital ended up providing the worst possible incentives to bankers. In contrast with the high-powered incentives that were built into Procapte to keep fiscal cost low, Fobaproa seemed purposefully planned to transfer most bank losses to the taxpayer.

Finally, my choice of Argentina and Mexico as exploratory cases was not due to my a priori perception of their policy responses, but to the fact that while Argentina could be depicted as a consolidated, albeit imperfect, democratic regime by 1994, Mexico was still in the midst of transition towards full electoral contestability by the time the crisis hit. My main theoretical claim is that democracies are better able to withstand pressures to transfer losses to disorganized taxpayers simply because the latter can make their voice heard during elections. In this regard, one could imagine that facing elections in the near future would have the opposite effect to the one posited here, i.e., that elected politicians fear the wrath of their constituents and are therefore likely to extend the lives of insolvent banks if elections are close in the horizon. In Argentina, before the Easter presidential decrees that ended the deposit run were implemented, there was indeed some speculation that the government could ignore the problem until after the elections. Politicians in democratic regimes may well choose to engage in regulatory forbearance in expectation of an electoral contest and therefore increase taxpayer costs, but in order to validate my theoretical claim the relevant counterfactual scenario is not that of a democratic regime without elections in the immediate future, but that of an election-less authoritarian regime or, more likely, one with limited electoral accountability.

An obvious candidate mechanism to explain why democracies may be less prone to bailouts is the existence of multiple veto points. The idea that democratic regimes with very different institutional features can be usefully compared through analysis of the number of veto players in assemblies and the executive power has been developed by Tsebelis (2002). From a theoretical point of view, it is not entirely clear whether we should expect veto points to increase or decrease the probability of bailouts. While it is possible that veto players with different policy positions could slow down attempts to respond to a banking crisis, this configuration could presumably also lead to checks-and-balances that might improve policy-making (Haggard and MacIntyre 1998). I find no reason to believe that a veto points argument could help understand Argentina's response. Congressional participation in revamping financial laws was minimal at best and, as was common during his tenure, President Menem passed many relevant reforms by decree. In Mexico, President Zedillo's administration avoided immediate major reforms and coordinated the bailout effort through the Ministry of Finance and Fobaproa. But in line with a veto point logic, a major effort to review bailout policies and revamp financial losses was put in motion once midterm elections in 1997 returned a more fractious lower Chamber. At that point, though, financial losses derived from bank insolvency had been apportioned and Mexican taxpayers had already acquired hefty obligations.

Suggestive as it may be, the paired Argentina-Mexico comparison is ultimately limited for two main reasons: First, as in many qualitative analyses, it is difficult to guarantee that these two cases are representative of the ways in which democracies and autocracies react to banking crises. One cannot rule out the possibility that the policy reactions of Argentina and Mexico are outliers within the populations of, respectively, democratic and semi-authoritarian regimes. Second, even if Argentina and Mexico in 1991 through 1999 were typical cases within the populations of democracies and authoritarian regimes, we are still unable to confidently attribute variations in their observed responses to differences in their political regimes. Political regime is one of the attributes that varies across these cases, but it is certainly not the only meaningful difference between these two countries. Consequently, throughout the rest of the book I base inferences about regime effects on inspection of a larger set of cases.

5

Variation in Government Bailout Propensities

Chapter 4 dissected the policy response to systemic banking crises during the mid-1990s of two governments, a democratic regime that carried out policies close to the Bagehot ideal-type and a semi-authoritarian regime that pursued policies closer to Bailout. The analysis in that chapter is consistent with the main proposition of this book, namely, that politicians in democracies react differently than politicians in autocracies whenever they confront wide insolvency in the banking sector. However, Argentina and Mexico were different not only in their political regimes, but also along dimensions that may help account for their policy choices, from the institutional setup of the monetary authority to the structure of their banking systems. Some of these factors—like supervisory stringency, or extension of crony links among entrepreneurs, bankers, and government—are theorized to follow from variations in political regime, but some others—like international openness or institutional constraints on the monetary authority—are not. Unfortunately, one cannot control for potential confounding variables in a paired comparison.

To make progress in estimating the effects of political regimes on banking policies, I follow a different strategy over the next chapters. Basically, I consider variation *across* governments to assess the degree to which political regimes matter in understanding policy responses to widespread bank insolvency. Based on theory presented in Chapter 3, the political regime under which governments operate should have an impact on the probability of observing a bank bailout. In line with Proposition 1, I expect democracies to be more successful in limiting burden-sharing with taxpayers upon suffering a banking crisis. Aside from validating this hypothesis, the analysis in this chapter and the next sheds light on other seldom-explored aspects of management of banking crises, like the relative political expediency of alternative policies and the potentially multi-dimensional character of government response. To fully present the evidence that substantiates Proposition 1, I break down the analysis into two chapters. In Section 5.1 of this chapter I first describe the data on which the analysis is based, a small sample of forty-six documented instances of policy response to banking crises. In Section 5.2 I detail the modeling assumptions that allow me to reach inferences about bailout proclivities based on the peculiar characteristics of observed data. In particular, I rely on item-response theory models to build and analyze an indicator of the bailout propensity of different governments. Section 5.3 closes with a preliminary analysis of the effect of political regime on the decision of governments to pursue Bagehot or Bailout, and Section 5.4 considers whether recent instances of bailouts in democratic regimes provide enough evidence to cast doubt on the existence of a democratic advantage. I build a case for a *causal interpretation* of the impact of political regimes on bank bailouts in Chapter 6. I conclude there that democratic regimes are indeed less likely to carry out onerous bailouts.

5.1 Crisis-Management Policies

I argued in Chapter 1 that the concept of "bank bailout" is only useful if we consider it as a theoretical continuum between the ideal-types of Bagehot and Bailout, where outcomes closer to the latter extreme correspond to higher burden-sharing with taxpayers. Every government redistributes losses derived from bank insolvency to some extent; consequently, even the thriftiest government ends up burdening taxpayers with at least some portion of financial losses produced by the behavior of economic actors. To validate Proposition 1, I assess the *bailout propensities* of different governments—i.e., the degree to which these governments sheltered banks from the consequences of insolvency. Recall that Proposition 1 states that democracies are more likely to adopt harsher closure rules to deal with distressed banks.

The empirical analysis is based on a sample of government responses to forty-six separate banking crises observed from 1976 to 2003. Most of these were compiled, coded, and disseminated by Honohan and Klingebiel (2000); I have complemented their database with information from Del Villar, Backal and Treviño (1997) and from secondary sources through Lexis-Nexis (see Appendix A.2.3). These forty-six events are a subset of a larger collection of episodes recognized by policy experts as systemic banking crises (see Chapter 7). Though the subset of $N = 46$ is relatively small and presumably favors banking crises that were relatively well publicized, no obvious selection bias is evident in the sample. In other words, democracies are not over-represented over autocracies, corrupt over non-corrupt regimes, or open over closed economies; in preliminary tests, not reported here, none of these factors were significant predictors of the inclusion of a banking crisis in the sample (see Rosas 2006). The only partial exception is that poorer economies tend to be slightly under-represented, in the sense that real per capita GDP is a statistically significant, albeit substantively unimportant, predictor of whether a systemic banking crisis will appear in the sample. Thus, these 46 banking crises are to a large extent representative of the wider universe of events. This need not mean that policy responses themselves are representative, nor do I make the claim that the distribution of treatment (democracy) and control conditions across these observations is random. I will return in Chapter 6 to the problem of making causal inferences based on observational data, where the mechanism assigning treatment (democracy) and control (non-democracy) is not known.

Honohan and Klingebiel provide details about governmental responses to banking crises. Among other indicators, they code whether any of seven policies commonly used to address bank *solvency* and *liquidity* problems were implemented during a systemic banking crisis; they build a dichotomous score for each of these seven policies within each banking crisis in the sample. Table 5.1 reproduces their coding scheme. As can be gleaned from this table, the seven binary indicators can be directly traced to the five policy issue-areas—exit policy, liquidity support, asset resolution, liability resolution, and bank capitalization—detailed in the Bagehot-Bailout classification scheme of Table 2.3. For example, *bank liquidity* is an indicator of government response regarding protection of bank depositors that is coded "1" for governments that extended emergency liquidity support during at least twelve months, with overall support exceeding the total amount of banking capital (Honohan and Klingebiel 2000). Table 5.1 shows how the other six indicators (*forbearance*, *public asset management*, *debt relief*, *explicit guarantees*, *deposit freeze*, and *recapitalization*) relate to policy issue-areas in Table 2.3. The last two columns of Table 5.1 display counts of the number of governments that enacted each of the seven policies and the number of missing values in each category. By far, the most popular interventions are provision of liquidity through heavy last resort lending (23 cases) and regulatory forbearance (28), whereas flagrant cases of debt relief for corporate borrowers or bank recapitalization with public funds are less common.

5.2 An Item-Response Theory Model of Bailout Propensity

We can exploit variation in the frequency with which these policies were implemented to elicit information about the underlying bailout propensities of different governments; in fact, better inferences about bailout propensities follow from consideration of *all* seven indicators as a set, rather than from examination of a handful, provided that these data are combined in a principled

Table 5.1: Seven crisis-management policy indicators. The last column displays the number of governments (out of 46) that implemented the corresponding policy in response to a banking crisis (missing values in parentheses).

Indicator (Proxy for …)	Coded 1 if …	#1 (MV)
Regulatory forbearance (Exit policy)	Government relaxes or fails to enforce regulation for at least one year. Bank competition is restricted. Government fails to shut down distressed banks after three months. Government allows insolvent banks to continue under original management.	28 (2)
Bank liquidity (Liquidity support)	Government provides liquidity support larger than total banking system capital to insolvent banks for at least one year.	23 (2)
Public asset management (Asset resolution)	Government transfers non-performing bank loans to a centralized public asset management corporation.	18 (1)
Debt relief (Asset resolution)	Government sponsors debt relief for corporate borrowers, through exchange rate guarantees or direct rescue.	10 (5)
Explicit guarantees (Liability resolution)	Government issues explicit deposit guarantee. State-owned institutions hold 75% of total banking deposits.	19 (2)
Deposit freeze (Liability resolution)	Government freezes deposits in intervened banks for at least one year.	18 (2)
Recapitalization (Bank capitalization)	Government recapitalizes banks through one-shot support scheme. Government recapitalizes banks through repeated rounds.	12 (1)

manner.[1]

I model government responses to banking crises using tools from item response theory (IRT). These models are extremely flexible tools to analyze limited dependent variables, particularly the kind of data—dichotomous variables—described in Table 5.1.[2] The basic setup of IRT models makes them ideal tools to analyze policy problems in which a set of dichotomous variables can be interpreted as manifest indicators of some latent policy construct. In this case, I construe the seven policies laid out in Table 5.1 as manifest indicators of a government's latent bailout propensity. We can then use IRT models to make inferences about unobserved tendencies that push politicians to enact alternative policies. In this section, I relate informally the various assumptions underlying IRT models of bank bailouts, abstracting from more technical issues about identification and estimation. I fit several models to the data described in Table 5.1; these models vary mostly in the amount of information they incorporate about government characteristics and the assumptions they make about the seven crisis-management policies, but they all start from the premise that government i's unobservable *bailout propensity* θ_i drives the distribution of observed policy responses $y_{i,j} = \{0, 1\}$ (i is the government index, j is the policy index). The unit of analysis is thus a government's response to a banking crisis, with seven dichotomous policy indicators per observation. Many countries suffered multiple banking crises during the period under inspection, but only five of these—Argentina, Indonesia, Malaysia, Mexico, and Turkey—provide more than one observation to the dataset.[3]

To understand how an IRT model helps us extract information from these data, recall from Table 5.1 that the number of governments that implement each of the seven crisis-management policies varies a great deal, from a minimum of ten countries pursuing *debt relief* to a maximum of 28 countries adopting *regulatory forbearance*. These differences speak to the relative ease with which governments can pursue different policies; in other words, it is reasonable to assume that the sample frequency of these policies reveals the degree to which these policies are politically expedient. For example, *regulatory forbearance* often starts with low-level bureaucratic decisions that do not immediately invite oversight from, or require the benediction of, elected government officials. Even when regulatory forbearance is the result of direct

---

[1]Previous research has used some of these dichotomous variables as indicators of selected aspects of Bagehot-Bailout (for example, Keefer 2002 uses *forbearance* and Nava-Campos 2002 combines *explicit guarantees*, *bank liquidity* and *forbearance* in an additive index).

[2]See Rasch (1980) for an introduction to IRT models and Johnson and Albert (1999, ch. 6) for IRT models in a Bayesian framework.

[3]I count each banking crisis as an independent observation, i.e., observations are not clustered within governments. This is not unreasonable given that banking crises do not occur within the same government, even if they occur within the same country.

intervention from "up high," this policy is relatively easy to implement, as it requires a passive "response." Instead, policies such as *debt relief* or *bank recapitalization* often require legislative intervention or concerted action by a variety of agencies, and are therefore relatively difficult to pursue, even by governments with high bailout propensity. Moreover, these two policies create immediately recognizable outlays that must be met with taxpayers' money. Relatedly, provision of *bank liquidity* is generally the province of a nation's central bank, which may or may not be autonomous from politicians. In any case, crisis-management policies are subject to political constraints of varying importance. In an IRT model, the overall political expediency of enacting each of the seven policies would be captured by a set of parameters α_j, which are appropriately labeled *difficulty* parameters.

5.2.1 Inferences Based on Frequency of Policy Implementation

With these definitions in place, consider now the model of bailout propensities across governments conveyed by Equations 5.1 and 5.2:

$$y_{ij} \sim Bernoulli(\pi_{ij}) \qquad (5.1)$$

$$\pi_{ij} = \Phi(\theta_i - \alpha_j) \qquad (5.2)$$

In Equation 5.1, each dichotomous policy item $y_{i,j}$ is modeled as a random draw from a Bernoulli distribution with parameter $\pi_{i,j} \in [0, 1]$—i.e., we assume that $y_{i,j}$ will take on a value of 1 with probability $\pi_{i,j}$. Equation 5.2 then considers parameter $\pi_{i,j}$ to be a function of item difficulty α_j and government bailout propensity θ_i: The probability of observing policy j in response to a banking crisis increases with the political expediency of the policy (lower values of α) and with the bailout propensity of the government (higher values of θ). These are the two core assumptions of the IRT model.[4] The main goal in this case is to estimate *bailout propensities* θ_i for all 46 governments based on observable policy choices $y_{i,j}$; however, the model requires estimation of *difficulty* parameters α_j as well. Incidentally, notice that item parameters vary across policies but are constant across governments, whereas bailout propensities appropriately vary across governments.

In this baseline setup, the IRT model requires estimation of 46 bailout propensities and seven item difficulty parameters, based on information from 46×7 observed policy values, so there is in principle sufficient information to uniquely estimate model parameters. Note however that parameters θ and α are invariant to changes in scale and rotation, and therefore the model as

---

[4]This model assumes a probit link for the Bernoulli parameter π_{ij} (Φ is the standard normal cumulative distribution function). Bear in mind that α and π are parameters of a statistical model; these are not the same as the *democracy weight* and *risk profile* in Chapter 3.

expressed in Equations 5.1 and 5.2 is not identified. In other words, θ and α could be multiplied by any constant value and model fit would remain unchanged. One advantage of the Bayesian estimation of IRT models is the possibility of using prior probabilities on parameters θ and α to identify the model. In the baseline setup, I fix the scale of bailout propensities by stipulating a standard normal prior distribution on parameters θ as is customarily done in this kind of model (Johnson and Albert 1999). This prior solves scale invariance by constraining the bailout propensity of the average government to be 0 and all other values of θ to fall within a narrow range around 0 (i.e., we assume a priori that 95% of all bailout propensities will fall within –2 and 2). By the same token, I stipulate that the prior distribution of difficulty parameters α is normal with mean 0 and standard deviation $\sqrt{2}$.[5] This prior distribution ensures that policies with average degrees of difficulty or political expediency will get a score of $\alpha \approx 0$, and it also allows the posterior distribution of difficulty parameters of all policies to be lower (or higher) than the lowest (largest) bailout propensity. The latter condition implies admitting a priori that some policies might not be extremely informative about bailout propensities. In other words, we could in principle see a policy that is so politically expedient (α_j lower than the lowest θ_i) that *all* governments stand a better than even chance of implementing it, regardless of how bailout-prone they are. Note that though prior probabilities on parameters θ and α are informative, this information is added to the model with the sole purpose of achieving identification. Inferences about θ are still largely data-driven and not overtly dependent on selection of priors.

Estimates of difficulty parameters for the model based on Equations 5.1 and 5.2 appear in the first column of Table 5.2 (the point estimate corresponds to the median of the posterior distribution, the standard deviation of the posterior distribution appears in parentheses). The conclusions that follow from the baseline model about the comparative expediency of alternative crisis-management policies are not surprising given knowledge of the frequency with which they have been adopted, but they confirm the basic adequacy of the IRT model.[6] Recall that a policy with parameter $\alpha \approx 0$ corresponds to a policy with "average" difficulty in the sample. Consistent with their relative frequency in the sample, policies with difficulty parameters well above 0—

---

[5]Note that this model is still invariant under rotation, so all θ and α parameters could be multiplied by -1 and fit would remain identical. To identify the model, I placed a non-positive constraint on the bailout propensity of Argentina 1995, along with a non-negative constraint on Mexico 1994 (cf. Jackman 2000). This implies that Mexico 1994 cannot have a lower bailout propensity than Argentina 1995, an assumption entirely supported by the analysis in Chapter 4.

[6]Estimates in Table 5.2 are based on 1,000 draws thinned every 10th draw after apparent convergence from the joint posterior pdf of parameters. I ran two chains for 1,000 iterations as burn-in for every model and assessed convergence based on the Gelman-Rubin $\hat{R}$ statistic. Convergence in these models was swift and clean.

Table 5.2: Bayesian estimation of Bagehot-Bailout policy (α, β) and case (δ) parameters. Point estimates are the median of parameter posterior densities (standard deviation of parameter posterior densities in parentheses).

Parameters	Model 1	Model 2	Model 3	Model 4
$\widehat{\alpha}_{AM}$	0.302	0.377	0.370	0.339
	(0.257)	(0.317)	(0.319)	(0.322)
$\widehat{\alpha}_R$	0.797	0.904	0.889	0.908
	(0.271)	(0.325)	(0.323)	(0.342)
$\widehat{\alpha}_G$	0.203	0.292	0.255	0.245
	(0.251)	(0.311)	(0.286)	(0.302)
$\widehat{\alpha}_{FB}$	−0.452	−0.443	−0.450	−0.452
	(0.258)	(0.233)	(0.256)	(0.251)
$\widehat{\alpha}_L$	−0.822	−0.062	−0.052	−0.059
	(0.240)	(0.202)	(0.190)	(0.190)
$\widehat{\alpha}_D$	0.802	0.714	0.679	0.689
	(0.268)	(0.225)	(0.213)	(0.221)
$\widehat{\alpha}_F$	0.245	0.235	0.232	0.229
	(0.254)	(0.196)	(0.201)	(0.199)
$\widehat{\beta}_{AM}$		1.389	1.342	1.399
		(0.468)	(0.418)	(0.453)
$\widehat{\beta}_R$		1.306	1.182	1.278
		(0.412)	(0.401)	(0.412)
$\widehat{\beta}_G$		1.400	1.192	1.288
		(0.445)	(0.442)	(0.482)
$\widehat{\beta}_{FB}$		0.673	0.589	0.724
		(0.365)	(0.335)	(0.412)
$\widehat{\beta}_L$		0.221	0.079	0.244
		(0.218)	(0.258)	(0.201)
$\widehat{\beta}_D$		0.275	0.186	0.313
		(0.243)	(0.302)	(0.242)
$\widehat{\beta}_F$		0.254	0.238	0.310
		(0.222)	(0.281)	(0.217)
$\widehat{\delta}$ (democracy)			−0.324	−0.198
			(0.192)	(0.189)
DIC	395.74	374.28	371.73	374.84
pD	41.16	39.80	38.67	39.37

Model 3 based on dichotomous, 4 on continuous, democracy index

L = liquidity, D = debt relief, AM = asset management agency, R = recapitalization,

G = explicit guarantees, F = deposit freeze, FB = forbearance

Figure 5.1: Estimates of difficulty and bailout propensity parameters in a common space. Point estimates are medians of the marginal posterior density of each parameter (*FB = forbearance, L = liquidity, G = explicit guarantees, D = debt relief*).

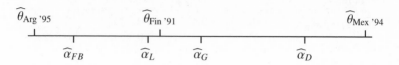

debt relief and *bank recapitalization*—are relatively hard to implement; in contrast *regulatory forbearance* is comparatively easy. In other words, many governments find it expedient to engage in *regulatory forbearance*, even those that do not have particularly high bailout proclivities. Instead, a policy like *bank recapitalization*, which requires investment of hefty public resources to keep insolvent banks in operation will be approached with trepidation even by the most bailout-prone government. Thus, the ease with which different governments enact these policies does not necessarily refer to the number of bureaucratic levers that need to be pulled, or the complexity of the process that needs to be set in motion, though admittedly this kind of mechanisms are probably at the heart of variation in policy difficulty. Instead, "relative ease" should be interpreted as the extent to which governments with different bailout propensities would choose these policies. Regulatory forbearance is very common in the sample, which makes this an "easy" policy item; therefore, observing that a government engages in forbearance only tells us that the government's bailout propensity is probably not extremely low. This also suggests why sole reliance on *regulatory forbearance* to infer the bailout propensity of governments would lead to incorrect inferences: Since *regulatory forbearance* is comparatively easy, many governments that are not particularly prone to Bailout still implement this policy; by inspecting just one indicator, we would be characterizing even these governments as reckless spendthrifts that place large financial burdens on taxpayers. By a similar argument, inspection of a subset of these seven indicators cannot be preferable to a principled analysis of the full set.[7]

To illustrate how the IRT model helps us make sense of government

---

[7]Incidentally, the posterior distribution of α tends to be wider for policies with more missing values, as one would expect. The data-augmentation step proposed by Albert and Chib (1993) to estimate the IRT model in a Bayesian framework allows multiple imputation of missing values within the updating algorithm itself. This imputation process is valid under the assumption of ignorable missingness (see Little and Rubin 1987; Rubin 1976).

proclivities, Figure 5.1 displays the spatial position of policy difficulty parameters and bailout propensities for selected governments. The graph shows point estimates (medians of the posterior distribution) of difficulty parameters for four policies: *regulatory forbearance* (α_{FB}), *liquidity* (α_L), *explicit guarantees* (α_G), and *debt relief* (α_D). Alongside these parameters, I plot point estimates of the bailout propensities of three governments that faced banking crises during the 1990s: Argentina 1995, Finland 1991, and Mexico 1994. Mexico appears as a government with extreme bailout propensity, consistent with multiple accounts of this crisis and with the thrust of the analysis in previous chapters. Also consistent with those views, Argentina comes very close to fulfilling the spirit of Bagehot's prescription by obtaining a very low θ score. Based on Figure 5.1, we would expect a government with the bailout propensity of Mexico in 1994 to enact all four of the policies plotted in the graph; a government with the characteristics of Argentina in 1995 would not be very likely to implement any of these policies. In contrast, governments with average bailout propensity ($\theta \approx 0$, like Finland in 1991) would be expected to implement *liquidity* and *forbearance*, but not *debt relief* or *explicit guarantees*.[8]

5.2.2 Inferences Based on Varying Policy Discrimination

The model based on Equations 5.1 and 5.2 is still unnecessarily restrictive in some important ways. One implicit assumption of this model is that all crisis-management policies are equally good at distinguishing among governments with different bailout propensities. In this context, the *discrimination potential* of a given policy can be understood as its ability to separate Bailout-prone from Bagehot-prone governments. A policy with high discrimination potential would offer a crisp cutpoint in the policy space represented in Figure 5.1; governments with bailout propensities to the right of this cutpoint would implement the policy with very high probability. In contrast, policies with low discrimination potential do not allow us to distinguish the policy effects of different bailout propensities with great precision. Another way of interpreting the discrimination potential of a policy is as follows: The probability that a government will adopt policy j that has average difficulty ($\alpha_j \approx 0$) is about even, regardless of the government's bailout propensity, if its discrimination potential is nil ($\beta_j \approx 0$). As discrimination potential becomes larger, the policy provides more information about underlying bailout

---

[8]These statements should be properly interpreted in a probabilistic fashion. Indeed, we can use draws from the joint posterior distribution of all parameters to provide educated guesses about the probability of observing different events of interest. For example, based on the baseline model, the probability that a government with Mexico's bailout propensity will implement all seven policies would be about 0.63. The probability that a government with Finland's characteristics would implement *liquidity* is estimated at around 0.33.

propensity. The assumption of equal discrimination is not necessary for identification purposes, and as I show below it receives no support from data. Consequently, I extend the baseline predictor in Equation 5.2 so that it now depends on a second policy-specific discrimination parameter β_j, as shown in Equation 5.3:

$$\pi_{i,j} = \Phi(\beta_j\theta_i - \alpha_j) \tag{5.3}$$

I expect all item discrimination parameters to be non-negative, which suggests that governments closer to the Bailout ideal-type are in principle more likely to implement the policies captured by the seven dichotomous indicators. Consistent with this expectation, I stipulate a normal prior distribution on β centered at 1 and with standard deviation 2. The prior mean of 1 implies a moderate level of discrimination for items that have average difficulty. A prior standard deviation of 2 assigns high probability to positive values of β_j while still placing enough probability mass on negative numbers to allow the possibility that some policies might actually have negative discrimination after updating. For example, finding that *regulatory forbearance* had negative discrimination would imply that Bailout-prone governments are *less* likely to adopt this type of policy, which would of course be contrary to theoretical expectations.[9]

Estimates based on Equation 5.3 are summarized in the second column of Table 5.2 (Model 2). To understand how policy parameters α and β translate into predictions about policy implementation consider Panel a in Figure 5.2, which plots *item response curves* of *explicit guarantees* and *bank liquidity* based on estimates of Model 2. The graph suggests that *explicit guarantees* and *bank liquidity* have very different potential to discriminate among governments with varying bailout propensities, even though both of these policies have average difficulty parameters. Figure 5.2 also plots estimates of the bailout propensities of Argentina and Mexico, along with predicted probabilities of enacting these policies. Based on estimates of the difficulty and discrimination parameters of *explicit guarantees* from Model 2 (i.e., $\hat{\alpha}_G$ and $\hat{\beta}_G$), one would expect a government with bailout propensity similar to that of Mexico in 1994 ($\widehat{\theta}_{\text{Mex '94}} \approx 1.31$) to implement this policy with probability 0.7. The probability that a country like Argentina ($\widehat{\theta}_{\text{Arg '95}} \approx -0.93$) would enact this policy is essentially 0. Contrast these results with those that obtain from considering *bank liquidity*: Despite obvious differences in the bailout propensities of Argentina and Mexico, the probability that these governments would implement generous *bank liquidity* policies is not that different (0.13 and 0.25, respectively). The discrimination potential of bank

---

[9] Incidentally, this prior distribution solves the problem of rotational invariance: Governments with high values of θ are now unarguably governments with high bailout propensity.

Figure 5.2: Item response curves for *explicit guarantees* and *bank liquidity* and predicted probabilities of implementation for Argentina and Mexico, and probabilities of enacting crisis-management policies conditional on political regime (bars represent 50% Bayesian credible intervals)

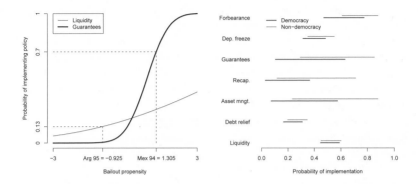

liquidity is very low, as one can see from the value $\hat{\beta}_L = 0.221$ in the second column of Table 5.2.

The extended model reveals that the discrimination parameters for *asset management corporation*, *recapitalization*, *explicit guarantees*, and *regulatory forbearance* are bounded away from 0.[10] These policies, particularly the first one, are very sensitive to differences in the bailout propensity of governments. Three other policy items—*liquidity provision*, *debt relief*, and *deposit freeze*—fail to display much discriminating power, as their posterior distributions are very close to 0. These three policies are all aimed at ameliorating bank cash-flow problems by either lending at a discount (*liquidity provision*), preventing further drain on banks' liabilities caused by indiscriminate depositor runs (*deposit freeze*), or supporting bank debtors so that they can continue to make payments on outstanding loans (*debt relief*). In other words, rather than aiming to restore *solvency* in a distressed banking system, these policies could be best understood as measures to manage *liquidity* problems during a banking crisis. In Chapter 6, I consider the possibility that a second liquidity dimension underlies government action, and explore whether political regimes also determine bailout propensities along this second dimension.

---

[10]Minor changes in the estimates of parameters α obtain in Model 2—particularly in the case of *bank liquidity*—upon estimation of parameters β.

5.3 Bagehot, Bailout, and Political Regimes

I devote extensive attention to the estimation of item-specific parameters α and β both to emphasize the usefulness of IRT models and because these parameters allow better understanding of some aspects of crisis management. However, the main objects of interest in this chapter are the varying bailout propensities of the forty-six governments in the sample. Figure 5.3 provides some sense of cross-government variation in bailout propensities by plotting point and interval estimates of θ for all governments in the sample. To provide some sense of how consequential these propensities are—aside from a further check on their validity—consider their association with fiscal costs of addressing banking crises. Several authors provide estimates of fiscal costs and show that they tend to increase with some of the seven crisis-management policies analyzed here (cf. Honohan and Klingebiel 2000; Keefer 2007). A regression of *fiscal cost* (log scale) on point estimates of the *bailout propensity* scores of these governments yields a slope coefficient estimate of 0.73 (SD = 0.28), which suggests that, on average, an increase of one standard deviation in a government's bailout propensity leads to an increase of about 7% of GDP in fiscal costs.[11]

Estimated bailout propensities corresponding to Models 1 and 2 in Table 5.2 appear in the top panels of Figure 5.3. Across these panels, note that by admitting varying degrees of discrimination among the seven policy items we are in fact able to recover finer gradations in the bailout scale. In this regard, even a cursory glance at these plots suggests that bailout propensities may indeed be driven by political regimes. Open circles in the graphs identify the bailout propensities of governments operating under a democratic regime. To keep things simple, the graphs use the dichotomous indicator of political regimes of Przeworski, Alvarez, Cheibub and Limongi (2000), as updated by Cheibub and Gandhi (2004).[12]

Even under the more stringent assumptions that inform the baseline model (Model 1), it would appear that governments in democratic regimes are better represented among those with lower-than-average bailout propensities (i.e., those with $\widehat{\theta} < 0$). This conjecture is corroborated after expanding the baseline model to include policy-specific discrimination parameters (Model 2). After accounting for varying degrees of discrimination among the seven policy

---

[11]The intercept estimate is 1.88 (0.20). These are Bayesian regression estimates based on 38 full cases and multiple imputation for eight missing values of *fiscal cost*—added uncertainty because of missing values is thus correctly accounted for, though uncertainty from estimation of bailout propensities is not, because I use point predictors as covariates.

[12]A government is coded as democratic if recognized as such by these authors during the starting year of a banking crisis. Przeworski et al. provide data for 140+ countries until 1990, and Cheibub and Gandhi (2004) update these data through 2000. Throughout the book, I reverse the original coding so that democracies receive a score of 1.

Figure 5.3: Bayesian estimates of government bailout propensities (median and 80% Bayesian credible intervals of the posterior distribution of θ). Democracies are identified with an open circle.

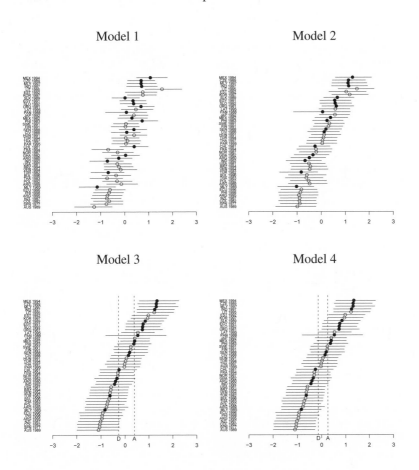

NOTE: Governments are arranged from most to least Bailout-prone based on Model 3: Mexico 1994, Czechoslovakia 1989, Malaysia 1997, Indonesia 1997, Lithuania 1995, Estonia 1992, South Korea 1997, Sri Lanka 1989, Egypt 1991, Slovenia 1992, Uruguay 1981, Latvia 1995, Panama 1988, Japan 1992, Mexico 1982, Philippines 1983, Sweden 1991, Finland 1991, Senegal 1988, Côte d'Ivoire 1988, Hungary 1991, Turkey 1994, Thailand 1997, Paraguay 1995, Chile 1981, France 1994, Norway 1987, Ghana 1982, Argentina 1980, Indonesia 1992, United States 1981, Brazil 1994, Venezuela 1994, Turkey 1982, Bulgaria 1996, Thailand 1983, Poland 1992, Argentina 1989, Malaysia 1985, Ecuador 1996, Philippines 1998, Argentina 1995, New Zealand 1987, Colombia 1982, Spain 1977, Australia 1989.

items, we do see a clearly defined group of democratic polities in the lower end of the graph, while non-democratic regimes appear to be plentiful towards the upper end. These results are encouraging and call for proper estimation of the effect of political regime on bailout propensities. Though one could use estimated bailout propensities as dependent variables in a regression framework, it is arguably best to *directly* assess the effect of political regimes within the IRT model by building a hierarchical model for bailout propensities θ. In this context, I incorporate information about the political regimes under which governments face banking crises by assuming that bailout propensities are a function of *democracy*. Equation 5.4 incorporates this extension:

$$\theta_i \sim \mathcal{N}(\mu_{\theta_i}, 1) \tag{5.4}$$
$$\mu_{\theta_i} = \delta \cdot democracy$$

The more general model is thus described by Equations 5.1, 5.3, and 5.4. In this model, the distribution of government-specific parameters θ_i is conditioned on a "hyperparameter" μ_{θ_i}, which is itself a function of the political regime under which governments confront a banking crisis. Parameter δ captures the average effect of *democracy* on a government's bailout propensity. If democracies enact solutions closer to the Bagehot ideal-type, the posterior density of δ should be negative.[13] The last two columns of Table 5.2 display estimates of the general model based on two different indicators of political regime: Estimates in Model 3 are based on Przeworski et al.'s dichotomous indicator of democracy-authoritarianism, whereas Model 4 reports estimates based on a continuous measure of political regime, namely, the Polity IV index, that takes integer values between -10 and 10.

The basic message conveyed by these models is that, regardless of indicator, political regimes are statistically associated with different bailout propensities.[14] This is most clearly seen in the model based on the dichotomous regime indicator (Model 3), whose coefficient is estimated to lie entirely to the left of 0. In the model based on the dichotomous *democracy* indicator (Model 4), δ can best be interpreted as a difference of means between the bailout propensities of democratic and non-democratic governments. This difference in means is portrayed graphically in the lower-left panel of Figure 5.3: On the horizontal axis, the point labeled "D" (at $\theta_D = -0.27$) corresponds to the mean bailout propensity of all democratic regimes, whereas "A" captures mean propensity among authoritarian regimes ($\theta_A = 0.38$). The average mean

---

[13]I do not estimate an intercept, consistent with the fact that the *democracy* indicators are mean-centered and the prior distribution of δ is centered at 0. The prior distribution of δ is normal with mean 0 and precision 0.01, which is not particularly informative given the scale on which bailout propensity is measured (the scale remains unchanged, as can be seen from distribution assumptions about θ in Equation 5.4).

[14]In Rosas (2006), I show that this association holds for a variety of democracy indicators.

Table 5.3: Posterior predictive distribution of the implementation of seven crisis-management policies. Cell entries correspond to the expected frequency (%) with which each policy is adopted under democracy and non-democracy.

Policy	Democracy	Non-democracy
Asset management	29	64
Recapitalization	16	52
Explicit guarantees	29	62
Regulatory forbearance	47	74
Bank liquidity	42	60
Debt relief	25	32
Deposit freeze	32	48

difference between democracies and non-democracies is −0.65; considering that the bailout propensity scale has standard deviation 1 by construction, this difference is far from trivial. Admittedly, the estimated political regime effect seems muted when we consider a continuous measure of *democracy*, as in Model 4. In this case, the posterior distribution of parameter δ even has some probability mass to the right of 0. Thus, based on estimates in Model 4, I calculate the probability that democracies have *larger than average* bailout propensities to be about 0.23, which is not a trivial amount. As a consequence, the effect of political regimes on bailout propensities displayed in the lower-right panel of Figure 5.3 is smaller. Since the *democracy* indicator used in column 4 is continuous, points labeled "D" and "A" correspond in this case to the sample interquartile range of the Polity indicator.

The degree of association between *political regime* and *bailout propensities* is put in its proper context once we consider the interaction between parameters θ, on the one hand, and the difficulty and discrimination parameters α and β of different policy items, on the other. The rightmost panel in Figure 5.2 portrays interval estimates of predicted probabilities of implementation of the seven policy issues conditional on the political regime under which a government confronts a crisis. Though political regimes are consequential in determining the bailout propensity of different governments, the low discrimination potential of some items means that the effect of democracy on *liquidity*, *debt relief*, and *deposit freeze* is relatively small. For all other policy items, political regimes make a huge difference even when we take into account uncertainty in the estimation of parameters, as Figure 5.2 does. To see this, notice that despite overlap in the credible intervals of these parameters we can still estimate probabilities of policy enactment under alternative

political regimes with relative precision. Table 5.3 summarizes results of a
simulation in which I predict implementation of the seven crisis-management
policies under the two political regimes.[15] For example, we would expect
democratic governments to implement *regulatory forbearance* in response
to a banking crisis about half the time (47%), whereas authoritarian regimes
would implement the same policy 3 times out of 4 (74%). Even for policies
with low discrimination parameters, like *bank liquidity* or *debt relief*, we still
find that democracies implement these policies 2 times out of 5 and 1 time
out of 4, respectively, as opposed to non-democracies, which implement these
policies about 3 times out of 5 and 1 time out of 3. Since the bailout propensities of governments correlate with the fiscal cost of restoring solvency to
distressed banking systems, it is arguably cheaper to be a taxpayer under
democratic than under authoritarian regimes.

5.4 Incorporating Information from Recent Bailouts

Consistent with a view of crisis-management policy as a continuum going
from Bagehot to Bailout ideal-types, I estimated IRT models that recover
differences in the bailout propensities of governments from principled analysis
of dichotomous policy indicators. The ancillary parameters of these models
confirm the expectation that not all of these policies are equally likely to
be enacted, i.e., crisis-management policies vary in their degree of political
expediency. Furthermore, inspection of these parameters suggests that large
differences in the bailout propensities of governments may have little impact
on implementation of some of these policies. This finding should increase
awareness that these policy indicators need to be considered in tandem, lest
one ends placing too much stock on policies that in the end provide too
little information about the underlying bailout propensities of governments.
This finding also suggests that relaxing the assumption of unidimensional
bailout propensities might be worthwhile; some of the policy items with weak
discrimination parameters may in fact help us separate Bailout from Bagehot
cases if we only allow for a more complex model. I investigate this scenario
in Chapter 6.

The main focus of the analysis, though, was assessment of Proposition 1.
The argument according to which democracies are less likely than authoritarian regimes to bail out insolvent banking systems is plausible, as suggested
by analysis of a sample of 46 government responses to as many banking
crises. Indeed, democratic governments are statistically less bailout-prone

---

[15]The percentages in Table 5.3 obtain from drawing 100 samples from the joint posterior
distribution of parameters, then substituting them in Equations 5.1, 5.3, and 5.4. The percentage
corresponds to the frequency with which the given policy was implemented (i.e., $\hat{y} = 1$).

than authoritarian regimes, and their effect on choice of different policies appears to be substantively important as well. This last statement, for which I provide more support in Chapter 6, might ring hollow given the observation of recent bank bailouts, particularly in the United States and Great Britain, the two countries with the longest-running history of democracy on record. As I mentioned before, the observation of bank bailouts in democracies is neither extraordinary nor definitive proof that my argument about the representation of taxpayers' interests in this type of regime is misplaced. However, reasonable skepticism is warranted about the degree to which these recent bailouts alter inferences about democratic effects. To couch the question in the vocabulary of Bayesian inference, how does our knowledge about the effects of democracy on bank bailouts change after updating based on these new data?

To face problems of insolvency and illiquidity, a variety of governments around the world have recently taken actions to prop up their banking systems. Though the shape that these interventions will take, the degree of relief that they will bring to distressed banks, and the changes that they will effect on banking systems remain to be seen, it is possible to carry out a preliminary assessment based on information available at the time of writing. To guarantee a minimum of coherence and comparability, I base this assessment on the *Financial Times* (FT) characterization of government responses to the subprime-mortgage financial crisis as of October 17, 2008.[16] This source summarizes government decisions along six policy areas in 29 countries that have been affected by the recent financial meltdown: liquidity and lending guarantees, bank deposit guarantees, bank recapitalization, asset purchase, interest rate moves, and crackdowns on short selling. The first four areas in this list correspond closely to *liquidity, explicit guarantees, recapitalization,* and *asset management agency*; under bank deposit guarantees, furthermore, this source reports one government, Ukraine, that has enacted a *deposit freeze.* This source does not consider *debt relief* or *regulatory forbearance* as policy categories, which does not necessarily mean that these policies have not been implemented; however, for the purpose of this preliminary exercise, I consider these policies as missing values. I use the FT information to construct dichotomous indicators for five of the seven policies I have thus far considered and I allow previous estimates of item parameters to be updated based on these data. Admittedly, the correspondence between the FT characterization

---

[16]http://www.ft.com/, last accessed on December 12, 2008. The 29 countries are: Australia, Austria, Belgium, China, Denmark, Finland, France, Germany, Great Britain, Greece, Hungary, Iceland, Indonesia, Ireland, Japan, South Korea, New Zealand, Netherlands, Norway, Portugal, Qatar, Russia, Saudi Arabia, Spain, Sweden, Switzerland, United Arab Emirates, United States, and the Ukraine. I code China, Qatar, Russia, Saudi Arabia, and United Arab Emirates as non-democracies.

of policy and the coding decisions of Honohan and Klingebiel (2000) is not perfect, but these preliminary data nonetheless allow a further empirical test of the existence of a democratic advantage.[17]

To update knowledge about the influence of democracy on bailout propensities, I re-estimate the IRT specification that corresponds to Model 3 in Table 5.2. Since all relevant knowledge about effect parameters that we can get from the original sample of $N = 46$ cases is already contained in the posterior distributions reported in that model, we need only use these as prior distributions in a new round of Bayesian updating.[18] Thus, I use the posterior distributions reported in Model 3 (Table 5.2) as a summary of the state of knowledge about bailout propensities. For example, the democratic effect parameter δ is normally distributed with mean -0.324 and standard deviation 0.192; this is the prior information for the democratic effect parameter whose distribution I update based on new data.

After incorporating the new information, the updated results mostly suggest changes in item difficulty parameters; recall that these parameters reflect how common different types of policies are, and may provide a clue as to the political expediency of these policies.[19] Among discrimination parameters, the new information leads to changes that are hardly consequential: *asset management*, *recapitalization*, and *guarantee* are still the policies most likely to be implemented by governments with high bailout propensity, whereas *deposit freeze* and *liquidity* still show parameters that are substantively minute. The main parameter of interest is δ, corresponding to the democratic effect. The posterior distribution of this parameter, based on the new information, is centered on -0.267, with standard deviation 0.165. This suggests a slightly reduced effect, but still one that leads credence to the proposition that democratic governments are less likely to engage in bailouts. This effect continues

---

[17]I code a policy as present whenever FT mentions its implementation, with one exception: I only code *explicit guarantees* as implemented if the policy extends existing deposit insurance schemes to *all* deposits in the banking system. Due to lack of comparable data, I eschew information on interest rate moves and short selling crackdowns (these are outright prohibitions to engage in the practice of "shorting," or selling stock that the seller holds on loan at the time of the transaction).

[18]Bayes theorem guarantees that the "final" posterior distributions based on this two-stage updating method will be identical to the posterior distributions obtained by re-running all models on an expanded sample of $N = 46 + 29$ (DeGroot and Schervish 2002, 72–73). This attractive property of Bayesian estimation implies that we can continue to update our knowledge about the effect of democracy on bank bailouts as new information continues to appear in the months to come.

[19]Mean and standard deviation of the posterior distribution of difficulty parameters are: $\widehat{\alpha}_{AM}$: 0.80 ± 0.23; $\widehat{\alpha}_{R}$: 0.59 ± 0.24; $\widehat{\alpha}_{G}$: 0.37 ± 0.22; $\widehat{\alpha}_{L}$: -0.22 ± 0.15; $\widehat{\alpha}_{F}$: 0.64 ± 0.16. The corresponding statistics for discrimination parameters are: $\widehat{\beta}_{AM}$: 0.80 ± 0.23; $\widehat{\beta}_{R}$: 0.59 ± 0.24; $\widehat{\beta}_{G}$: 0.37 ± 0.22; $\widehat{\beta}_{L}$: -0.22 ± 0.15; $\widehat{\beta}_{F}$: 0.64 ± 0.16. Since I add no new information about *debt relief* or *forbearance*, knowledge about these parameters is not updated.

to obtain even after considering evidence from mostly democratic countries that have implemented bailout policies to prop up their banking systems.

Be this as it may, it is not in general possible to provide a causal interpretation of the political regime effect δ when this parameter is estimated based on observational data. As I argued before, the original sample of 46 government responses is broadly representative of the universe of registered banking crises between 1975 and 2000, but the mechanism of assignment of governments to treatment (democracy) and control (non-democracy) is obviously not known. Under these circumstances, causal interpretation of coefficient δ is only possible under very stringent assumptions about ignorability of the treatment assignment and appropriateness of model specification. In Chapter 6, I make efforts to substantiate a causal interpretation of the effect of democratic regimes on bank bailout policies.

6

Political Regimes and Bailout Propensities

This chapter contributes several necessary extensions to the analysis presented in Chapter 5. The purpose of these extensions is twofold: First, I intend to throw further light on the process that leads governments to implement bank bailouts. Second, and more importantly, I plan to convince the reader that the restraining effect of democratic regimes holds after controlling for other obvious determinants of government policy choice, and after correcting for *covariate imbalance* and potential *endogeneity* of political regimes. In short, my goal is to build a case for a causal, rather than strictly correlational, interpretation of the effects unveiled in Chapter 5.

To do so, I divide the chapter in four sections. Section 6.1 considers alternative explanatory factors that might impinge on the propensity of governments to bail out insolvent banks. One such factor stands out as an important potential confounder, namely, the level of autonomy of a nation's central bank. A second factor—the existence of crony links between bankers and politicians—should be an important predictor of government bailout propensities, but the argument in Chapter 3 leads me to consider this factor as a direct consequence of the level of democracy in a country. In short, I believe that extensive crony networks are endogenous to democratic representation and accountability. Cronyism in this account is a "post-treatment" variable that should not be controlled for in an analysis of the causal effects of political regime, lest the effect of democracy be estimated with bias. Even then, my view of cronyism as endogenous to democracy may be incorrect. Therefore, I consider initially an indicator of corruption among the set of desirable controls in a regression setup. Aside from these two factors, I consider co-variates such as the degree of capital account openness of a country, its level of economic development and inequality, and the relative importance of the domestic banking sector as a crucial link in a country's payments system in order to approximate the stringent assumption of conditional independence.

Sections 6.2 and 6.3 include these controls in the IRT model specifications first presented in Chapter 5, first without and then with corrections for covariate imbalance and endogeneity. The main message of these sections is that political regimes matter even after making allowances for the observational nature of the sample. Finally, Section 6.4 considers a two-dimensional extension to the basic unidimensional IRT model of Chapter 5. Section 6.4 thus explores whether governments make "disjoint" choices along two different policy dimensions, one corresponding to bank *solvency* considerations, the other to *liquidity* concerns. I do so because preliminary results in Chapter 5 suggest that policies to redress solvency and liquidity problems may not necessarily correlate. It follows from this finding that political regimes may only affect one set of policies—i.e., solvency or liquidity policies—rather than both of them. I conclude that political regimes have little effect, if any, on liquidity policies.

6.1 Alternative Explanations

The theoretical argument in Chapter 3 points to the existence of a *democratic effect* in the way in which governments respond to banking crises. The mechanism behind this effect is governmental anticipation of the policy preferences of the median voter, which leads to more conservative closure rules in the event of a banking crisis.

In Chapter 5, I estimate a political regime parameter (δ) in a regression-like framework and posit that its size and sign are consistent with Proposition 1. This interpretation is not strictly correct: For δ to reflect a true *democratic effect*, its estimation would require random assignment conditions that can only be approached, at best, through experimental manipulation. In the absence of true random assignment in an experimental setting, a causal interpretation of δ depends on very stringent assumptions about the process that generated assignment of governments into the *democracy* and *non-democracy* categories, assumptions that can only be approximated with careful modeling choices. The first and perhaps most important of these assumptions is *conditional independence*, also known as ignorability of the treatment assignment or selection on observables. The most obvious way to think about conditional independence is as a requirement to control for confounding covariates that may be associated both with political regimes and bailout propensities.

Needless to say, building an exhaustive catalog of all such potential confounding covariates is well-nigh impossible. However, political economists have studied a variety of factors that may be consequential in understanding government bailout propensities. More importantly, the theoretical argument explored in Chapter 3 points to several obvious confounding factors. Previous theoretical knowledge suggests that *central bank independence*, importance of the *domestic banking sector*, the level of *economic openness* of a country, and its level of *economic development* should be controlled for to approximate conditional independence. I consider each of these potential confounders in the following sections.

6.1.1 Central Bank Independence

The theoretical argument in Chapter 3 is premised on the assumption that governments are not constrained in their ability to provide loans to distressed banks upon observation of large liquidity shocks. In other words, I assume that politicians control the levers of monetary policy. However, this assumption is not entirely tenable in countries where central banks are autonomous from political pressures. More problematically, many polities have moved in recent decades towards the adoption of charters that secure independence for central banks and allow them to pursue monetary stability with minimal political meddling (Maxfield 1997). It is well understood that politicians may be tempted to rely on easy money in hard economic times (Kydland and Prescott 1977; Sargent and Wallace 1975); hence the relevance of policy advice to get politicians' hands off monetary policy. Indeed, the proposition that institutionally-autonomous central banks are less likely to produce high bouts of inflation has received ample empirical confirmation in observational studies (Cukierman 1992; Cukierman, Miller and Neyapti 2002; Cukierman, Webb and Neyapti 1992; Desai, Olofsgård and Yousef 2003; Franzese 1999; Grilli, Masciandaro and Tabellini 1991).

The stabilizing effect of autonomous central banks is relevant in an analysis of bank bailouts because these institutions are also called to perform the function of lending of last resort (cf. Bagehot 1873; Goodhart and Illing 2002). From the point of view of the monetary authority, banking crises may present a stark choice between an expansive policy to aid illiquid banks and conservative use of the monetary tool to preserve price stability. Even independent central banks could decide, however, to bail out banks rather than preserve the value of the national currency. After all, institutional independence from political pressures only guarantees that politicians will not control the money supply; it does not necessarily mean that central bankers will always err on the side of preserving price stability. Still, because of legal stipulations to pursue low inflation that are often found in central bank charters, independent central bankers should be less likely, all else constant, to act as overly generous lenders of last resort to the banking system during a crisis, let alone to accommodate fiscal expansion to bail out banks. Inasmuch as central bank autonomy entails tighter monetary policy, it should also curtail a politician's ability to carry out bank bailouts.

Despite its likely effect on bailout propensities, central bank autonomy should be considered a relevant confounding variable only if it is also associated with political regimes. Evidence and theory suggesting elective affinities between democracies and autonomous central banks are less plentiful. Part of the problem is that the literature on the political determinants of institutional variation in the status of central banks has focused largely on advanced market economies, which are by-and-large democratic. For example, Bernhard argues that variation in intraparty or intracoalitional conflicts explains incentives to delegate monetary policy to independent central banks, an argument he substantiates by analyzing central bank reform in advanced democratic regimes (Bernhard 2002). Relatedly, some contributions consider the effect of veto players on the adoption (Hallerberg 2002) and effectiveness (Keefer and Stasavage 2002, 2003) of different monetary policy arrangements. An implication of these arguments is that adoption of central bank independence may be related to political regimes, as democracies are more likely to count with checks-and-balance mechanisms captured by the notion of veto players. Perhaps Boylan (2001) and Broz (2002) present the clearest theoretical arguments substantiating the possibility of a correlation between central bank status and political regime. Boylan contends that authoritarian regimes that carry out deep market-oriented economic reform may provide autonomy to the monetary authority in anticipation of transition to democracy. By doing so, market-friendly dictators secure their economic legacy by limiting the ability of profligate democratic governments to spend their way into fiscal crises. By this account, independent central banks ought to be over-represented among democracies with recent authoritarian pasts. Broz (2002) also suggests that political regimes and central bank independence may be correlated. In his argument, countries signal commitment to a low-inflation monetary policy by choosing a fixed exchange rate regime (a transparent signal) or central bank independence (an "opaque" commitment technology). In democracies, the political process is itself transparent, and so resorting to central bank independence signals commitment; autocracies instead can only resort to fixed exchange rates. Democracies can take advantage of central bank independence as a commitment mechanism because they are transparent regimes Other arguments about central bank independence discount the possibility of affinities between political regimes and central bank status. For example, Maxfield (1997) considers the adoption of central bank independence among middle-income economies to be a consequence of a country's need for international credit and investment, regardless of political regime; in her account, central bank independence sends a credible signal of credit-worthiness to international investors.

Be this as it may, the institutional status of central banks is perhaps the most important confounding variable in my analysis, so regardless of its theoretical links with political regimes I include it as a covariate. I resort to the index of legal central bank independence created by Cukierman, Webb and Neyapti (1992) and updated by Cukierman, Miller and Neyapti (2002) and Polillo and Guillén (2005) as an indicator of the institutional status of the monetary authority. The correlation between Przeworski et al.'s dichotomous regime score and the index of legal central bank independence based on 39 full observations is 0.25, which indeed suggests that democratic politicians tend to have less influence on the conduct of monetary policy.

6.1.2 Economic Development and Inequality

It is important to control for the effect of economic variables for two reasons. First and foremost, my argument about the constraining effects of democracy is premised on the idea that different economic structures affect the probability that governments will engage in bailouts. Recall that the argument in Chapter 3 suggests that bailouts are relatively more onerous to the median voter in unequal societies. Therefore, inequality should be *negatively* associated with a government's bailout propensity. In principle, this effect should also be seen with regards to level of economic development. As we saw in Chapter 3, a government's closure rule becomes more conservative (i.e., the government will have lower bailout propensity) as the average level of economic well-being in society increases. The effect of economic development, however, occurs only through the spread parameter σ in the Pareto distribution that I use to approximate patterns of economic inequality. Therefore, after controlling for inequality, a country's level of economic development may have little effect on its government's bailout propensity.

Second, recent advances in political economy suggest that both *level of economic development* and *economic inequality* may affect a society's opportunities to develop a sustainable democratic regime. In the case of economic development, an old debate that in its most recent incarnation can be traced back to modernization theory concerns the links between democracy and wealth. Some argue that democracies are simply more likely to survive under conditions of economic affluence (Przeworski et al. 2000), whereas others provide evidence that wealth directly engenders democracy (Boix and Stokes 2003). In either case, it is evident that richer countries are more likely to have democratic political regimes than poorer countries, so in fact there is a high correlation between these two variables. When it comes to economic inequality, democracies might be more unlikely to emerge and survive in economies with grave patterns of inequality (Acemoglu and Robinson 2005; Boix 2003). Underlying this insight is the proposition that the policy preferences of the median voter in unequal societies are for greater redistribution from the very rich. Anticipating that these preferences will be decisive under democratic rule, economic elites oppose transition to a more open political regime; instead, they might be more willing to accept democracy if the median voter prefers less redistribution, as happens in principle in egalitarian societies.

In other words, it is unlikely that political regimes are independent of patterns of economic inequality and development. Inequality and development are likely to be correlated with the main independent variable,[1] and as argued in Chapter 3 they should also affect bailout propensities. If we were not to control for these two variables, we might mistakenly attribute part of their influence on bailout propensity to a country's political regime. I use the real per capita GDP of a country (log scale) as an indicator of level of development; for economic inequality, I use Gini indices from the United Nations University's World Income Inequality Database, as corrected by Desai, Olofsgård and Yousef (2003).

6.1.3 Crony Capitalism

The theoretical importance that many scholars grant to crony capitalism as a factor that explains bank bailouts is undeniable. As reviewed in Chapter 1, several scholars have studied the links between politicians and entrepreneurs/bankers, and conclude that these are economically consequential. At the firm level, Faccio (2006) and Faccio, Masulis and McConnell (2006) study the performance of firms that count politicians among their large shareholders or as board members and compares it with the performance of non-connected firms. Faccio does not assume explicitly the existence of any *quid pro quo* in the relationship between politicians and entrepreneurs, but her research finds that political connectedness provides firms with better debt financing, higher tax benefits, and larger market power. Politically-connected firms are also more inefficient, as they tend to generate lower returns-on-equity, lower market-to-book ratios, and lower stock prices. More tellingly, politically-connected firms are more likely to be bailed out in case of financial distress. In the realm of banking, Bongini, Claessens and Ferri (2001) find that banks with crony links were more likely to suffer financial distress based on bank-level data from the East Asian financial crisis, even though crony links were not significant predictors of bailouts. There is also some evidence that government-owned banks are routinely used to bolster political fortunes. Dinç (2005) finds that government-owned banks in emerging markets increase their lending in election years compared to private banks and Khwaja and Mian (2005) explore loan-level data from Pakistan to discover that public banks make larger loans to connected firms, that returns on these assets are

---

[1] The sample correlations between *inequality* and *GDP per capita*, on the one hand, and the dichotomous democracy score, on the other, are −0.086 and 0.495. Sample correlations with the continuous Polity IV score are −0.139 and 0.556, respectively.

lower, that connected firms are more likely to default, and that recovery rates conditional on default are lower for connected firms. Moreover, stronger politicians (based on information about their electoral prowess) are more likely to get larger loans.

Crony capitalism should also be related to a country's political regime, a conclusion I arrive at in my theoretical analysis. In Chapter 3, politicians in democratic regimes purport to implement the policy preferences of the median voter. Since these preferences are for less onerous bailouts, politicians strive to reduce the impact of financial distress on taxpayers, and they do so by, among other things, limiting the extent of crony links with entrepreneurs. Incidentally, Haber (2002*a*) provides a theory about crony capitalism that starts from different assumptions but reaches similar implications. In his theory, democracy and cronyism are functional equivalents in that either of these factors gives credibility to the ruler's commitment not to expropriate investments. The difference between these factors is that where democracy makes this commitment credible by creating checks on arbitrary rule, cronyism solves the commitment problem by allowing the ruler to share in the rents created by entrepreneurial action, thus reducing the ruler's temptation to expropriate.

In any case, I expect democracy and cronyism to be negatively correlated, but I also believe with Haber that there is a strong causal link flowing from political regime to cronyism. Consequently, any proxy for crony capitalism should be appropriately considered a "post-treatment variable" according to the argument laid out in Chapter 3. As such, its inclusion is not advisable in a model that purports to estimate causal effects of political regimes. The inclusion of post-treatment variables in a regression framework works at cross-purposes with the inclusion of pre-treatment variables. Whereas controlling for pre-treatment variables like economic development or economic inequality helps one approximate the ideal condition of comparing "like" units, introducing a proxy for a post-treatment variable all but guarantees that "treated" and "control" units will be fundamentally different (Gelman and Hill 2007, 188–190). If my theoretical argument is correct, including a crony capitalism variable in the regression analysis would radically change the interpretation of the political regime coefficient. In this case, the coefficient of *democracy* would represent a difference in bailout propensities among observations that vary along the political regime dimension, but also along the crony capitalism dimension. Be this as it may, my theoretical framework may be mistaken in assuming that crony capitalism is endogenous to democracy. If in fact cronyism is not endogenous to democracy, the empirical correlation between indicators of political regime and cronyism would mandate inclusion of the latter among the set of controlling factors in a regression setup. To cover all bases, I estimate models with and without an indicator of crony capitalism. As I show below, the estimated coefficient of political regime on bailout propensity is substantively smaller when including the crony capitalism indicator, as is to be expected, but in general not too different from estimates of the regime effect in the absence of a crony capitalism indicator.

Kang (2002) notes in his study on East Asia how difficult it is to measure intrinsic features of crony capitalism. In contrast with him, I do consider that indicators of corruption provide a reasonable approximation to the measurement of cronyism at the country level. Admittedly, cronyism and corruption are not synonyms, but it is reasonable to expect that where corruption is low the chances are also low that politicians, bankers, and entrepreneurs will be consistently enmeshed in the kind of crony arrangements suggested in Chapter 3. I build an indicator of relative lack of corruption, *transparency*, from commonly employed data (Knack and Keefer 1998; Transparency International 2002). I expect the ensuing *transparency* measure to be negatively associated with bailout propensity.[2]

6.1.4 Other Controls

To approximate conditional independence, it is important to control for at least two other factors: *capital openness* and *importance of the domestic banking sector*. I consider the possibility, hinted at but not considered explicitly in Chapter 3, that the optimal closure rule may be a function of the importance of banks within a country's financial sector. Where financial markets are primarily organized around banks, then bank closures threaten severe economic disruptions as the ensuing credit crunch threatens entrepreneurial projects. Undoubtedly, some of these projects should be terminated, especially if they contributed to bank insolvency, but bank closures also derail viable projects. Politicians may find it too costly to terminate banks if their failure threatens high negative externalities. In other words, I acknowledge that redressing bank insolvency at minimum public cost might entail postponing the exit of insolvent banks from the banking system. To control for this factor, I include the ratio of total deposits in the banking system to gross domestic product (Beck, Demirgüç-Kunt and Levine 1999). *Deposit share* is a proxy for the relative importance of banks as intermediaries within a nation's financial system.

Domestic institutions that hinder cronyism are not the only potential constraints on a politician's decision to bail out banks. Instead, international factors impinge upon domestic policy-making. In an era of global integration of capital and goods markets, the ability of politicians to carry out independent

---

[2] Treisman (2000) shows that TI and ICRG (Knack and Keefer 1998) indices are very highly correlated. Hence, I standardize these two measures to a common 1–10 metric and use their average as an indicator of transparency.

public policies can be constrained by the possibility of capital flight (Andrews 1994; Cooper 1968; Oatley 1999). Though opening up a nation's borders to capital flows and increased trade opportunities improves a country's access to cheaper credit and allows specialization close to comparative advantage, it might also mean foregoing the use of Keynesian tools of demand management. As Obstfeld (1998) argues, globalization has the beneficial side-effect of disciplining governments, forcing them into a path of sustainable budgets and price stability. With respect to bank bailouts, globalization might exert a similar downward pressure on fiscal profligacy. Politicians may choose policies closer to Bagehot to the extent that their countries are more thoroughly integrated into the world economy through capital markets. Therefore, I include an indicator of *capital openness* as a further control (Chinn and Ito 2002).

As argued before, one can potentially think of a host of factors that might determine a government's bailout propensity and that may correlate with political regimes. However, omitted variables pose a threat to causal interpretation (a) when they correlate with the dependent variable, and (b) when they are causally prior to the independent variable whose causal impact one aims to gauge, in this case regime type. This is the case for all controls discussed in the previous sections. I also considered several other covariates in alternative specifications, which are reported in an exploratory paper (cf. Rosas 2006). Among these, I included a dummy for the existence of a stand-by agreement with the IMF on the starting year of a banking crisis, an indicator of bank concentration, the market share of foreign banks, the micro- vs. macro-economic origin of banking crises, and the country's degree of trade openness. Though some of these indicators were significant predictors of bailout propensity, they did not alter the estimated effect of political regime in a substantive way. Furthermore, I could not find theoretical arguments that would allow me to construe these indicators as *pre-treatment* factors associated with democracy, which explains my preference for more parsimonious model specifications.

6.2 Controlling for Observable Predictors

Table A.2.2 in the Appendix contains summary information about all indicators used in the analysis.[3] The control variables discussed in the previous

---

[3] As Table A.2.2 makes clear, there are missing values in some covariates. Throughout the book, I deal with missing values in *independent variables* in a principled way. First, I obtain multiple imputations of missing values in a Bayesian MCMC context under the assumption of random missingness (Van Buuren and Oudshoorn 2000). I then estimate all models based on five *complete* datasets, which contain as many imputations for each missing value. Reported estimates are based on a combination of the five resulting samples from the posterior distribution; using

sections are added as predictors of government bailout propensities, that is,

$$\mu_{\theta_i} = \delta_0 \cdot democracy_i + \delta_1 \cdot central\ bank_i + \cdots + \delta_7 \cdot deposit\ share_i \quad (6.1)$$

The hierarchical specification of Equation 6.1 adds a series of control variables to the basic setup of Equation 5.4. In other words, the new specification recognizes that governments in the sample differ along dimensions other than just their political regimes; some of these dimensions may be consequential in understanding the bailout propensities of governments as they react to banking crises. I estimate four versions of this model.[4] Table 6.1 displays Bayesian estimates of effect parameters δ; estimates of item discrimination (β) and difficulty (α) parameters are omitted for the sake of space, but in all cases are very similar to those reported in Table 5.2.

Models 1 and 3 in Table 6.1 confirm the negative association between continuous and dichotomous political regime indicators, on the one hand, and *bailout propensity*, on the other, that I had uncovered before, this time after controlling for theoretically-relevant factors and the "post-treatment" *transparency* indicator. In fact, estimates of the effect parameters of *democracy* in both models are about similar in magnitude to the ones in Chapter 5. In the case of the dichotomous indicator (Model 3), the posterior distribution of the effect parameter for *democracy* is clearly centered away from 0 and on the negative orthant (its 95% credible interval is –1.106, –0.199); when switching to the continuous Polity IV score (Model 1), the 95% credible interval for the effect parameter still straddles 0, as was the case in Chapter 5, though most probability mass still appears to the left of 0. It is also noteworthy that estimated coefficients for other control variables are signed according to expectations. Especially in Model 3, the posterior distributions of coefficients on *central bank independence* (95% CI: –0.686, 0.109) and *income inequality* (95% CI: –0.774, 0.069) have little probability mass to the right of zero, suggesting that countries with high levels of central bank autonomy and high levels of economic inequality are less prone to engage in bailout policies, all else constant. The negative sign on the *central bank* coefficient is consistent with accumulated theoretical knowledge about the

---

this procedure, one can appropriately factor uncertainty derived from the multiple imputation process into coefficient estimates. Missing values in dependent variables are still imputed as a by-product of the MCMC sampling process (see fn. 7 in Chapter 5). This process can be regarded as an iterative multiple imputation procedure that properly reflects uncertainty due to missing values (see Gelman et al. 2004, 519–520).

[4]These models are identified using restrictions similar to those employed in Chapter 5. In particular, I avoid rotational invariance by assuming a priori that discrimination parameters can only take on non-negative values. As in Chapter 5, all indicators are standardized; since they have mean 0 and the prior distribution of θ is also centered at 0, I do not estimate an intercept. The prior distribution on each coefficient δ is $\mathcal{N}(0, 0.001)$, a diffuse and rather uninformative prior.

Table 6.1: Bayesian estimation of covariate coefficients (δ). The point estimate is the median of the parameter's posterior density (standard deviation of the posterior density in parentheses). Models 1 and 2 are based on the continuous Polity IV democracy indicator; Models 3 and 4 are based on the dichotomous regime indicator in Przeworski et al. (2000).

	Model 1	Model 2	Model 3	Model 4
Democracy	−0.239	−0.251	−0.609	−0.534
	(0.254)	(0.238)	(0.254)	(0.262)
Central bank	−0.146	−0.179	−0.274	−0.257
	(0.211)	(0.221)	(0.243)	(0.226)
GDP per capita	0.184	−0.108	0.389	0.031
	(0.379)	(0.281)	(0.402)	(0.288)
Income inequality	−0.311	−0.445	−0.351	−0.502
	(0.244)	(0.225)	(0.260)	(0.251)
Capital openness	−0.064	−0.023	−0.154	−0.101
	(0.263)	(0.251)	(0.260)	(0.277)
Deposit share	−0.041	0.044	−0.010	0.022
	(0.251)	(0.226)	(0.266)	(0.228)
Transparency	−0.210		−0.203	
	(0.389)		(0.388)	
DIC	376.70	374.90	376.10	374.20
pD	38.99	36.69	38.50	36.77

restraining effect of autonomy of the monetary authority. The coefficient on *income inequality* is in line with predictions flowing from Chapter 3 about the unwillingness of politicians to have generous closure rules in countries where the median voter is relatively poorer.

Other control variables have coefficients that are *not* entirely distinguishable from 0, but are in most cases signed in the right direction. In the case of *GDP per capita*, my theoretical expectation was either a nil effect or a negative effect. Recall from Chapter 3 that the "location" parameter of a country's economic distribution (μ) drops out of the politician's calculus as she entertains whether to support an illiquid bank or not. Given that we identify this parameter with the overall level of wealth of a country, this theoretical result would lead one to expect a nil effect. However, given the specific assumptions I made about the theoretical distribution of income in an economy, the "spread" parameter (σ corresponds more closely to economic inequality) also affects overall levels of wealth (higher values of σ correspond to higher average wealth). In this interpretation, we would then expect a negative association between *GDP per capita* and bailout propensity. Either way, the point estimate for *GDP per capita* shifts signs depending on whether *transparency* is also controlled for, an artifact of high sample correlation between these two variables; the posterior distribution of this parameter is extremely wide and leaves ample probability mass to the left and right of 0. For all purposes, I conclude that the coefficient of *GDP per capita* is not distinguishable from 0. The same argument leads me to disregard *deposit share* as a relevant predictor of *bailout propensity*.

The coefficients on *transparency* and *capital openness* are signed according to expectations—they are both negative, suggesting that more transparent and open economies are less likely to suffer bailout-prone governments—but again their coefficients have posterior distributions with wide standard deviations that straddle 0. Incidentally, excluding *transparency* from the analysis, as I do in Models 2 and 4, has discernible effects on the estimates of *GDP per capita* but not on the political regime coefficients, which remain largely unchanged. Recall that the rationale for the exclusion of *transparency* is the post-treatment character of crony capitalism in my theoretical account of bank bailouts.

Models 1 through 4 confirm that democratic regimes are associated with lower bailout propensities, even after accounting for potential confounders. The mechanism linking political regimes to bank bailouts is anticipation of the policy preferences of the median voter. The negative sign on *income inequality* is consistent with this interpretation; after all, the median voter in an economically inegalitarian society carries relatively higher costs and enjoys relatively lower benefits from banks that are restored to solvency using taxpayers' money. This evidence leads me to believe that the posited mechanism is indeed responsible for the degree of association between political regimes and bailout propensities. Further evidence comes from dissecting democracy into two of its main characteristics. Indeed, while I have emphasized representation of the policy preferences of the median voter/taxpayer—which is enabled by accountability of democratic politicians to the electorate—as the relevant mechanism, democratic regimes are also characterized by strong systems of checks-and-balances that may limit policy response. The positive association between bailout propensities and political regimes may be the consequence of democratic checks-and-balances rather than democratic accountability.

To distinguish the effects of these different features of democracy on bailouts, I decompose the Polity IV score into its three separate "concept variables" and use two of these to proxy for the *accountability* and *checks-and-balances* mechanisms of democracy. The relevant sub-indices are described as "the extent of institutional constraints on the decision-making powers of the chief executive" (*excons*) and "the openness of executive recruitment" (*exrec*). Though correspondences are far from perfect, *excons* embodies the idea of veto points, whereas *exrec* corresponds to the ease with which voters can replace the holder of executive power. In a specification identical to that of Models 2 and 4, the posterior distribution of *excons* is centered on −0.14 ± 0.24 (median ± SD); when I replace *exrec* for *excons* in this model, the posterior distribution lies more clearly on the negative orthant and is centered on −0.36 (±0.24). Finally, I resort to the *checks2* indicator from the Database of Political Institutions, which is a more obvious proxy for the number of veto points or legislative checks on executive behavior. The posterior distribution of *checks2* is centered on 0.21 (±0.20), which suggests that, if anything, more veto points are conducive to higher bailout propensities. These alternative estimates suggest that to the degree that political regimes are good predictors of bailout propensities, the transmission mechanism is more likely to be electoral accountability than checks-and-balances.

6.3 A Causal Interpretation of Regime Effects

Controlling for observed confounders is not the only obstacle in the way of a causal interpretation of the effect parameter of democracy. The analysis in this chapter is based on observational data, and therefore one must proceed with caution to reach valid causal inferences about the effects of political regimes on bailout propensities. I explore issues of *covariate imbalance* and *non-ignorable treatment assignment* in this section.[5] To motivate the discussion, consider the distribution of control variables across democracies and non-democracies based on the dichotomous indicator of political regimes (Table 6.2). Consistent with observed relations among wealth, income inequality, and political regimes in the contemporary world, we see that democracies in the sample are on average richer and have flatter income distributions than non-democratic regimes. Furthermore, and also consistent with previous theoretical knowledge, the democratic regimes in the sample tend to have higher *transparency* scores; they also have larger measures of *deposit share*, which is likely a consequence of the higher degree of development among democratic regimes. Instead, the difference between mean *central bank independence* scores across democratic and non-democratic regimes seems trivial.

Naturally, this lack of balance in the sample distribution of covariates provides an important rationale for including them as control variables in the bailout propensity models. After all, we know that researchers cannot assign

---

[5]These are problems that plague the search for causal effects regardless of the inferential framework that researchers adopt; that is, they need to be addressed in Bayesian analysis as much as in a frequentist setup.

Table 6.2: Sample means of control variables across democratic and non-democratic regimes, along with percent improvement in balance based on matched data

	Non-democracy	Democracy	% Balance improvement
Central bank autonomy	0.37	0.32	100.00
GDP per capita (log)	8.40	9.10	35.86
Income inequality	43.21	39.19	87.94
Capital openness	0.48	0.59	−7.35
Transparency	3.48	5.34	47.28
Deposit share	0.31	0.36	89.45
Propensity score	0.32	0.38	31.17
N	19	27	

political regimes randomly to countries, a situation that would automatically guarantee conditional independence across units. But even after controlling for these factors, the condition of covariate imbalance across political regimes poses a more subtle quandary to our ability to provide a causal interpretation of the regime effect. Because we tend to observe democratic regimes among countries that are richer, have more egalitarian income distributions, and more transparent business environments, there exists a real risk that the estimated effect of *democracy* on bailout propensity may be driven preponderantly by assumptions about the functional form of the model. In other words, we may not have enough data points corresponding to *democratic* regimes in poor, unequal, and corrupt settings on which to base an estimate of the average regime effect; in the absence of informative data, this estimate will be determined solely by the assumption of linearity of bailout propensities with respect to the effect parameter of *democracy*.

In order to assess the causal impact of political regimes we would like to observe paired governments identical in all respects except for their political regime. In this ideal setup, we would be closer to truly estimating the average causal effect of democracy on bailout propositions. Though a perfect pairing of democratic and non-democratic regimes is not possible, it is possible to limit the sample to a reduced set of observations that are closely "matched." By doing so, we can approximate conditions of randomization of observed

Figure 6.1: Propensity scores of democracies and non-democracies. Black dots are unmatched democracies, gray dots correspond to observations outside the region of common support.

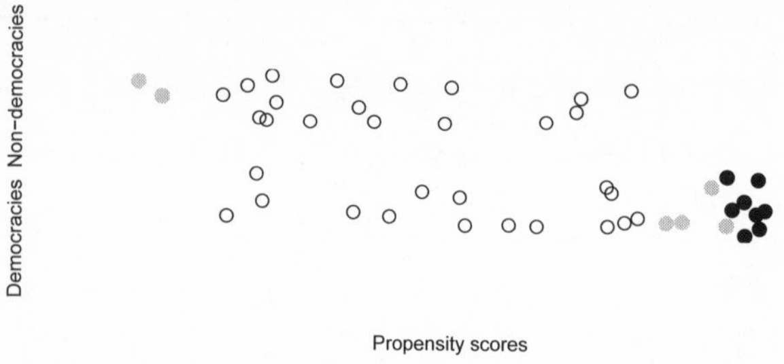

covariates across treatment and control groups.[6] To this effect, I use the technique of nearest neighbor matching based on propensity scores. In essence, I estimate propensity scores for each observation based on a logistic regression of *political regime* on the six relevant control variables of Table 6.2. Note that these "propensity scores" *are not* the same as the government "bailout propensities" shown in Figure 5.3. The propensity scores are the fitted probabilities derived from the logistic regression and consequently vary between 0 and 1, with higher numbers corresponding to observations that are more likely to be predicted as democratic regimes. Finally, each non-democratic regime in the sample is matched to the one democratic regime with the closest propensity score; matching proceeds until all non-democracies are matched to one and only one democracy.[7] Note finally that the matching exercise is not based on information about the dependent variable (i.e., the policy items). In building a matched dataset, ignoring values of the dependent variable guarantees that no information on outcomes determines which observations go into treatment and control groups, and thus approximates conditions of an experimental design.

Figure 6.1 provides a graphical illustration of how matching renders a more balanced sample of democracies and non-democracies. The graph plots

---

[6]Cf. Ho, Imai, King and Stuart (2007*a*); King and Zeng (2006); Rosenbaum and Rubin (1983).

[7]I use the MatchIt software of Ho, Imai, King and Stuart (2007*b*). Because of missing observations among some of the covariates in these logit models, I impute missing values *before* proceeding with propensity score matching. In practice, then, I carry out the matching exercise on five imputed datasets, identical in all respects except in the values of missing observations that were imputed.

the forty-six democratic and non-democratic governments on the vertical axis (jittered for display purposes) against each government's propensity score. Because the distribution of political regimes is not random with respect to control variables, the propensity scores of democracies tend to be higher than the propensity scores of non-democracies. After matching, some of the democratic regimes—corresponding to the black dots in the lower-right corner—are dropped from the analysis, which leaves 19 democracies matched with 19 non-democracies. The eight democratic governments that are dropped from the analysis are Finland 1991, Hungary 1991, Japan 1992, Korea 1997, New Zealand 1987, Norway 1987, Spain 1977, and Sweden 1991. This list of unmatched democracies confirms, for example, the outlier character of the Scandinavian democracies (Finland and Sweden have Gini scores that are more than one standard deviation below the sample mean), but some of these other countries are "unique" in other ways. As can be gleaned from Table 6.2, balance among covariates is much improved; the "% balance improvement" statistic is a measure of the distance between the sample distribution of covariates across democracies and non-democracies before and after matching. Except for *capital openness*, which is slightly more unbalanced after than before matching, there are notable improvements in the similarity of cases across political regimes when analysis is restricted to the matched sample. Thus, the sample of matched observations achieves maximum balance on covariates and keeps as many observations as possible in the analysis.

Parameter estimates based on the reduced matched sample of 38 governments appear in Table 6.3 (item parameter estimates, not shown, are similar to those in Table 5.2). The estimated political regime effects are slightly smaller than those based on the full sample (Table 6.1), but they are of similar magnitude (point estimates are –0.52 and –0.50, 90% credible intervals are –0.98 to –0.10 in Model 5 and –0.93 to –0.11 in Model 6). Model 5 includes relevant controls and confirms that the negative coefficient estimate for *democracy* is not overtly dependent on the functional form of the model. Model 6 omits controls and instead estimates a coefficient for the propensity score itself. It should in principle be sufficient to include propensity scores as the relevant control, because these measures already contain all possible information about covariate imbalance (Rosenbaum and Rubin 1983). However, the main condition for propensity scores to be a valid summary of covariates is that they are based on the "true" propensity model, which needless to say is an unverifiable assumption. Be this as it may, comparison of the coefficient estimates for *democracy* in Models 5 and 6 confirms that not much is lost by substituting control covariates with the propensity score; this finding will come handy in Section 6.4.

Returning to Figure 6.1, we can see that propensity score matching still

Table 6.3: Bayesian estimation of government-level parameters (δ) based exclusively on *matched* (Models 5–6) or *common support* (Models 7–8) cases, and *instrumental variables two-stage least squares regression* (Models 9–10). Point estimate is the median of the parameter's posterior density (standard deviation of the posterior density).

	Matched observations		Common support		2SLS	
	Model 5	Model 6	Model 7	Model 8	Model 9	Model 10
Democracy	−0.523	−0.503	−0.487	−0.437	−0.282	−0.141
	(0.270)	(0.249)	(0.303)	(0.239)	(0.110)	(0.149)
Central bank	−0.549		−0.837		−0.074	−0.049
	(0.299)		(0.356)		(0.095)	(0.096)
GDP per capita	0.192		0.362		−0.015	−0.060
	(0.288)		(0.345)		(0.108)	(0.109)
Income inequality	−0.699		−0.942		−0.170	−0.157
	(0.314)		(0.393)		(0.098)	(0.100)
Capital openness	−0.261		−0.113		−0.003	0.025
	(0.279)		(0.340)		(0.101)	(0.099)
Deposit share	0.034		0.022		0.041	0.041
	(0.246)		(0.248)		(0.102)	(0.100)
Propensity score		0.167		0.211		
		(0.228)		(0.234)		
DIC	301.2	301.6	255.0	256.0	99.8	220.0
pD	32.29	33.43	28.73	30.31	5.3	11.2
N	38	38	32	32	46	46

leaves some imbalance in the distribution of propensity scores. Even worse, the graph suggests that the overlap of propensity scores between democracies and non-democracies is far from perfect. Lack of complete overlap means that there are democracies in the sample which do not have a "counterfactual" observation, i.e., another observation alike in all respects but with a non-democratic regime. In Figure 6.1 I have identified six further observations, shown as gray dots, that lie outside the common support of propensity scores. These include four democracies (Argentina 1989, Australia 1989, Brazil, 1994, and France 1994) and two authoritarian regimes (Indonesia 1997 and Senegal 1988). When these are dropped from the analysis, the remaining sample is no longer perfectly matched (there are fifteen democracies and seventeen non-democracies), but is now based on observations with common support on propensity scores. Parameter estimates based on the "common support" sample with 32 observations appear in Models 7 and 8. Again, the estimated political regime effects are lower than in larger samples, but still remain within the same order of magnitude (point estimates are –0.49 and –0.44, 90% CI from −1.02 to −0.05 in Model 7 and −0.85 to −0.06 in Model 8). Based on these results, we can conclude that lack of balance among covariates—which bedevils many estimates of the effects of political regimes in realms other than banking policy because of the affinities among wealth, equality, and democracy—is of no great consequence in this sample. Consequently, for the remainder of the chapter, I will inspect information from the full sample of 46 observations.

Having concluded that covariate imbalance is not problematic, I now turn to the second quandary—the assumption of ignorability of the treatment assignment —which turns out to be more consequential. In part, I have already taken steps to approximate this assumption by including observed covariates in the models of bailout propensity. Taking this step guarantees that the effect of democracy is not vulnerable to the problem of selection on observables. However, there may well be other unobserved factors—the real extent of insolvency, the severity of an exogenous shock, or the lobbying power of bank shareholders, for example—that may correlate with political regimes and affect the ability of governments to deal with banking crises, thus affecting their bailout propensities. Though I have been careful to include as controls all factors that relate theoretically to political regime *and* bailout propensity, the basic inability to randomize treatment in observational studies means that one can never be sure that the effect of democracy is not biased by unobserved omitted variables. Keefer (2007, p. 632) for example wonders if the reduced propensity of democracies to engage in bailouts "could be driven by the possibility that precrisis financial policies are different in democracies and autocracies, affecting the probability that they experience crises or the nature of those crises and, as a consequence, their policy response once crisis occurs." There are several alternative ways of alleviating this problem in applied research. The approach I follow here is to provide an instrumental-variables estimate of the effect of democracy on bailout propensities based on two-stage least squares analysis.

In order to perform this estimation, it is necessary to count with a valid instrument for political regime. Recently, there have been a variety of attempts to interpret coefficients in observational political economy studies in a causal manner; it is little wonder then that several instruments of democracy have been recently proposed.[8] I considered oil exports, British colonial heritage, constitutional age of a country, number of prior transitions to democracy, and coastline length as potential instruments. Behind each of these instrumental variables there is a theoretical account that substantiates the assumption of ignorability of the instrument. Unfortunately, none of these potential instruments correlated highly with democratic status in the sample, therefore failing the basic condition of non-zero association between instrument and treatment variable. In the end, I resorted to the average level of *regional democracy* as an instrument for political regime. The correlation between political regime and the proposed instrument is 0.556.

Aside from this criterion of relevance, the validity of instrumental variables estimation hinges on two critical assumptions, namely, *monotonicity* and *exclusion restriction*. To assess the degree of verisimilitude of these assumptions, consider the rationale for employing *regional democracy* as an instrument for a country's regime type. We know empirically that authoritarian countries are more likely to transit to democracy if a majority of their neighbors are democratic (Gleditsch and Ward 2006). The "diffusion effect" of democracies may operate through a variety of mechanisms. Gleditsch and Ward (2006), for example, consider the possibility that the democratization of neighboring countries may change the regional distribution of power and/or the preferences of politicians and societal actors in an authoritarian regime. In this context, the assumption of monotonicity implies that a country in a region with high levels of democracy is at least as likely to be a democracy as it would be were it located in a region with low levels of democracy. This assumption is eminently plausible given ample evidence about the mechanisms behind diffusion of democracy. The second assumption, exclusion restriction, implies that a government's bailout propensity is not affected by *regional democracy* after controlling for its own political regime. In other words, any effect that *regional democracy* may have on bailout propensities is assumed to occur exclusively through its impact on regime itself. This assumption would be violated, for example, if democratic regimes in the vicinity of a financially-troubled democracy tended to lend a hand by providing funds

---

[8]See *inter alia* Keefer (2007); Persson and Tabellini (2003); Przeworski et al. (2000).

Figure 6.2: Posterior predictive distribution of bailout propensity scores for democratic and non-democratic regimes. The panel on the left is based on Bayesian regression estimates, the panel on the right on Bayesian IV-2SLS estimates.

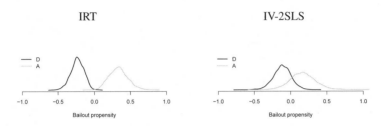

to bail out banks. Whereas support to manage banking crises may be available from international financial institutions or even other large countries, it does not seem plausible that neighboring countries would coordinate for this purpose.[9]

Before discussing the instrumental variables estimate of the *democracy* effect, one further caveat is in order. The estimates presented in Models 9 and 10 are not based on the extended IRT model I have discussed so far. To facilitate estimation, the dependent variable in these models is the point estimate of government bailout propensities derived from Model 4 in Table 5.2. These point estimates provide my best guess regarding the underlying propensity of each government to engage in bailouts, and are based on information from the seven crisis management policies and the political regime of each government. It is no wonder, then, that the Bayesian regression estimate of *democracy* in Model 9 is negative and clearly bounded away from 0, with a 90% credible interval from –0.47 to –0.11. I provide the instrumental variables estimate of the effect of democracy on bailout propensity in Model 10. I arrive at this estimate through two-stage least squares analysis in a Bayesian framework (WinBugs code is in Appendix A.3.3).

The instrumental variables estimate invites greater caution in gauging the empirical validity of Proposition 1. In fact, the IV estimate in Model 10 is about half the size of the regression estimate of Model 9 and has wider standard error (0.39, with 90% CI from –0.44 to 0.1). Figure 6.2 provides an illustration of these effects. These plots graph the posterior predictive

---

[9]The exclusion restriction is testable in an overidentified model. In other words, it would be necessary to include a second instrument to test this assumption. Given the paucity of relevant instruments, I am not able to carry out statistical tests of the validity of the exclusion restriction.

distributions of bailout propensity scores based on Models 9 (left plot) and 10 (right plot), while holding all other covariates fixed at their mean sample values. Based on the posterior predictive distributions in the left plot, I estimate the probability that autocracies have *lower* bailout propensities than democracies to be less than 0.01.

According to this model, democracies have average bailout scores of –0.23, whereas an average non-democratic regime would have a score of 0.33. In contrast, based on the IV model I estimate the probability that autocracies may have *lower* bailout propensity scores than democracies to be about 0.156, i.e., there is a non-negligible probability, though still relatively small, that authoritarian regimes are more contained than democracies in approaching crisis management. Based on the IV estimate, democracies (non-democracies) have an average bailout score of –0.12 (0.17).

Before wrapping up this section, it is important to recall what instrumental variables analysis allows us to say about the effect of instrumented predictors. An observational study can only inform about the average treatment effect for units whose treatment can be construed as having been somehow manipulated (Angrist, Imbens and Rubin 1996). The literature on causal inference refers to this as the *local average treatment effect*. In this case, the IV estimate is not based on countries that would be democratic even if surrounded by authoritarian countries ("always compliers" in the parlance of causal inference) nor on countries that would be authoritarian even if surrounded by democratic countries ("never compliers").

The IV estimate, as it were, is the average effect on bailout propensities of authoritarian regimes that could be compelled to transit to democracy by the sheer fact of being surrounded by democracies ("induced democracies") and of democratic regimes that could turn into non-democracies if surrounded by this type of country ("induced autocracies"). Instrumental variables analysis therefore provides consistent estimates of a more limited notion of causal effect than would obtain in a real experimental setting where treatment and control status could be assigned randomly.

I thus conclude with a more cautious note about the empirical validity of Proposition 1. If we construe the IV local average treatment effect estimates as a lower bound—and the substantively larger estimates obtained in Models 1 through 9 as an upper bound—on the true effect of democracy on bailout propensities, then we can say that democracies are much less likely than non-democracies to engage in crisis-management policies closer to the ideal-type of Bailout. However, the substantive effects of political regime on policy output, though positive, may not be as large as those originally reported in Table 5.3.

6.4 Distinct Solvency and Liquidity Bailout Propensities

Three of the seven policies inspected in Chapter 5—*liquidity provision, deposit freeze*, and *debt relief*—showed low capacity to discriminate among Bagehot and Bailout governments, as evinced by discrimination parameters that were not clearly centered away from 0. In a one-dimensional setting, these findings suggest that such policies provide little information about government bailout propensities beyond what is already provided by their sample frequency. However, these are consequential and costly policies meant to postpone the exit of distressed banks with immediate liquidity problems and that may very well be insolvent, as analyzed in Chapter 3. For this reason alone, it is not plausible that governments implement these policies haphazardly, more or less independently of their bailout propensities. Instead, the lack of discrimination power of these items along a single dimension may be due to the existence of a second policy dimension that has so far remained untapped.

To build intuition about the substantive policy content of this hypothesized second dimension, consider that *liquidity provision, deposit freeze*, and *debt relief* are policies that aim to control bank cash-flows. When banks face deposit runs, *liquidity provision* and *debt relief* keep them from having to liquidate assets in order to meet cash outflows. The first policy does so by providing ample support from the central bank, the latter by giving bank debtors the wherewithal to avoid defaults on their loans. *Deposit freezes* achieve the same objective through different means: By prohibiting cash outflows, governments remove the burden of asset liquidation from banks, buying time to rebuild their portfolios and restructure loan payments without facing immediate pressure from jittery depositors. Note finally that these three policies achieve the same objective—i.e., preventing asset liquidation to meet deposit runs—through antithetical means. In other words, these policies are almost perfect substitutes. Indeed, if deposits are frozen, it is not really necessary to provide discount loans to banks. For this reason, we seldom see implementation of *liquidity provision* or *debt relief* when a *deposit freeze* is in place. Out of the 46 observations in the sample, 41 governments enacted at least one of these three policies, but only 5 implemented *deposit freeze* along with either *debt relief* or *liquidity provision*, and only three governments implemented all three of these policies concurrently. I refer to these cash-flow management actions as *liquidity* policies.

Because Bagehot's maxim of lending on good collateral to solvent banks implies providing ample support to some financial intermediaries, one may be tempted to construe implementation of these policies, particularly *liquidity provision*, as a signal of a more restrained bailout propensity. However, Honohan and Klingebiel (2000) make it clear that they code governments as having engaged in *liquidity provision, debt relief,* and *deposit freeze* only if they hold these policies in place for a long period (see Table 5.1). In the case of *debt relief,* governments get a "1" if they extend a helping hand to large corporate borrowers. In no case are these policies coded "1" as a result of a limited "market-upholding" intervention by a Bagehot policy-maker. Consequently, implementation of these policies suggests policy action closer to the Bailout ideal-type.

To sum up, it is understandable that the three liquidity policies do not help discriminate Bagehot from Bailout governments when one assumes the existence of a single policy dimension. But should we expect liquidity and solvency dimensions to be correlated? As discussed in Chapters 1 and 3, policies to redress solvency and liquidity need not correlate. On the one hand, systemic bank insolvency need not produce large panic deposit runs if, for instance, depositors are protected by a credible system of deposit insurance. On the other hand, liquidity problems in a banking system need not be the consequence of generalized bank insolvency. For this reason, if solvency and liquidity policy dimensions were close to uncorrelated, a one-dimensional model would fail to capture variation in government propensity to engage in bailout practices along *both* solvency and liquidity fronts.

To explore the possibility that liquidity policies are indeed informative about government types but not reducible to a single Bagehot-Bailout underlying dimension, I expand the IRT model considered so far to admit two different dimensions, θ_1 and θ_2, that capture bailout propensities in the realms of solvency and liquidity, respectively. The relevant change to Equation 5.3 appears in Equation 6.2:

$$\pi_{i,j} = \Phi(\theta_{S,i}\beta_{S,j} + \theta_{L,i}\beta_{L,j} - \alpha_j) \qquad (6.2)$$

As can be seen from Equation 6.2, introducing a second dimension increases the number of parameters to estimate and complicates identification of the model. With two underlying dimensions, the identification problems described in Chapter 5 become more insidious, as there are now two different sources of rotational and scaling invariance.[10] It is thus necessary to impose additional constraints on the two-dimensional model to achieve identification.

To do so, I place "spike" priors on some item discrimination parameters in either dimension 1 or 2. This decision is informed both by theory and by results from the one-dimensional fit. Thus, the discrimination parameters β for *liquidity provision, debt relief,* and *deposit freeze* are assumed to be 0

---

[10]To see how this extension compounds identification problems, consider that, once recovered, the two dimensions can be multiplied by (1,1), (−1,1), (1,−1), or (−1,−1), and this would not change the rank-order of governments' bailout propensities at all. In other words, the two-dimensional Θ space can be rotated in 2×2 different ways (Jackman 2001).

along the first dimension, whereas the remaining policy items are assumed to take on positive values. Along the second dimension, I stipulate that *asset management, recapitalization,* and *explicit guarantees* have $\beta = 0$; in addition, the discrimination parameter of *liquidity provision* is constrained to be positive to ensure that higher scores on the second dimension correspond to higher bailout propensities. Consider again the substantive meaning of these restrictions: I am effectively assuming that *asset management, recapitalization,* and *explicit guarantees* provide information *exclusively* about a government's propensity to address bank solvency problems by engaging in bailouts. This is in line with the evidence reviewed in Chapter 4, where these policies were shown to promote the restoration of solvency to distressed banking systems in Argentina and Mexico. I am also assuming that *liquidity provision, debt relief,* and *deposit freeze* provide information about a government's propensity to provide liquidity assistance, but not to address solvency problems. Finally, I allow *regulatory forbearance* to provide information about both dimensions. This is consistent with results from the one-dimensional model, where the discrimination parameter of this policy was positive, but substantively small. The solution I adopt overidentifies the model, in the sense that estimation could in principle be carried out with slightly less severe restrictions, but avoids imposing direct restrictions on governments' bailout propensities. Furthermore, with sample size unchanged at 46 observations, these additional constraints allow data to be informative about a relatively smaller number of parameters.

Table 6.4 displays summary information about the item parameters of a two-dimensional IRT model. Due to the multiplicity of parameters to estimate, I include only three government-level covariates in this specification: *democracy, central bank* and *propensity score.* The latter indicator is included in lieu of all other control variables in an effort to approximate the assumption of conditional independence. The *central bank* indicator is included here on account of the accumulated knowledge about the monetary effects of central bank independence reviewed in Section 6.1.1. Based on the central bank autonomy literature, I expect this indicator to correlate negatively with the *liquidity* dimension. As for the *democracy* indicator, I am again interested in testing the validity of Proposition 1 with regard to separate *solvency* and *liquidity* dimensions. The theoretical argument in Chapter 3 was premised on the assumption that the government controlled monetary policy. Flowing from this assumption, one would expect that *democracy* would also correlate negatively with *liquidity* in the two-dimensional model. However, governments may be limited in their ability to make decisions regarding cash-flow management in the presence of a politically-autonomous central bank. If this is indeed the case, then the effect of *democracy* on a government's *liquidity* score would be essentially nil.

Table 6.4: Bayesian estimation of Bagehot-Bailout policy discrimination (β) and government-level (δ) parameters. The point estimate is the median of the parameter's posterior density (standard deviation of the posterior density in parentheses).

	Solvency dimension	Liquidity dimension
Democracy	−0.535	0.063
	(0.261)	(0.301)
Central bank	−0.186	−0.468
	(0.222)	(0.332)
Propensity score	−0.247	0.265
	(0.251)	(0.303)
β_{AM}	1.228	
	(0.392)	
β_R	1.199	
	(0.340)	
β_G	1.171	
	(0.414)	
β_{FB}	0.510	0.259
	(0.323)	(0.413)
β_L		0.934
		(0.474)
β_D		0.490
		(0.349)
β_F		−0.942
		(0.473)
DIC	352.98	
pD	57.11	

L = liquidity, D = debt relief, AM = asset management agency,
R = recapitalization, G = explicit guarantees, F = deposit freeze,
FB = forbearance

Before commenting on the results, one indication that the one- and two-dimensional models are appropriately identified, even under different parametric restrictions, is that both yield similar posterior distributions for the

Figure 6.3: Bailout propensity scores of democratic and non-democratic regimes along solvency and liquidity dimensions

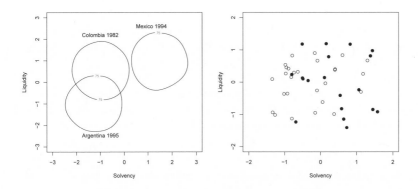

seven item difficulty parameters.[11] Naturally, these posterior distributions are narrower in the one-dimensional model, as that model requires estimation of a lower number of parameters. Thus, the one- and two-dimensional models reveal very similar information regarding the difficulty of implementing policies to address banking crises.

The posterior distribution of discrimination parameters confirms that the second dimension captures government propensities to engage in measures to alleviate liquidity problems in the banking system. Obviously, since the parameter on *liquidity provision* was purposefully constrained to be positive, I cannot invoke its magnitude and direction as corroborating the nature of the second latent propensity scale. Note however that *deposit freeze* has a negative discrimination parameter along the second dimension whereas *debt relief* has positive discrimination parameter, confirming indeed that freezing deposits is a policy that does not tend to occur simultaneously with policies to relieve bank debtors or with excessively generous central bank lending. As for *regulatory forbearance*, whose coefficient was not constrained a priori, parameter estimates suggest that this policy discriminates mostly along the solvency dimension. The posterior distribution of its discrimination parameter on the liquidity dimension is positive, but wide enough to straddle zero.

Confirming the narrative of Chapter 4, the left panel of Figure 6.3 portrays 75% credible intervals for the two-dimensional bailout propensities of the

---

[11]Point estimates (±SD) for difficulty parameters follow: $\alpha_{AM} = 0.36$ (±0.30), $\alpha_R = 0.91$ (±0.32), $\alpha_G = 0.23$ (±0.28), $\alpha_{FB} = -0.45$ (±0.25), $\alpha_L = -0.04$ (±0.26), $\alpha_D = 0.80$ (±0.26), $\alpha_F = 0.31$ (±0.27).

Argentine and Mexican governments during the *Tequila* crises (Colombia 1982 is also plotted for comparison). Consistent with knowledge about policy responses to these crises, the Argentine government of Carlos Saúl Menem scores very low on both bailout dimensions, whereas Ernesto Zedillo's is one of the most bailout-prone governments in the sample. Indeed, I estimate the probability that this government is the *most* bailout-prone in terms of solvency support to be about 0.15; in terms of liquidity support, this probability falls to 0.069. Instead, the chances that Argentina 1995 is the *least* bailout-prone government along these two dimensions are 0.11 and 0.067, respectively.

This model throws further light onto potential differences between democracies and non-democracies in the use of policy tools to manage banking crises. In this regard, the right panel of Figure 6.3 plots point estimates of bailout scores for the forty-six observations in the sample along the solvency and liquidity dimensions (incidentally, the correlation between the two dimensions is only 0.03, i.e., these dimensions are orthogonal for practical purposes). The plot distinguishes between democratic regimes (open circles) and non-democracies (solid circles). Consistent with results in Table 6.4, there is no readily distinguishable difference in the spread of democracies and authoritarian regimes along the liquidity dimension; we do see however that democracies tend to cluster on the lower ranges of the solvency dimension.

But how do these differences between political regimes translate into predicted probabilities of observing different types of policy interventions to manage banking crises? Table 6.5 suggests how different combinations of *political regimes* and *central bank status* yield rather different predictions about the crisis-management policies that we would expect to see. Based on the estimates of Table 6.4, we would expect a democratic government in a country where an independent central bank is in control of monetary policy to engage in *regulatory forbearance* about half the time (52%). Democratic regimes are a lot less likely to generously nourish banks back to solvency at the expense of taxpayers. For example, even where central banks are not independent from the political process, democratic governments are reluctant to establish public asset management corporations, which more often than not end up failing to recover more than a fraction of the face value of non-performing loans. Democratic governments are also less likely to issue explicit deposit guarantees over and above existing deposit insurance schemes (about 3 out of 10 times); they are also very unlikely to recapitalize banks using public funds (about 1 in 10 times). The chances that democratic governments will engage in this kind of policy are even lower where policy action is constrained by an independent central bank.

With the possible exception of *deposit freezes*, which are a bit less common under democracies, political regimes have very little impact on liquidity policies. This is of course consistent with the effect parameter of *democracy*

Table 6.5: Posterior predictive distribution of the implementation of seven crisis-management policies. Cell entries correspond to the expected frequency (%) with which each policy is adopted under different combinations of political regime and central bank independence (25th and 75th sample percentiles of *central bank independence*).

		Democracy	Non-democracy
	Asset management	26	68
	Recapitalization	13	50
	Explicit guarantees	30	68
Low CBI	Regulatory forbearance	61	80
	Bank liquidity	62	60
	Debt relief	27	27
	Deposit freeze	27	34
	Asset management	19	58
	Recapitalization	7	37
	Explicit guarantees	20	61
High CBI	Regulatory forbearance	52	73
	Bank liquidity	41	38
	Debt relief	20	17
	Deposit freeze	51	56

in Table 6.4, which is basically centered on 0. The existence of an independent central bank forces democratic and non-democratic governments alike to enact *deposit freezes* about half the time (deposit freezes are far less common when central banks are not autonomous). Governments of either stripe resort to *debt relief* rather sparingly (never more than 1 out of 3 times); this is the one policy where central bank status does not seem to have much of an effect. Instead, the impact of central bank autonomy appears to be substantial when it comes to *bank liquidity*: In the simulation, independent central banks engage in liquidity support 4 out of 10 times; non-autonomous central banks provide liquidity support 6 out of 10 times.

6.5 Concluding Remarks

Though the status of monetary policy-making is tangential to my theory of bank bailouts, the analysis in this chapter suggests that autonomous central banks have the potential to limit the extent to which taxpayers share in the burden of financial insolvency. Independent central banks may or may not be reluctant to play the Bagehot script of lending at a discount on good collateral, but they definitely appear to be reluctant to sink large amounts of money for long periods of time into illiquid banking systems. Even then, the evidence inspected in Chapters 5 and 6 is not inconsistent with Proposition 1—that is, governments in democratic regimes are less likely to implement generous bailout policies in response to banking crises—even after taking into account the constraining effect of central bank autonomy. This basic result survives the inclusion of control variables and corrections for covariate imbalance. In contrast, the instrumental variables estimate of the political regime effect and the two-dimensional model of liquidity and solvency bailout propensities invite more caution in assessing regime effects. Though the instrumental variables estimate still suggests the existence of a democratic effect, this effect is more muted than what obtains in models where we assume strict ignorability of political regime assignment. Similarly, the two-dimensional model of policy implementation suggests that democratic effects may be circumscribed to policies that aim to redress insolvency, rather than to those that alleviate liquidity pressures on banks. The latter type of policies are likely to be determined more by institutional limits on the conduct of monetary policy—specifically, by the degree of political autonomy of the central bank—than by any limits voters may place on socializing the costs of banking crises in democratic regimes.

7

Political Regimes and Banking Crises

The theory developed in Chapter 3 suggests that the salutary effects of democracy do not stop at limiting financial loss-sharing with taxpayers *after* the beginning of a banking crisis. Instead, rational forward-looking entrepreneurs and bankers should be able to anticipate that democratic governments have limited freedom to engage in onerous bailouts in bad times. This realization should lead them to take on lower risks in their investment and lending decisions. Furthermore, politicians in democratic governments understand that electoral accountability constrains their ability to pass on the costs of adjustment to taxpayers, and will therefore choose not to develop extended crony networks. As suggested by Propositions 2 and 3, both of these effects work in the direction of preventing financial distress under democratic regimes.

These propositions are at odds with alternative accounts of the effect of democratic politics on banking crises. As Keefer (2007, 617) argues, government incentives to enact strict prudential regulation of bank portfolios are weak, regardless of political regime, "given the often long time lags between weak regulation and crisis, and the rarity of crisis." Keefer correctly points out that banking crises are relatively infrequent, and goes on to suggest that the infrequency of crises, concurrent with the long lags between weak regulation and crisis, mean that elected and non-elected governments alike will lack incentives to invest in strict prudential regulation. In Keefer's account, political regimes may not exert a systematic effect on the choice of patterns of prudential regulation of banks. Evidently, this does not mean that banking regulation is unimportant in understanding banking crises, only that regulatory structures may not be systematically traced back to differences in political regime.

In contrast, my explanation emphasizes the credibility of the commitment not to (excessively) share losses derived from bank insolvency with taxpayers as the mechanism through which democracies limit financial distress. This mechanism is independent of a country's structure of prudential regulation of banks. Because I believe this is a strong mechanism that prevents the most onerous bank bailouts, I also expect it to have an effect on measures of financial distress. In addition, if politicians under democratic regimes understood that regulatory inaction increases the probability of banking crises, they might actually have incentives to initiate regulatory reforms conducive to minimize these risks. This alternative mechanism would only add to the direct effect of electoral accountability on banking outcomes, thus reinforcing the total effect of the credible commitment to minimize sharing of financial burden in a democracy. I insist though that the political choice of regulatory frameworks and the credibility imparted to "no bailout" rules by the electoral need to consider taxpayer preferences are two distinct mechanisms; the second mechanism should exert influence on the behavior of economic actors independently of regulatory frameworks.

Recall from Chapter 3 that both the probability of bank failure and the amount of risk taken by entrepreneurs are lower under democratic than under non-democratic regimes (Figure 3.5), though this effect tends to become muted as the signal about future endstates becomes clearer. I argue that these theoretical constructs have an empirical correlate in the degree of financial distress of banking systems. If my theory about electoral accountability has explanatory purchase, financial distress should be driven down in democratic regimes, or at the very least remain constant across regimes; in no case should we see that democracies are more prone on average to financial distress than non-democracies. I corroborate the degree of association between *political regimes* and *financial distress* through a two-pronged strategy. Because acute financial distress occasionally leads to outright banking crises, I make use of available crisis indicators to estimate the incidence of distress under different types of political regimes (Section 7.1).

Banking crises do not exhaust all instances of financial distress, however, so I extend this analysis to consider an alternative indicator built on balance-sheet accounting ratios measured at the bank system level (Section 7.2). In the absence of an aggregate-level indicator of market-value net worth, which would be the most appropriate indicator of overall financial solvency in a banking system, the accounting ratio I consider is a measure of aggregate book-value net worth. This second indicator of financial distress should be positively correlated with democratic regimes, suggesting that democratic regimes indeed exert a salutary effect on the levels of financial solvency of banking systems. None of these empirical indicators of financial distress in banking systems is perfect—measurements of social phenomena seldom are—but analyzing indicators that proxy for different aspects of financial distress increases confidence in inferences about the empirical association between banking crises and political regimes.

7.1 Expert Assessments of Banking Crises

In this section, I use expert scores of banking crises to estimate the probability of failure, and hence levels of financial distress, of banking systems across political regimes. Recall from Chapter 3 that the probability of failure is marginally higher under non-democratic regimes when the signal about future endstates is uninformative ($q = 0.5$). As the signal about future endstates becomes clearer, the effect of democracy on the probability of failure becomes less pronounced. Consequently, one would expect, at a minimum, that there would be no difference in the incidence of banking crises across regime types. I refer to this as the *weak interpretation* of political regime effects. At a maximum, we should see the incidence of banking crises to be reduced under democratic regimes; this is a *strong interpretation* of regime effects. This testable implication of the argument in Chapter 3 would be definitely invalidated if we were to find that the probability of failure is actually higher under democratic regimes.

From the mid-1990s onwards, policy experts have published assessments of banking crises around the world.[1] These datasets offer information aggregated at the country/year level, and are often coded dichotomously, though the dataset I employ includes three categories, as discussed below. In terms of geographic and temporal coverage, the broadest and most recently updated effort is the World Bank Database of Banking Crises (Caprio et al. 2005), which identifies the occurrence of banking crises based on a template set by Lindgren, García and Saal (1996). Basically, this template considers observation of four different types of events as evidence that a systemic banking crisis has occurred in country i in year t. These events are (i) generalized depositor runs on banks, (ii) accumulation of non-performing loans in excess of 10% of bank assets, (iii) government assistance to banks through suspension of financial activities (e.g., bank holidays or deposit freezes), and (iv) government support to banks through policies with fiscal costs that exceed 2% of GDP. These four criteria constitute an exhaustive list of "things that can go wrong" during a banking crisis. More importantly, these criteria allow recognition of banking crises even in environments where financial distress may not trigger *all* of these economic behaviors. In other words, any one of these four events signals the occurrence of a banking crisis. Policy experts need to use various criteria to identify banking crises because of variation in institutional settings and accounting rules across countries. For example, it is possible that a banking system is under severe financial strain without necessarily suffering

---

[1] Caprio and Klingebiel (1997); Demirgüç-Kunt and Detragiache (2000); Dziobek and Pazarbasioglu (1999); Glick and Hutchison (1999); Kaminsky and Reinhart (1999); Lindgren, García and Saal (1996). See Frydl (1999) and Eichengreen and Arteta (2002) for comparative analysis of some of these datasets.

generalized deposit runs. In such cases, generalized bank insolvency cannot be inferred from deposit runs, but it will be fathomed from the behavior of authorities or depositors. Thus, the four criteria are complementary: the first two criteria—bank runs and accumulation of bad loans—pick up instances of banking trouble that may or may not have prompted government action but have already caused changes in depositor or borrower behavior and should consequently be recognized as outright banking crises, whereas the two latter criteria—bank holidays and government support—capture events that may or may not prompt changes in the behavior of economic actors but confirm that governments have already taken steps to contain financial distress. The complementarity of different criteria is an undeniable advantage of expert scores.

Caprio et al. (2005) code "banking crises" based on these four criteria, and recognize "significant bank trouble" as any problem in a country's banking sector short of a bank crisis. For example, significant bank trouble may occur when a localized segment of a country's banking sector is under financial distress, or when a big bank carries a heavy load of non-performing loans. These events cannot be considered systemic banking crises, but nonetheless reveal a certain level of distress in the banking sector. To take full advantage of the amount of information contained in the coding decisions of Caprio et al. (2005), I depart from common practice and consider banking problems as a three-way ordered categorization, rather than a dichotomous variable.[2] I consider *banking crises* and *significant bank trouble* as symptomatic of banking sector difficulties in a given country/year. Consequently, I code the dependent variable in this analysis as an ordered category with the following labels: *no event* (1), *borderline crisis* (2), and *systemic crisis* (3).

7.1.1 Democracy and Financial Distress

As I move to understand whether levels of financial distress vary significantly across political regimes, it is necessary to address the problems of inference based on observational data that were identified in Chapter 6. I had suggested that one of the main quandaries in making inferences about the economic consequences of democracy based on observational data is lack of covariate imbalance. In fact, when analyzing data from the latter half of the twentieth century, prosperity, economic equality, and democracy appear hand-in-hand in

---

[2]The availability of banking crises expert scores has fueled efforts to develop "early warning systems" (cf. Demirgüç-Kunt and Detragiache 2000, Hardy and Pazarbasioglu 1998; see also Kaminsky and Reinhart 1999). The main thrust of these models is to find the best possible *predictors* of imminent banking crises, which is not the purpose I pursue here. This literature codes banking crises as dichotomous events, or ignores information about significant bank trouble, therefore eschewing valuable information about the intensity of bank distress.

Table 7.1: Distribution of events conditional on *political regime* (dichotomous index) and *level of development* (countries with per capita GDP above/below sample mean). Observations are at the country/year level (58 observations lost due to missing values).

	Autocracies		Democracies	
	Rich	Poor	Rich	Poor
No event	287	555	455	231
	(0.83)	(0.89)	(0.84)	(0.89)
Borderline	13	6	17	7
	(0.04)	(0.01)	(0.03)	(0.03)
Systemic	45	65	67	23
	(0.13)	(0.10)	(0.12)	(0.09)
Total	345	626	539	261

many polities, whereas poor, inegalitarian economies tend to be governed by authoritarian regimes. Regardless of the reasons behind this "modernization syndrome," the coincidence of democracy and well-being around the world means that inferences about the effects of regimes might be driven more by *modeling assumptions* than by *observed data*. In other words, even if we find that democracies show, on average, lower levels of financial distress, this finding may rest on a sample of cases with few poor, unequal democracies and few prosperous, egalitarian non-democracies. We would still be able to arrive at inferences about the effects of democracy across all types of societies (rich and poor, egalitarian and unequal), but these inferences would be extremely dependent on the linearity assumption that underlies regression models.

When we further consider that samples are limited by data availability on crucial variables, it follows that using all available information need not be the best way of arriving at solid inferences about regime effects. As I did in Chapter 6, I base my analysis of the occurrence of banking crises on a reduced sample of observations that are as closely matched as possible in relevant respects, but that differ in their political regimes. That is, the following analysis is based on a balanced sample of democratic and non-democratic regimes. I start with a set that includes all countries for which Caprio et al. (2005) have registered at least one event (i.e., borderline or systemic crisis) and for which covariate data are available. I then use propensity scores to match observations at the country/year level. The implicit assumption underlying this exercise is that *any* country/level observation can be matched to any other observation in the sample, so in principle the year *t* observation for country *i* could be a close match for the year *t* + 1 observation for that same country. This procedure yields a set of matched observations at the country/year level, that is, it contains countries such that, *when analyzed at the country/year level*, there exists one-to-one matching between democracies and non-democracies. After pre-processing the sample to match democracies and non-democracies as closely as possible, the usable balanced sample contains sixty-three countries observed annually from 1975 to 2003.[3]

Before proceeding to the full analysis, consider the breakdown of the dependent variable—the count of country/years coded as *no event, borderline,* or *systemic crisis*—by *political regime* and *level of development* in Table 7.1. Political regimes are coded using the dichotomous *regime* indicator of Prze-worski et al. (2000), as updated by Cheibub and Gandhi (2004); the level of development variable simply divides observations between those above (rich) and below (poor) the median sample value of *GDP per capita.* The preliminary view of Table 7.1 suggests that the weak interpretation of political regime effects is in fact correct, as the incidence of systemic banking crises and borderline events does not seem to be markedly lower under democratic regimes. If anything, the sample frequency of observations in the borderline or systemic categories is slightly larger under democracies (0.143) than under autocracies (0.133), though admittedly systemic events are slightly less frequent under democratic regimes.[4] This preliminary breakdown also suggests that the frequency of borderline and systemic crises varies across levels of development. The incidence of some type of banking event (either crisis or bank trouble) is 0.114 in *poor* country/years and 0.161 in *rich* country/years.[5]

The preliminary breakdown of Table 7.1 does not control for other confounding variables nor does it take into account the structure of dependence among observations that are nested within countries and within years. In the next paragraphs I explain how these data characteristics can be accommodated in a hierarchical model of financial distress. Let us start with the distributional assumptions about the dependent variable. The three categories reported in Table 7.1 correspond to ordered degrees of financial distress; we can therefore conceive of these ordinal categories as limited indicators of what is in essence

---

[3]This procedure leads to the elimination mostly of rich democracies and ex communist regimes. Sampled countries appear in Appendix A.2.4.

[4]In the unbalanced data, the sample frequency of systemic banking crises was 0.14 under democracy and 0.22 under autocracy, which is more consistent with a strong regime effect.

[5]This frequency seems high for several reasons: First, the "rich" countries in the sample are actually middle-income economies, which in the 1990s seemed particularly prone to endure this type of events. Second, the sample includes countries that suffered through at least one bank crisis or bank trouble year in the period under investigation. This set is rather large—it includes 126 countries—but there are a few banking systems that are not reported as ever having suffered significant bank trouble, let alone a banking crisis.

a continuous unobserved probability of failure or financial distress score. An ordinal logit model is appropriate for this kind of indicator. This model is represented in terms of cumulative probabilities $\theta_{itk} = p_{it1} + \cdots + p_{itk}$, where θ_{itk} is the probability that observation i,t will be in category k *or lower* (with $k = 1$ representing *no event* and $k = 3$ *systemic crisis* in this case). To estimate the effect of covariates, we specify these cumulative probabilities as a logistic function of an underlying score Y_{it}^* and cutpoints γ_c, as in Equation 7.1; the latent variable Y_{it}^* corresponds to the level of financial distress of country i at year t:

$$\log\left(\frac{\theta_{itk}}{1 - \theta_{itk}}\right) = \gamma_c - Y_{it}^* \quad \text{for } c = k + 1 \tag{7.1}$$

As is customary in ordered logit models, the first and last cutpoints are assumed to be $\pm\infty$; two further middle cutpoints, γ_2 and γ_3, are needed in order to accommodate three categories. To be able to estimate an intercept, which is required in order to account for the multilevel structure of observations, I fix $\gamma_2 = 0$ and leave γ_3 as a free parameter to be estimated from data.

Having laid bare the auxiliary aspects of the model, I now describe my modeling decisions regarding the unobserved financial distress score Y^*, which should be either unaffected by (weak interpretation) or negatively associated with a polity's democracy indicator (strong interpretation of regime effects). I start with the problem of approximating conditional independence. The purpose of fitting this model *is not* to build a predictive model that would help develop an "early warning system" of impending banking crises. The purpose is to verify that political regimes exert influence on financial distress after controlling for relevant covariates. Relevant covariates are those that correlate with political regimes and financial distress and that are considered to be, for theoretical reasons, pre-treatment variables. Aside from *political regime*, I control for several other covariates to approximate conditional independence. The theoretical argument in Chapter 3 suggests inclusion of *per capita GDP* (log scale) and *economic inequality* (Gini coefficient) as relevant covariates. Furthermore, perhaps the single most relevant omitted variable in a predictive model of banking crises would be the rate of economic growth. Because of its effect on bank balance sheets, low economic growth should lead to higher probability of observing banking crises. However, it is possibly the case that the causal link tying banking crises and economic growth runs in both directions, i.e., banking crises may have a negative impact on economic growth. Therefore, I include lagged values of *GDP growth* to mitigate the impact of simultaneous causation.

Aside from these confounding covariates, countries with few capital controls may suffer more drastically from sudden reversals in capital flows (Rodrik 1998). In consequence, I also include an index of capital openness as a predictor of financial distress (this is the same Chinn and Ito (2002) index used in Chapter 6). Unfortunately, I lack data for *economic inequality* for several years in the observation window. Gini indices of economic inequality are either not comparable when one considers a long annual series, or limited to a handful of years when they are directly comparable. Even the coding scheme employed by Desai, Olofsgård and Yousef (2003)—which I used to measure inequality at limited points in time in Chapter 6—does not prevent a high attrition rate due to missing values. To palliate the problem of limited information, I use within-country averages of available data as a single, time-invariant indicator of *income inequality*. In doing so, the implicit assumption is that Gini indices do not vary drastically within countries across the period under inspection. This is also true for *transparency*, which I include in some specifications with the caveat that this should be considered a post-treatment variable according to my theoretical argument. I do acknowledge the time-invariant character of these indicators through appropriate hierarchical modeling of country intercepts.

If data on borderline and systemic banking crises lacked a time-series cross-sectional structure and if all covariates were measurable at the data level (i.e., as country/year observations), a reasonable model of financial distress would take the form of Equation 7.2, with disturbances ε assumed uncorrelated across countries and years:

$$Y_{it}^* = \alpha + \beta_1 X_{1it} + \cdots + \beta_q X_{qit} + \varepsilon_{it}. \tag{7.2}$$

However, observations in Table 7.1 are not independent draws from some process that generates banking crises, but are strongly patterned in time and space, with events recorded for country i at year t. Where data points are clustered within countries and within years the assumption of independence of observations is not tenable. There are several reasons why the time-series cross-sectional structure of the data limits the amount of information provided by these observations. For example, consider the case of political regime indicators. In principle, scores of democracy/autocracy could change every year, but political regimes are in fact very persistent. Also note that there are variables that in principle fluctuate annually, but for which indicators that vary at such frequencies are difficult to find, as discussed above for the case of inequality. More importantly, errors cannot be assumed to be uncorrelated in time. In fact, the impact of the temporal dimension on inferences about financial distress is twofold, as one should worry both about *serial correlation* within each country and *contemporaneous correlation* across countries.

Consider the case of serial correlation first. All else constant, we would expect disturbances at time t to be correlated with disturbances at $t - 1$ in a process such as the one that underlies financial distress. That is, knowing that a banking system suffered high levels of economic distress at $t - 1$ tells us that financial distress is also likely to be high at t, even after conditioning on independent variables at time t. To deal with this issue, I model financial distress as an autoregressive process and estimate a serial correlation parameter ϕ from data.[6]

Similarly, contemporaneous correlation can occur in this case if financial distress was contagious from country to country or if countries were subjected to common shocks in any given year; both of these are rather reasonable assumptions in a world of relatively open capital flows across countries.[7] To deal with this concern, I estimate annual random effects, i.e., I estimate varying intercepts δ_t for each year in the observation window to acknowledge the fact that the global incidence of banking crises may well change throughout time. In this regard, my main concern is with the temporal trend towards democratization across the globe, which has run parallel to an increase in the global integration of capital markets over the last three decades. Finding that democracy and banking crises are *positively* correlated without controlling for the fact that democratization and financial instability both *increased* during the observation period would be suspect. In this case, a changing incidence of financial distress may be spuriously attributed to changes in political regimes, even if one controls for other covariates at the country/year level, when it is instead the product of a shifting worldwide incidence of banking crises that is driven by changes in the architecture of international finance following the breakdown of Bretton Woods.

Bringing all of these elements together, the model I estimate is described by Equation 7.1, and extended in Equations 7.3 and 7.4:

$$Y_{it}^* = \delta_t + \alpha_i + \beta_1 X_{1it} + \cdots + \beta_q X_{qit} + \varepsilon_{it} \tag{7.3}$$

$$\alpha_i \sim \mathcal{N}(\mu_{\alpha_i}, \sigma_\alpha)$$

$$\mu_{\alpha_i} = \lambda_0 + \lambda_1 \text{Inequality}_i \tag{7.4}$$

As can be seen in Equations 7.3 and 7.4, I also estimate varying country-specific intercepts α_i in this hierarchical model. Estimating these intercepts is tantamount to admitting that there may be systematic differences in the propensity of different countries to suffer financial distress that are not captured by their political regime or economic makeup. For example, if countries differ in the quality of their bureaucratic or regulatory structures, or in the makeup of their banking systems, and if these features have an impact on

---

[6]The assumption is $\varepsilon_{it} = \phi \varepsilon_{i,t-1} + \epsilon_{it}$, where ϵ_{it} is random error. The prior distribution on ϕ is $\mathcal{N}(0, 1)$, which places ample probability mass on negative values and on values beyond -1 and 1.

[7]Rosas (2002) shows that the annual count of worldwide banking crises is overdispersed; in any given year, occurrence of a banking crisis increases the probability that more crises will follow elsewhere.

the possibility of banking crises and correlate with political regimes, failing to control for these unobserved characteristics would potentially bias estimates of the political regime effect.[8] For these intercepts, I fit two alternative specifications. I model them first as random-effects or unmodeled varying intercepts (Gelman and Hill 2007). In this case, I posit simply that different countries, regardless of their political regime, may have different propensities to generate financial distress that follow from country-level features that remain unobserved. In the second specification, I model varying intercepts as a function of country-specific levels of *inequality*, as in Equation 7.4, i.e., a covariate that changes across, but not within, countries (cf. Shor et al. 2007).[9]

7.1.2 Results

Table 7.2 displays results from several versions of the model contained in Equations 7.1, 7.3, and 7.4, using the continuous Polity IV score as an indicator of *democracy*.[10] The first three models estimate the effects of *democracy* on probability of failure assuming ignorability of treatment assignment. In other words, these three models treat the political regime covariate as if it were truly exogenous and assigned randomly to different country/years. Model 4 includes an instrument for political regime in order to approximate this latter assumption empirically. To instrument for *democracy* in country i at year t, I use the year-t average Polity IV score of all countries in i's region, excluding country i in a first-stage regression where I also include all control variables (results not shown). This instrument is essentially identical to the one employed and justified theoretically in Chapter 6. All models lead to similar inferences about the effect of *democracy*; though the effect seems substantively larger in the instrumental variables model, the posterior distribution of this effect parameter in Model 4 is also wider. Among the models that assume ignorability of treatment assignment, Model 1 does not

---

[8]There is a theoretical rationale to include *central bank independence* as a predictor of bailout propensities (autonomous central banks are less likely to submit to political pressure to provide liquidity to distressed banks), but it is not obvious that this same rationale extends to the case of financial distress. In any case, the indicator of *central bank independence* that I use is unfortunately very limited in its geographic coverage. The Cukierman index of central bank autonomy is up-to-date only through 2000 (Polillo and Guillén 2005).

[9]Prior distributions on parameters are as follows: $\phi \sim \mathcal{N}(0, 1), \beta_q, \delta_m \sim \mathcal{N}(0, 0.1)$, and $\gamma_3 \sim \mathcal{N}(0, 0.001)^+$. All covariates have been standardized to speed up the MCMC simulation process. Estimates are based on thinned draws from the posterior distribution after apparent convergence, with 10K to 15K burn-in iterations. WinBugs code is reproduced in Appendix A.3.5.

[10]I treat the 58 country/year missing values in the dependent variable as parameters to be estimated under the assumption of random missingness. These missing values stem from inconclusive coding in Caprio et al. (2005). For example, when this source reports "banking problems in the early 1980s" for some country, I code the year 1983 as a banking crisis observation, but consider the previous and following two years to be data missing at random. See fn. 7 in Chapter 5.

Table 7.2: Hierarchical ordinal logit model of banking crises. Point estimates are the median of parameter posterior densities (standard deviation of parameter posterior densities in parentheses).

	Model 1	Model 2	Model 3	Model 4
Country/year level				
Democracy	−0.343	−0.360	−0.337	−0.934
	(0.282)	(0.325)	(0.300)	(1.186)
Openness	−0.639	−0.647	−0.679	−0.613
	(0.234)	(0.241)	(0.240)	(0.231)
Growth	−0.780	−0.785	−0.840	−0.837
	(0.166)	(0.151)	(0.168)	(0.159)
GDP per capita	0.605	0.636	0.631	0.526
	(0.608)	(0.650)	(0.564)	(0.659)
Transparency		0.059	0.057	0.050
		(0.185)	(0.193)	(0.186)
Country level				
Intercept			−5.344	
			(0.864)	
Gini			−0.127	
			(0.539)	
Ancillary parameters				
Cut (γ_3)	0.529	0.515	0.517	0.531
	(0.080)	(0.081)	(0.074)	(0.078)
AR (ϕ)	0.922	0.929	0.900	0.933
	(0.018)	(0.021)	(0.019)	(0.021)
N	1,827	1,827	1,827	1,827
Countries	63	63	63	63
pD	179	180	175	186
DIC	888	891	882	5,215

Figure 7.1: Posterior distribution of year- and country-specific intercepts
(median and 80% Bayesian credible intervals of the posterior distribution of
δ and α)

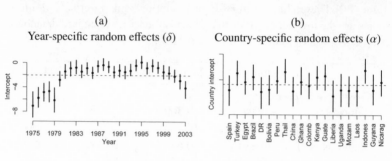

control for *transparency*, which is assumed to be endogenous to political
regime and therefore a post-treatment variable in empirical analysis. Inclusion
of this confounding covariate in Models 2 through 4 does not change the
basic finding about the association between political regimes and probability
of failure or financial distress, namely, that higher levels of *democracy* are
associated with lower levels of financial distress.

Before commenting on the statistical and substantive importance of estimated regime effects, I ponder briefly on some other conclusions that are
supported by these models. Recall that I estimate country-specific and year-
specific random effects in all models, though these are not reproduced in
Table 7.2 for the sake of space. Figure 7.1 (Plot a) displays year-specific random effects based on results from Model 4 (inferences about these parameters
remain essentially identical across models). As can be gleaned from this plot,
year effects vary substantially throughout time, accounting for the fact that
the cross-country incidence of banking crises varied during the observation
period. In particular, the mid-1990s were years with more banking crises
than average, though the incidence of critical events declined relatively fast
in later years. The mid-to-late 1990s were, however, not an outlying period.
This distinction corresponds to the early years in the observation window,
i.e., the late 1970s, during which the number of crises around the world was
much lower. Note also that there exists variation in the propensity to fail
across countries that is not captured by included covariates. Figure 7.1 (Plot
b) displays summaries of the posterior distribution of a random sample of 20
country-specific intercepts. As can be seen from this plot, some countries are
slightly more prone to suffer banking crises during the observation period
than others, even after accounting for their regimes, economic makeup, and

financial openness. In particular, Turkey, Thailand, and Indonesia appear as countries with higher-than-average propensities to suffer banking crises. Outside of the countries included in this plot, other countries with random-effect intercepts that lie almost entirely above average are Malaysia, Mexico, and South Korea. Though these are, incidentally, countries that at least during some years throughout the observation period were non-democracies, their political regimes do not fully account for their increased propensities to suffer banking crises.

Despite the inclusion of year- and country-specific intercepts in all of these models, several covariates at the data level show coefficients that are statistically different from zero. This is the case of *openness*, *growth*, and *GDP per capita*. Consistent with Table 7.1, relatively rich countries in the sample are associated with higher levels of financial distress. Recall that "rich" countries in this sample are not advanced industrial democracies, as most of these have been removed from the balanced sample, but middle-income economies with the level of development of, say, Mexico. The lagged value of GDP growth is a negative predictor of the probability of failure (i.e., higher rates of economic growth are associated with lower propensities to suffer financial distress a year later), and *openness* of a country's capital account is also negatively associated with the probability of failure. The latter result holds after accounting for the time-varying incidence of banking crises across countries. In contrast, *Gini* and *transparency* do not appear to be relevant predictors of financial distress. In Models 2 through 4, the posterior distribution of the coefficient on *transparency* is centered on the positive orthant, but the spread of this parameter is simply too wide to be considered as anything other than irrelevant. The same can be said of the coefficient for *Gini* in Model 3; though the point estimate is negative, consistent with the argument in Chapter 3, the posterior distribution of this parameter is wide enough to be practically centered on zero.

Compare now the inferences about the effects of political regimes that follow from different models. Figure 7.2 provides a more intuitive sense of the substantive importance of these regime effects. Consider first the posterior predictive distributions of underlying financial distress $\widehat{Y}^*$ that obtain from estimates in Model 2 (left plot) and Model 4 (right plot). The posterior predictive distributions correspond to the values of the underlying financial distress score that we would expect to obtain at low (25th) and high (75th sample percentile) values of the Polity IV indicator while holding all other covariates constant at mean sample values. Higher values of $\widehat{Y}^*$ correspond to higher latent financial distress and therefore higher probability of suffering a banking crisis. The spread of these distributions conveys a good deal of uncertainty about the substantive importance of this effect. As can be seen from the left plot, the predictive distributions of $\widehat{Y}^*$ under democratic and

Figure 7.2: Posterior predictive distribution of financial distress $(\widehat{Y^*})$ across democratic and non-democratic regimes

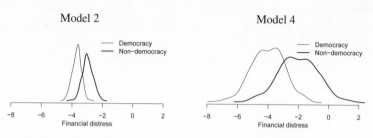

non-democratic regimes are more or less distinct, but this effect is muddled when we consider the predictive distribution of $\widehat{Y^*}$ based on the instrumental variable estimates of Model 4. Even though the overlap in the predictive distributions of $\widehat{Y^*}$ corresponding to high and low values of *democracy* is more extensive, we can still interpret these results as substantiating a positive regime effect.

Admittedly, the plots in Figure 7.1 do not include uncertainty derived from estimation of other parameters in the model (random effects, for example). More importantly, though one can see substantial differences in the distribution of financial distress scores $\widehat{Y^*}$ across regimes, it is difficult to build an intuitive understanding of the size of these differences, or to translate them into relevant quantities, such as the probability of observing *significant bank trouble* and *banking crises* under alternative political regimes. Contrary to predictions about financial distress, which is a linear function of levels of democracy, predictions about the *frequency* of systemic and borderline banking crises depend as much on values of *democracy* scores as on the values at which we hold other covariates constant. This follows from the non-linear relation between probabilities θ_{itk} and financial distress scores $\widehat{Y^*_{it}}$ (Equation 7.1).

To provide better intuition about the substantive effects of political regimes, consider Table 7.3, which displays the predicted frequency of *borderline* and *systemic* crises based on draws from the posterior distribution of parameters from Model 4. The counts in this table correspond to the number of times, out of 100, that we would expect to see instances of *borderline* or *systemic* events in an average country/year.[11] To convey the level of uncertainty about the effect of regimes, this table also includes 80% credible intervals of the

---

[11] The average year intercept corresponds to 2001, the average country intercept to Colombia's.

predicted count of borderline and systemic crises. These predicted counts are calculated at different combinations of *political regime* and *level of development* (in all cases ±1 SD from sample means), while holding constant all other covariates at mean sample values.[12]

Consider then the predicted frequency of different types of events in an average year. For example, based on the simulations of Table 7.3, I would expect poor democracies to suffer between 2 and 8 years of *systemic crisis* in a period of 100 years with probability 0.8. Among richer economies, the incidence of borderline crises in the simulation is already a bit higher among authoritarian than democratic regimes (5 vs. 3), but the effect of democratic regimes appears in full force when considering systemic crises: whereas "rich" democratic regimes are expected to suffer between 6 and 13 crisis years in a century, "rich" authoritarian regimes can expect to suffer between 21 and 33. These relatively high counts obtain from more pronounced differences in the probability of observing systemic banking crises on an average year, which I estimate as 0.29 for authoritarian regimes and 0.09 for democracies. At these rates, richer authoritarian regimes can expect to go about three and a half years without a banking crisis, whereas richer democracies would be expected to see a crisis every eleven years. This calculus is however premised on the assumption that banking crises always last one year, when in fact the typical length of systemic bank crises in the sample is about 2 to 3 years. As can be gathered from this exercise, differences in the incidence of financial distress across political regimes are far from trivial even after factoring uncertainty about regime effects into the analysis. The analysis confirms that democracies are less likely to suffer high levels of financial distress or, alternatively, that they enjoy much lower probabilities of systemic failure. This result is in line with a "strong" interpretation of political regime effects.

Lest it be thought that the regime effect is an artifact of the "modernization syndrome" alluded to at the beginning of this section, recall that these results are based on a balanced sample, and therefore less likely to be model-dependent than an alternative analysis based on an unbalanced sample of all available observations. In other words, the impact of democracy uncovered in this analysis is not based on a sample of rich democracies on the one hand, and poor autocracies on the other, but on a sample that includes relatively rich and relatively poor democracies alongside relatively rich and relatively poor authoritarian regimes. Furthermore, the estimates I present correspond to an instrumental variables specification that seeks to isolate the truly exogenous component of variation in the *political regime* variable.

---

[12]Recall the caveat about "poor" and "rich" countries; a country like Bolivia in this case would be 1 SD below the average *per capita GDP* in the sample, and therefore epitomizes a "poor" country, while a country like Mexico would be considered "rich" at about 1 SD above the sample average.

Table 7.3: Predicted frequency of *borderline* and *systemic crises* under alternative political regimes and levels of economic development (point estimate is the median of the posterior predictive distribution, interval estimate is the 80% credible interval)

	Autocracies		Democracies	
	Rich	Poor	Rich	Poor
Borderline	5	4	3	2
	(2–8)	(2–7)	(1–5)	(0–4)
Systemic	26	18	9	5
	(21–33)	(13–23)	(6–13)	(2–8)

Though these effects are not estimated in a design with random assignment of countries to treatment and control, the model specifications inspected here seek to reasonably approximate these conditions based on observational data.

7.2 Accounting Ratios as Indicators of Financial Distress

Expert scores constitute the most common way to measure incidence of banking crises, and therefore underlying financial distress. Be this as it may, these indicators are not without flaw. One problem with expert scores follows from their binary nature, which makes it difficult to use them to convey relative magnitudes. In fact, in the comparison of Argentina and Mexico in Section 7.1, part of the reason why Mexico obtains higher levels of financial distress than Argentina may be the fact that banking crises have tended to last longer in Mexico, i.e., runs of consecutive 1's in the Caprio et al. (2005) database are longer in that country than in Argentina. To see how this might affect the conclusions of the previous section, consider the latent financial distress score Y_{it}^*: This value will tend to increase when Y_{it} is coded 1 and to decrease when it is coded 0. If a banking crisis lasts one year, Y_{it}^* will tend to increase for one period to capture this information; however, if a banking crisis lasts several years, Y^* will keep increasing to account for the string of consecutive years within a country coded as 1. Countries with *longer* banking crises (i.e., with longer runs of 1's) will then appear to be countries with *harsher* financial distress. Harsher financial distress may indeed lead to longer banking crises, in which case inferences about the preventive effects of political regimes will remain unchanged. But what if this relationship does not hold?

Table 7.4: Aggregate balance of a nation's banking system (IFS series number in parentheses)

Assets	*Liabilities*
Claims on other actors (22A-G)	Demand deposits (24)
Reserves (20-D)	Time deposits (25)
Foreign assets (21)	Other deposits (26A-G)
	Capital (27)

Complicating this issue, the dichotomous coding of intrinsically continuous variables magnifies measurement error, particularly in cases that are close to a coding cutpoint. For example, a banking system that reduces its ratio of non-performing loans from 11% to 9% in two consecutive years is hardly out of the woods, but receives scores of 1 and 0, respectively, because these values are on either side of the 10% cutpoint used by experts to decide that a country's banks are in critical condition. This is a drawback of any attempt to aggregate intrinsically continuous data into discrete indicators. In the case of banking crises, the problem is compounded by the fact that information about underlying continuous indicators is not always very precise. For example, there are at times important differences in the tally of fiscal costs of banking crises that are derived from the inability to put a market value on the size of losses. By the same token, it is difficult to gauge relative improvement or worsening in a banking sector that experts have tagged as being in critical condition. A case in point is that of Mexico's banking system in the 1980s. Insolvent private banks were taken over by the government in 1982, slowly nursed back to solvency, and reprivatized in the early 1990s, but there is no way of assessing how healthy the banking sector progressively became throughout the 1980s by relying exclusively on a dichotomous score.

For these reasons, it is worth looking at alternative indicators of financial distress. In this section, I use one such indicator built for this purpose from information in the International Monetary Fund's IFS. The IFS publishes information on several categories of bank assets and liabilities aggregated at the bank-system level. Though the indices are published on a quarterly basis, I aggregate them annually to correspond with the frequency at which independent variables are observed. Table 7.4 provides details about the relevant IFS series used to construct the accounting indicators, and suggests how these series correspond to different elements of, as it were, the balance

Figure 7.3: *Net worth* series for Argentina and Mexico (Capital/Assets). Series are built from the IMF-IFS and are laid over banking crises (gray bars) identified by Caprio et al. (2005).

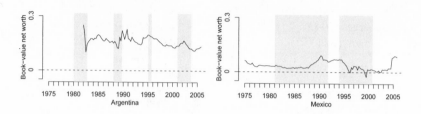

sheet of a country's entire banking sector (see Chapter 2). Keep in mind that by the rules of double-entry bookkeeping, assets should be equal to the sum of liabilities plus capital.[13]

From the series in Table 7.4, I consider the ratio Capital/Assets as a system-wide measure of financial activity and refer to it as *net worth*. This index has some resemblance to, but is not identical to, the regulatory capital-asset ratio that one would ideally use to gauge bank insolvency. In fact, the "capital" series in the IFS does not correspond to shareholders' capital, but is simply a measure of the book value of all assets in the national financial system compared to the book value of all liabilities. Because the IFS reports these series at current values based on local currency units, the only way to insure comparability across time and space is to consider this measure as a proportion of total assets. The resulting ratio can be interpreted as measuring the book-value net worth of a banking system. The index can take negative values—corresponding to situations in which the book value of liabilities outstrips the book value of assets and the banking system therefore has negative net worth—though this kind of flagrant insolvency is infrequent in the data.

To familiarize the reader with this series, Figure 7.3 displays the time-path of *net worth* in Argentina and Mexico, along with periods of systemic banking crisis as recognized by experts. For reasons noted above, the correlation between dichotomous scores and continuous indicators will be far from perfect. However, as can be gleaned from this plot, it is possible to find

---

[13]The banking sector in the IMF-IFS series includes deposit-taking banks and savings and loans, but not other financial intermediaries like insurance companies or mutual funds administrators. The approach I take here is based on Ishihara (2005), who uses a similar method to identify the occurrence of different types of financial crises.

Table 7.5: Mean and standard deviation of *net worth* conditional on *political regime* (dichotomous index) and *level of development* (countries with per capita GDP above/below sample mean). Observations are at the country/year level and are multiplied by 100.

	Autocracies		Democracies	
	Rich	Poor	Rich	Poor
Net worth	9.42	13.14	10.36	11.21
	(6.24)	(7.58)	(5.16)	(6.03)
N	251	364	435	175

correspondence between periods of systemic banking crisis identified by experts and movements of the *net worth* variable. Consider for example the series for Argentina, which follows recognized periods of banking crisis relatively closely, with dips in the series in 1988–1989, 1994–1995, and at the beginning of 2002. In the case of Mexico, we can see a gradual improvement in aggregate net worth in the late 1980s in the period preceding bank privatization, and then a precipitous decline starting in 1994, with a further drop in net worth around 1998–1999.[14]

As I did previously, I try to build as strong as possible a case for a causal interpretation of the political regime effect. To do so, I draw again a sample of countries that ensures sufficient covariate balance across types of political regime (see Section 7.1.1). Because the sample of countries for which the IFS provides information is not identical to the sample of countries included in Caprio et al.'s tally of banking crises, the set of countries on which I base the analysis in this section is smaller (*N* = 51) and slightly different from that of Section 7.1.[15]

I expect democratic regimes, on average, to be associated with higher values of *net worth*, which would correspond to lower levels of financial distress. Table 7.5 breaks down the distribution of *net worth* across political regimes and across levels of economic development based on information from the

---

[14]The *net worth* series are stationary for all countries, as confirmed by KPSS stationarity tests (Baum and Sperling 2001; Kwiatkowski, Phillips, Schmidt and Shin 1992).

[15]See Appendix A.2.5. Coverage of the IFS series is uneven across countries. Lack of information in some IMF-IFS series led to loss of data for India, Israel, Japan, Norway, Senegal, Singapore, and United Kingdom. These countries were not considered in the matching procedure. For other countries, data exist at quarterly frequency from 1975 to date, but there are some gaps in the series. Missing values of the dependent variable are assumed missing at random and updated through the estimation process (84 values are missing among 1,173 country/year observations).

balanced sample. As in Table 7.1, Table 7.5 uses categories corresponding to above and below mean income for level of development and the *regime* indicator of Przeworski et al. (2000) for democratic and non-democratic regimes. The cross-tabulation does not support my expectations, as the category with *highest* average *net worth* is that of poorer non-democratic regimes. Furthermore, average *net worth* across all democracies, regardless of level of development, is 10.6 (SD = 5.4), as opposed to 11.5 (SD = 7.4) across non-democracies; though substantively small, this difference is statistically significant at the 95% confidence level. A skeptical reader of these data would remark on the fact that banks do not always face incentives to report their real financial status to domestic authorities, and that these incentives are less powerful precisely in poorer non-democratic countries. If this interpretation were indeed accurate, we would expect the *regime* coefficient to be biased *against* the hypothesis that I purport to verify—a far less complicated situation than the alternative, since any results that obtain in the expected direction can only be presumed to be larger in the absence of measurement error. In any case, recall that the matching process that I employ to obtain a more balanced sample of observations does not take into consideration the values of the dependent variable of interest, so sample choice was in no way guided by the distribution of *net worth* across regimes.

To build a reasonable model within which to estimate regime effects, one must make several assumptions about the process that drives *net worth*. More fundamentally, building a model of the association between political regimes and *net worth* in a context of time-serial cross-sectional data requires appropriate assumptions about underlying dynamics. Consider then a model where *net worth* in country i at time t is drawn from a normal distribution— i.e., net worth$_{it} \sim \mathcal{N}(\mu_{it}, \sigma_i^2)$—where μ_{it} has an autoregressive distributed lag (ADL) structure, as in Equation 7.5:

$$\mu_{it} = \alpha_i + \beta_0 \text{Net worth}_{it-1} + \beta_1 \text{Regime}_{it} + \beta_2 \text{Regime}_{it-1}$$

$$+ \sum^{k} (\gamma_{1k} X_{itk} + \gamma_{2k} X_{it-1k}) \quad (7.5)$$

As DeBoef and Keele (2008) point out, this model is identical to an error correction model but relies on a different, more intuitive, parameterization. The ADL model is particularly useful when theory provides little guidance about the lags at which independent variables affect the dependent variable. In this case, the hypothesis of interest is that the effect of political *regime* on *net worth* is positive, but it is not clear from the theory in Chapter 3 whether we should expect this effect to be spent out contemporaneously (which would be captured by β_1) or whether *regime* continues to affect *net worth* after a 1-period lag (captured by β_2). Furthermore, we can calculate a "dynamic multiplier" effect from this model, i.e., an estimate of the long run or total effect of *regime* on *net worth* distributed over future time periods.[16] The value of *net worth* for country i at year t is also a function of other covariates measured at the country-year level (X_{it}), whose effects are also partitioned into contemporaneous (γ_1) and lagged (γ_2) effects. I rely on the same battery of covariates as in the previous exercise: *capital openness, GDP growth*, and *per capita GDP.* I also estimate random country intercepts α_i because banking systems differ systematically in their average levels of *net worth* throughout the period under study, likely a consequence of unobserved covariates—like regulatory regimes or central bank status. Note also that I consider the possibility of heteroscedasticity, i.e., that the variance of *net worth* scores may be different across countries. By estimating country-specific variances σ_i^2, I admit the possibility that countries may have different patterns of year-to-year book value net worth.[17]

7.2.1 Results

Table 7.6 reproduces coefficient estimates from various specifications of the basic model described in Equation 7.5. To convey the main results of the analysis, I discuss first the simplest specification (Model 1). This model includes random country-level intercepts and country-specific variance parameters (not shown for the sake of space). In this specification, the strongest positive predictor of system-wide *net worth* is a country's lagged level of development, captured by per capita GDP (log scale). Values of average economic growth are, contrary to expectations, negatively correlated with *net worth*, whereas *openness*, which captures the degree to which capital is able to flow across country borders, has a contemporaneous positive short term association with the dependent variable in line with results in Section 7.1.[18] Across the different specifications, there are no relevant changes in estimates of the coefficients for the main control variables.

I offer several models based alternatively on Przeworski et al.'s dichotomous regime indicator (Models 1 and 3) and the continuous Polity IV indicator of democracy (Models 2 and 4); both indicators are coded so that higher val-

---

[16]Based on the notation of Equation 7.5, the dynamic multiplier is $k = (\beta_1 + \beta_2)/(1 - \beta_0)$.

[17]WinBugs code appears in Appendix A.3.6. To complete the description of the model, I stipulated diffuse prior distributions on parameters: $\beta, \gamma \sim \mathcal{N}(0, 0.01)$, $\alpha \sim \mathcal{N}(0, 0.001)$, $\sigma \sim \text{Uniform}(0, 100)$. The dependent variable is rescaled by a factor of 100 and independent variables are standardized to aid convergence. Descriptions of the posterior distribution of parameters are based on 500 to 1,000 draws from two separate chains, thinned every 10th iteration, after apparent convergence. Convergence was swift and clean and was monitored using the Gelman-Rubin $\widehat{R}$ statistic.

[18]To be precise, higher degrees of *openness* are associated with lower probabilities of banking crises (Table 7.2) and higher values of net worth (Table 7.6).

Table 7.6: Autoregressive distributive lag models of aggregate net worth. Point estimates are the median of parameter posterior densities (standard deviation of parameter posterior densities in parentheses). Statistic k is the dynamic multiplier effect of *regime*.

Indicators	Model 1 REG	Model 2 Polity IV	Model 3 REG	Model 4 Polity IV
Country/year level				
Net worth$_{t-1}$	0.823	0.822	0.878	0.881
	(0.018)	(0.019)	(0.016)	(0.016)
Regime$_t$	0.084	0.135	0.085	0.153
	(0.116)	(0.155)	(0.112)	(0.160)
Openness$_t$	0.173	0.250	0.158	0.243
	(0.121)	(0.135)	(0.128)	(0.126)
Growth$_t$	−0.123	−0.129	−0.122	−0.123
	(0.093)	(0.097)	(0.091)	(0.093)
GDP pc$_t$	0.043	0.140	−0.376	−0.486
	(0.434)	(0.019)	(0.449)	(0.459)
Regime$_{t-1}$	0.225	0.189	0.174	0.092
	(0.117)	(0.157)	(0.115)	(0.167)
Openness$_{t-1}$	−0.097	−0.151	−0.103	−0.170
	(0.120)	(0.138)	(0.127)	(0.139)
Growth$_{t-1}$	−0.024	−0.018	−0.001	0.027
	(0.088)	(0.090)	(0.086)	(0.091)
GDP pc$_{t-1}$	0.729	0.628	0.391	0.485
	(0.430)	(0.461)	(0.456)	(0.451)
Country level				
Intercept			1.489	1.462
			(0.235)	(0.248)
Inequality			0.070	0.012
			(0.227)	(0.237)
Transparency			−0.121	−0.184
			(0.322)	(0.327)
k	1.753	1.819	2.131	2.054
	(0.371)	(0.442)	(0.513)	(0.513)
N	1,122	1,122	1,122	1,122
Countries	51	51	51	51
DIC	5,096	5,102	5,078	5,084
pD	108	108	111	111

ues correspond to democratic regimes. Across these different specifications, the coefficients of main concern are those that correspond to immediate (t) and lagged ($t - 1$) effects of *regime* on *net worth*. In Model 1, for example, the contemporaneous effect is positive, but straddles 0 (0.084 ± 0.12), whereas the posterior distribution of the lag effect has most probability mass to the left of 0 (0.225 ± 117). These two parameters capture the short-term effect of political regime on a banking system's book-value *net worth*. Aside from this immediate effect, the dynamic multiplier k statistic at the bottom of the table reveals the long-run effect of *regime* on *net worth*.

Across all four specifications, the short- and long-run effects of political regime are consistently positive, though there are admittedly noteworthy variations in the estimated size of these effects and in the degree of uncertainty that surrounds them, especially in the short run. The dynamic multiplier statistic suggests that average *net worth* over the long run can be several points higher in democratic than in non-democratic regimes. For example, based on coefficients for Model 1, the long-run difference in *net worth* between democratic and non-democratic regimes is 3.57 (± 0.76) points, which is not a trivial amount considering that the standard deviation of the unconditional distribution of *net worth* is 6.48. Similar estimates of the long-run positive impact of democracy on *net worth* follow from the rest of the models.

These long-run effects are the result of slow accumulation, as in the short run the estimated effects of *regime* are more uncertain and much smaller in terms of substantive magnitude. In particular, Models 3 and 4 reveal a smaller *regime* coefficient; these models include average *inequality* and *transparency* measures at the country level and provide a slightly better fit based on the deviance information criterion reported in the last row of Table 7.6.[19] Since they provide the most conservative estimates of the *regime* coefficient, I focus on Models 3 and 4 to gauge the substantive importance of this variable as a predictor of *net worth* in the short run, that is, considering the *regime* variable fixed during two consecutive years. For this purpose, the left panel in Figure 7.5 plots the posterior predictive distribution of *net worth* for the two values of the political regime dichotomous indicator while holding all other variables at their mean sample values. As can be gleaned from this graph, the posterior predictive distributions of *net worth* under these two regimes overlap. In fact, they overlap to such an extent that there is a non-negligible probability (≈ 0.14) that non-democratic regimes may have higher *net worth* in the short run. In substantive terms, the average regime effect based on

---

[19]Country averages of *inequality* and *transparency* are based on available information for each country. They are added as predictors of country intercepts, i.e., $\alpha_i = \delta_0 + \delta_1$Transparency + δ_2Inequality. The coefficient of *inequality* is basically centered on 0; the posterior distribution of the coefficient of *transparency* has most probability mass to the left of 0, but also straddles this value.

Figure 7.4: Posterior predictive distribution of *net worth* across democratic and non-democratic regimes (a) and partial regression of country-specific *net worth* variance on average regime scores (b)

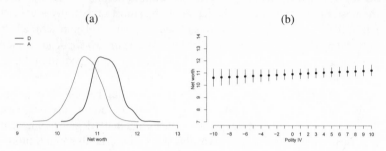

the scenario of the left plot of Figure 7.5 can be summarized as follows: Within two years, the banking system's book-value *net worth* of an average authoritarian country would lie between 10.28 and 11.15, and between 10.82 and 11.62 under an average democratic regime (80% credible intervals).

The right panel of Figure 7.5 displays a similar exercise corresponding to Model 4, which is based on the continuous Polity IV score as the relevant indicator of democracy. In this graph, point estimates correspond to the median of the posterior predictive distribution of *net worth*. In Model 4, the contemporaneous regime effect is 0.15 (±0.16) and the lagged effect is 0.09 (±0.17); the posterior distributions of these effects are centered on positive values, but wide enough to straddle 0. Consequently, the plot suggests a barely noticeable upward trend in the posterior predictive distribution of *net worth*; at the left end of the scale, an average country with the least-democratic Polity IV score of −10 would be expected to have net worth between 9.90 and 11.34, whereas an average country with the most-democratic Polity IV score of 10 would have a net worth range between 10.81 and 11.72 (again, these are 80% credible intervals). The positive, albeit small, short-run effects of *regime* in these models are still consistent with long-run dynamic multipliers of 2.13 (±0.52) and 2.05 (±0.51), respectively.

Aside from understanding regime effects on *net worth* levels on a short- and long-run basis, these models offer a glimpse into potential association between political regime and overall *net worth* stability. To do so, we can analyze cross-country patterns of variability of the *net worth* series. Recall that the models reported in Table 7.6 include unmodeled country-specific intercepts (α_i) and variance (σ_i^2) parameters. The first set of parameters captures the average level of *net worth* in each country throughout the obser-

Figure 7.5: Partial regressions of country-specific *net worth* intercept (α) and variance (σ) parameters on *average regime scores* and *average GDP per capita*, based on Model 4 in Table 7.6

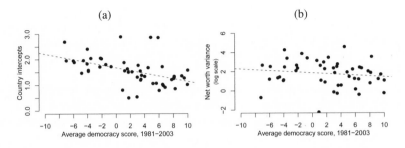

vation period, whereas variance parameters capture the amount of variability around this average level. Figure 7.5 displays added-variable plots of point estimates of country-specific intercepts (Plot a) and country-specific variance parameters (Plot b) as a function of a country's average level of democracy, based on Model 4. As can be seen in Plot a, countries with *higher* average levels of democracy throughout the observation period tend to have slightly lower average *net worth*, as suggested by the category breakdown of Table 7.5. Plot b reveals no systematic effect of average levels of democracy on country-specific variation in *net worth*. Though the association between country-specific variances and average levels of democracy is negative, suggesting that democratic regimes have more stable patterns of *net worth*, this result is not statistically relevant.[20]

7.3 Concluding Remarks

I have sought to understand in this chapter whether the effects of democratic regimes on banking policy extend beyond limiting government propensities to implement bailout policies. This enterprise is complicated because the theoretical concepts that one would like to measure are intangible probabilities of failure and solvency status of banking systems. I have resorted to banking crises indicators and measures of the book-value net worth of banking systems as tangible indicators of these theoretical concepts. Furthermore, the observational nature of the data limits our ability to make causal inferences

---

[20]In contrast, I find that "richer" countries (again, due to the use of a balanced sample these tend to be middle-income economies) have conspicuously less volatile net worth series (results not shown).

about parameters. As I did in Chapter 6, I built a case for causal interpretation of model parameters. To do so, I have resorted to matching methods that correct for covariate imbalance and techniques such as instrumental variables that contribute to isolate truly exogenous variation in a crucial regressor to comply with the assumption of ignorability of treatment assignment. Based on these assumptions, I conclude that democratic regimes limit the possibility of financial distress and bolster the overall solvency status of banking systems, though the true size of the effect is difficult to gauge. This finding is in line with Propositions 2 and 3.

The analysis in this chapter rounds up the empirical evidence that I marshal to substantiate an optimistic view of democratic accountability. The evidence presented in this chapter is consistent with a view according to which economic actors look forward and rationally anticipate government policy output, incorporating these expectations into current behavior. In my view, democracy reins in politicians and forces them to consider the welfare of taxpayers when devising programs to redress banking crises. Bankers and entrepreneurs understand the effect of this constraint on government action, and thus discount the probability of generous bailouts funded by taxpayers. This knowledge affects their economic decisions enough so that the probability of bank failure and the book-value net worth of banking systems are noticeably lower under democracies than under authoritarian regimes.

Conclusion

The term "bailout" has an unmistakable pejorative connotation in banking policy. This connotation builds up with every instance of government support to failing banks, regardless of the extent of this support and its stated policy objectives. Bank bailouts violate innate norms of fairness because they suggest that governments protect powerful actors from their own greed and folly at the expense of common citizens. And yet, banks are indeed special; they are highly leveraged, intricately intertwined, and suffer to a larger extent than non-financial firms from mismatches in their asset/liability structure. Not only do these features subject the best-managed institutions to the possibility of failure, but failure of even a small bank threatens ample ripple effects that may destroy trust in the basic solvency of a country's financial system.

We can understand government policies to contain banking crises within a dual economic and political logic. The economic logic behind public support builds on Bagehot's doctrine, a rule that requires a lender of last resort to provide liquidity to distressed banks. This kind of forceful intervention is necessary to restore stability to a country's financial system and, if done right, can strengthen the banking sector by pruning the weakest institutions. After all, Bagehot's doctrine also calls upon governments to force the orderly exit of insolvent banks. When government interventions are limited to following Bagehot's precepts, it is hard to construe them as examples of robber baron capitalism gone awry. The lender of last resort is meant to temporarily "fill in" for the market mechanism: it sorts banks out according to quality, lends freely to solvent banks, and shuts insolvent banks down. Taxpayers do not stand to lose because last resort loans are doled out at a penalty rate and on good collateral.

Be this as it may, governments very often overstep the boundaries of Bagehot's doctrine and provide support to banks that hardly deserve it. Bagehot's doctrine is often criticized because it is in practice difficult for regulators and politicians to perform the kind of triage on which it is premised. After all, if information about the financial status of banks is sufficiently unclear that it prevents markets from allocating liquidity to deserving banks, what guarantees that government agencies will be any better at separating distressed but fundamentally solid institutions from those fated to the dustbin of history? Under conditions of extreme asymmetric information, government agencies are as helpless as other economic actors in reaching correct conclusions about the true financial status of banks. When one adds concerns about systemic risk—i.e, about the possibility that insolvency of one or a handful of banks will extend to other institutions—it is easier to see how even reluctant governments will seem eager to extend a helping hand to banks.

This book has shown that there exists wide variation in the kind of policies that governments put together to manage banking crises, and that an important part of this variation can be traced back to differences in political regimes across countries. Banking crises can only be avoided at very hefty cost, for example by mandating extremely high rates of capitalization and forcing banks to invest in safe and liquid assets. Needless to say, these options would also eliminate a banking system's ability to allocate credit to desirable projects and would very likely slow down a country's pace of economic growth. Barring such extreme policies, it is foreseeable that banks will continue to fail every now and then. Banks, like other actors in financial markets, are in business for the *promise* of future returns; these promises cannot always be kept, even under the best intentions.

I have argued that the political logic that underlies bailouts may help tame the more costly aspects of banking policy. I consider that democratic regimes are better than authoritarian regimes at countering pressures from organized groups that face concentrated losses in the event of a banking crisis. Democracies achieve this effect by subjecting governments to meaningful periodic elections. Though electoral accountability might not always make for a high-powered set of incentives pushing governments toward implementing the policy preferences of unorganized voters, it certainly constrains democratic governments enough to keep them away from the most blatant and intrusive forms of bank bailout. In this regard, the evidence reviewed in Chapters 5 and 6 confirms that governments in democratic regimes have on average lower bailout propensities than governments in authoritarian regimes. By showing that the bailout policies put forth by democratic governments tend to be less expansive, I engage a debate on the possibility and limits of a "democratic advantage" in policy-making, a debate that has been pursued in many fields of inquiry within political economy, for example in research on foreign direct investment (Jensen 2006), sovereign debt (Saiegh 2005; Schultz and Weingast 2003), credit risk assessments (Archer, Biglaiser and DeRouen 2007; Vaaler and McNamara 2004), and monetary policy (Desai, Olofsgård and Yousef 2003). My contention that democratic regimes tend to enact less intrusive bailouts than non-democracies should not be construed as a full endorsement of democratic policy-making. To do so, one would need to show that banking policy output under democratic regimes is optimal according to some uncontroversial yardstick. Given the amount of uncertainty that surrounds policy choice during banking crises, finding such an uncontroversial yardstick is difficult at best. Building that yardstick would require answers to the following questions: Is the decision to pass some financial losses on to taxpayers the optimal way to safeguard the banking system? If so, what is the minimum amount of financial losses that must be socialized in order to guarantee the stability of a country's banking system? Thus, an important limitation of my research is that is not meant to answer questions about the optimality of democratic policy-making in the midst of banking crises. In other words, though I can say with a high degree of confidence that democratic regimes are less prone than non-democratic regimes to implement policies that socialize financial losses, I cannot say how close or far away democratic regimes are from solving banking crises in an optimal manner. In the face of current financial distress in the banking systems of core democratic economies, it would be extremely important to understand the institutional conditions under which electoral accountability has the largest impact on limiting government intervention to the bare minimum. This of course implies a nuanced understanding of banking policy among countries that have enjoyed stable democratic governance in the recent past.

My analysis also supports the view that the salutary effects of electoral accountability extend beyond simply limiting the propensity of governments to bail out troubled banks. The theoretical argument is premised on the recognition that rational actors are capable of anticipating government policy choices. If bankers, entrepreneurs, and even bank creditors and debtors anticipate that bailouts will not be forthcoming in case of financial distress, this realization ought to change their economic behavior. A direct test of this argument would require inspection of the risk-taking behavior of entrepreneurs and bankers under different political regimes. Given the difficulty of carrying out such a test in a large number of countries, I chose to corroborate testable implications of this argument. First, I inspected the frequency of banking meltdowns under alternative regimes. I found that democratic regimes tend to suffer lower counts of banking crises than authoritarian regimes. Second, I inspected the level of association between political regimes and accounting ratios that more directly reflect the book-value net worth of banking systems. In this case, I also found that democratic regimes have a positive effect on the aggregate net worth of banking systems, especially in the long run. Again, I do not mean to dress up this conclusion as support for the proposition that democratic accountability *suffices* to prevent banking crises; it clearly does not, as is obvious from the fact that the subprime-mortgage crisis started in the core democratic nations of the global financial system.

These findings are premised on a number of assumptions about the inner workings of politics and financial intermediaries and about the characteristics of observed samples. I have strived to make explicit all the assumptions that underlie the empirical sections of the book. My conclusions about the salutary effects of democratic regimes on banking policy ultimately stand on analysis of *observational* data. Under ideal circumstances, one would be able to randomly assign treatment (in this case, democratic accountability) to different polities, thus complying with *necessary conditions* required to estimate causal effects (Holland 1986; Rubin 1974). When random treatment assignment is not possible, as is common in many fields of scientific research, estimates of causal effects are only as good as the effort spent in approaching these necessary conditions. Effort must be spent in controlling for relevant covariates, obtaining balanced samples, and above all approximating the assumption of exogenous independent variables that underlies causal analysis. In the analysis of observational data, careful statistical modeling is still the best way to approximate a causal interpretation of effect parameters. I believe that my analysis complies with the extant conditions required to provide such an interpretation of regime effects; ultimately, the results stand on the verisimilitude of these assumptions, which explains my insistence in vetting them thoroughly.

I have also laid out clearly all theoretical assumptions about the interaction between governments, entrepreneurs, and bankers. I have been careful to select these assumptions so that they correspond with accumulated knowledge about politics and policy choice. Some of these assumptions, like the assumption of rational choice and expected utility maximization, are ubiquitous and more or less consensual in applied work in political economy. Wherever necessary, I provide theoretical justification for all the other assumptions that underlie the main argument—assumptions about order of play, agent payoffs, and exogenous parameters. There are, however, a number of assumptions that have remained implicit in my analysis. In my view, future work should aim to revisit and perhaps relax these assumptions.

First, I have not considered certain institutional aspects of banking regulation in great detail. I have given short consideration to issues such as autonomy of bank regulators, transparency in bank accounting standards, and distribution of supervisory and regulatory functions among more than one agency. In particular, *autonomy of bank regulators* stands out as a factor that may affect the bailout propensity of governments. Satyanath, for example, considers that the ability of developed democracies to get away with liberal capital controls without succumbing to major banking crises may result from independence of regulators from political pressures (Satyanath 2006). Indeed, if bank regulators have a preference for stringent regulation and if they are indeed autonomous from politicians, it certainly follows that they will be successful in preventing banking crises.

There are however reasons to suspect that this explanation is incomplete. To begin with, governments undergoing banking crises have great incentives to revamp their banking agencies and regulatory structures, so these institutions are more aptly seen as endogenous to the political process. Furthermore, even autonomous regulators may have an incentive to engage in forbearance. After all, the objective of a competent autonomous regulator is to ensure that banks are solvent by monitoring them continuously and preventing financial distress. Bank closures, even if justifiable, are an unequivocal signal that the bureaucrat failed in her mission to prevent insolvency. Finally, even if one argues that "better" regulatory agencies have a beneficial impact on banking policy, one should provide an answer to the question of where the political impetus or willingness to supply appropriate regulatory frameworks comes from. In my opinion, the decision to supply better regulation is mostly determined by links of political accountability. It may well be that mature democracies have an advantage in counting with independent regulators, but that is only because they have had ample time to learn that such institutional settings make for better banking outcomes. Many young democracies may simply have failed to discover the benefits of such regulatory structures. Once they undergo a financial crisis, and therefore understand how devastating these events can be, the incentives to adopt these institutions may very well increase. Such incentives seem to be at work even in older democracies, like the United States, where the subprime-mortgage crisis of 2007 and 2008 has brought about urgent calls to regulate financial products that have been largely out of the purview of banking agencies in the past. At the end of the day, the best regulatory schemes cannot dissipate entirely the temptation of economic actors to increase risk-taking *if these actors can count on shifting part of the downside risk to society at large*. In this regard, non-democratic regimes provide economic actors with reasons to anticipate larger degrees of socialization of bank losses.

A second implicit assumption concerns the close identification I make between banks and banking systems, i.e., between the components of a system and the system as a whole. My theoretical argument considers the interaction between a set of entrepreneurs and a decision-maker, with a single bank that plays the passive role of gathering deposits and lending them to entrepreneurs in exchange for interest payment. I have then considered this single bank as an example of how governments react vis-à-vis the whole banking system. In short, I have obviated consideration of the problem of aggregation. The "single bank" assumption, I believe, has been extremely productive in generating testable implications, and is in fact defensible if one considers this bank to be a representative agent. However, even a cursory reading of Chapter 4 suggests that banking systems cannot always be reduced to the sum of their component units. For starters, banks come in different sizes and attitudes towards risk, and belong in different categories that may receive unequal policy treatment. More importantly, banking crises usher in periods of consolidation in which larger banks are often called upon (and subsidized) to take on smaller banks. Under these circumstances, it is worthwhile to consider whether the very structure of a country's banking sector may have an impact both in producing widespread insolvency and in fostering certain types of crisis-management policies. On the one hand, what we know about the logic of collective action suggests that more concentrated banking sectors may be better able to push for bailouts in case of financial distress.[1] On the other hand, an oligopolistic organization of banking systems might diminish incentives for cutthroat competition in the banking industry and might produce more cooperative outcomes in times of distress.

A third implicit assumption has to do with the consideration of national banking as a closed system. This assumption has two consequences. First, of course, the possibility of financial contagion has been discussed extensively in the literature and remains an active area of research. I have not explicitly considered channels of financial contagion across countries, but I made an effort to allow the possibility of variable correlations across countries within the same time-period. I am more interested about a second potential consequence of this implicit assumption. I have analyzed national banking systems as if these operated within self-contained polities, an assumption that becomes less accurate as banks, particularly those based in developed economies, continue to increase their reach beyond national borders. This phenomenon is not new, but the pace at which international banks take up market share in the retail banking sector of many economies is staggering. At the same time, bank regulation and supervision is failing to keep up with the pace of this process. Admittedly, international efforts enshrined in the Basel Accords have helped standardize "best practice" banking regulation around the world; these efforts have been interpreted as the fruit of coordination among sovereign states to prevent negative externalities from a banking crisis in one country from spilling over to other countries (Kapstein 1994). However, the crux of the problem is that as large banks deepen their commitment to act globally, banking regulation continues to be essentially a national endeavor. In fact, an alternative interpretation of the Basel Accords suggests that US regulators pushed for it in an effort to drag down the competitiveness of foreign banks gaining market share on American banks (Oatley and Nabors 1998; Singer 2007). In this interpretation, far from helping authorities keep up with the global reach of banks by endowing an international authority with regulatory

---

[1] Be this as it may, an indicator of bank concentration fails as a predictor of bailout propensities (Rosas 2006).

capacity, these efforts at international coordination may simply increase the occurrence and severity of banking crises. It is thus important to expand our understanding of the conditions under which national governments, regardless of their political regime, can coordinate effectively to deal with banking crises.

Appendices

A.1 Mathematical Proofs for Chapter 3

DERIVATION OF EQUATION 3.1. Set the Lagrangean equation

$$L = \pi(R(\pi) - 1 - r) - (1 - \pi)w + \lambda(R(\pi) - 1 - r).$$

I disregard the possibility that the constraint is binding, i.e., $R(\pi) - 1 = r$, as there is no reason to assume that an entrepreneur would be content with risking capital in exchange for a return that barely covers interest payments in the good state. Therefore, the first-order necessary condition requires compliance with the following conditions: $\partial L/\partial \pi = 0$, $\lambda = 0$, and $R(\pi) - 1 > r$. Satisfying the first-order condition implies that $E(U_E)' = 0$, which obtains when $R(\pi^*) + \pi^* R'(\pi^*) = 1 - r - w$. To show that π^* is an interior solution, consider $\pi = 0$ and $\pi = 1$ as candidate solutions. In the first case, the first-order condition would be rewritten as $R(0) = 1 + r - w$, but this equality cannot hold because $R(0) > 1$ and $1 + r - w < 1$. In the second case, the first-order condition would be $R(1) + R'(1) = 1 + r - w$. By assumption, $R(1) = 1$ and $R'(1) \leq -1$, so $R(1) + R'(1) \leq 0$, while $1 + r - w > 0$. This shows that the endpoints 0 and 1 cannot be solutions. To show that equilibrium choice π^* is a maximum, note that the second-order condition is $2R'(\pi^*) + \pi^* R''(\pi^*) < 0$, which holds because $R' < 0$ and $R'' < 0$ by assumption (see fn. 4).

PROBABILITIES OF DIFFERENT ENDSTATES CONDITIONAL ON SIGNALS. Using Bayes' rule, the probabilities for the different endstates of the game upon observing signal $s \in \{s_0, s_1\}$ are

$$\Pr(R_1|s_1) = \frac{\Pr(R_1)\Pr(s_1|R_1)}{\Pr(s_1)} = \frac{\pi^* q}{\pi^* q} = 1$$

$$\Pr(R_0|s_1) = \frac{\Pr(R_0)\Pr(s_1|R_0)}{\Pr(s_1)} = \frac{(1 - \pi^*) \cdot 0}{\pi^* q} = 0$$

178

$$\Pr(R_1|s_0) = \frac{\Pr(R_1)\Pr(s_0|R_1)}{\Pr(s_0)} = \frac{\pi^*(1-q)}{\pi^*(1-q) + (1-\pi^*)}$$

$$\Pr(R_0|s_0) = \frac{\Pr(R_0)\Pr(s_0|R_0)}{\Pr(s_0)} = \frac{(1-\pi^*)}{\pi^*(1-q) + (1-\pi^*)}$$

PROOF THAT $\partial c_d^*/\partial \sigma > 0$. The formal proof that democratic governments are less likely to engage in forbearance in less egalitarian societies follows from signing the partial derivative of c_d^* with respect to σ, which parameterizes inequality, as positive. Applying the chain rule, the relevant derivative is

$$\frac{\partial c_d^*}{\partial \sigma} = \frac{\partial c_d^*}{\partial \bar{y}/y_m} \frac{\partial \bar{y}/y_m}{\partial \sigma} \tag{A.1}$$

Writing $a = \pi^* r$ and $b = (1 - \pi^*)(1 - q)(1 - w)$, the first term in Equation A.1 is

$$\frac{\partial c_d^*}{\partial \bar{y}/y_m} = \frac{(b-a)b}{(a + b(\bar{y}/y_m - 1))^2},$$

which is negative if $a > b$. This will be the case if $\pi^* r > (1 - \pi^*)(1 - q)(1 - w)$, that is if $\pi^* > (1 - q)(1 - w)/(r + (1 - q)(1 - w))$, which is guaranteed to hold. To see this, assume that $\pi \le (1 - q)(1 - w)/(r + (1 - q)(1 - w))$; this implies that $c_d \le 0$, which in turn means that $F(c_d) = 0$, which finally leads to 0 expected utility for the entrepreneur. But the entrepreneur can guarantee herself a positive payoff by choosing $\pi > (1 - q)(1 - w)/(r + (1 - q)(1 - w))$. Thus, the numerator is negative, the denominator positive, and the entire expression negative.

From the definition of the Pareto distribution, write $\bar{y}/y_m$ as $\sigma((\sigma - 1)2^{1/\sigma})^{-1}$. The second term in Equation A.1 is

$$\frac{\partial \bar{y}/y_m}{\partial \sigma} = \frac{(\sigma - 1)\left(2^{-1/\sigma} + 2^{-1/\sigma}\log(2)\sigma^{-1}\right) - 2^{-1/\sigma}\sigma}{(\sigma - 1)^2}$$

$$= \frac{\sigma(\log(2) - 1) - \log(2)}{\sigma(\sigma - 1)^2 2^{1/\sigma}}$$

Since $\sigma > 1$, the denominator of this expression is positive. The numerator, however, is negative because $\log(2) > \sigma(\log(2) - 1)$. To see this, rearrange terms and rewrite this latter expression as $1 + \frac{\sigma}{\log(2)} > \sigma$, which always holds because $\log(2) < 1$. Consequently, the partial derivative of c_d^* with respect to σ is positive, which implies that as inequality decreases (i.e., σ increases), democratic governments have more incentives to forbear.

PROOF OF CONDITION 3.9. The entrepreneur's problem is to set

$$\kappa^* \equiv \underset{\kappa}{\text{argmax}} \ \mathsf{E}_{cd}(U_G).$$

The first order condition obtains when

$$\frac{\partial \mathsf{E}_{cd}(U_G)}{\partial \kappa} = \pi^* Z'(\kappa) - (1 - \pi^*)\alpha w \bar{y} = 0,$$

which readily yields Condition 3.9. There cannot be a corner solution at $\kappa^* = 0$, because this would imply $Z'(0) = \frac{1-\pi^*}{\pi^*}\alpha w \bar{y}$ and this violates the assumption that $Z'(0) = \infty$ (see fn. 22). However, a corner solution at $\kappa^* = 1$ is possible for some values of parameters w, σ, and π^*, and certain for $\alpha = 0$. The second-order condition for κ^* to be a maximum obtains because

$$\frac{\partial^2 \mathsf{E}_{cd}(U_G)}{\partial \kappa} = \pi^* Z''(\kappa) < 0,$$

which follows directly from assumptions about $Z(\cdot)$ (see fn. 22).

To show that the optimal choice of κ^* is increasing in σ and μ, it suffices to show that $\mathsf{E}_{cd}(U_G)$ has monotone comparative statics with respect to these two parameters (Ashworth and Bueno de Mesquita 2006). Monotone comparative statics obtain if the relevant cross-partial derivatives of $\mathsf{E}_{cd}(U_G)$ do not change signs. The relevant cross-partial derivatives are

$$\frac{\partial \mathsf{E}_{cd}(U_G)}{\partial \kappa \partial \sigma} = \frac{\partial \mathsf{E}_{cd}(U_G)}{\partial \kappa \partial \bar{y}} \cdot \frac{\partial \bar{y}}{\partial \sigma} = -\frac{(1-\pi^*)w\alpha}{(\sigma-1)^2},$$

which is negative for all values of π^*, α, w and σ, and

$$\frac{\partial \mathsf{E}_{cd}(U_G)}{\partial \kappa \partial \mu} = \frac{\partial \mathsf{E}_{cd}(U_G)}{\partial \kappa \partial \bar{y}} \cdot \frac{\partial \bar{y}}{\partial \mu} = -\frac{(1-\pi^*)w\sigma\alpha}{\sigma-1},$$

which is everywhere negative as well. Finally, we check that $\mathsf{E}_{cd}(U_G)$ has monotone comparative statics with respect to α, which is also the case because the relevant cross-partial derivative is negative:

$$\frac{\partial \mathsf{E}_{cd}(U_G)}{\partial \kappa \partial \alpha} = -(1 - \pi^*)w\bar{y}.$$

The government's expected utility function has *negative* monotone comparative statics with respect to parameters α, σ, and μ, which means that it has increasing differences with respect to κ, $-\alpha$, $-\sigma$, and $-\mu$ (Ashworth and Bueno de Mesquita 2006). In short, this suggests that the optimal choice κ^* is decreasing in α, σ, and μ.

A.2 Data Sources

A.2.1 Bank Exit in Argentina and Mexico (Chapter 4.2)

Indicator	Description (Source)	N
Argentina		
CAR	Capital-asset ratio (BCESWIN)	12,856
CB credit	Central bank loans (BCRA)	12,856
GDP change	Change in GDP from same quarter in previous year (MECON, Gellineau)	12,856
Loan concentration	Herfindahl index of concentration of bank loans across economic sectors (BCESWIN)	8,351
Mutual bank	Mutual bank ownership (BCESWIN)	12,856
Bank size	Log of total assets (BCESWIN)	12,856
Mexico		
CAR	Capital-asset ratio (CNBV)	1,104
CMHN	Membership in the Mexican Council of Businessmen (Teichman 1995)	1,104
CB credit	Central bank loans (IMF-IFS)	1,104
Foreign bank	Foreign-owned bank (CNBV)	1,104
GDP change	Change in GDP from same quarter in previous year (INEGI)	1,104
Loan concentration	Herfindahl index of concentration of bank loans across economic sectors (CNBV)	987
NPL ratio	Ratio of non-performing to total loans (CNBV)	1,093
Bank size	Log of total assets (CNBV)	1,104

A.2.2 Data Sources and Descriptive Statistics for Chapter 6

Indicator	Description (Source)	MV	Mean	SD
Central bank independence	Legal central bank autonomy index (Cukierman, Miller and Neyapti 2002; Cukierman, Webb and Neyapti 1992; Polillo and Guillén 2005)	7	0.34	0.11
Income inequality	Gini coefficient of income inequality (Desai, Olofsgård and Yousef 2003)	3	42.60	9.70
GDP pc	Natural log of per capita GDP (Heston, Summers and Aten 2002)	1	3.83	0.31
Capital openness	First principal component of measures in IMF's AREAER (Chinn and Ito 2002)	8	0.51	1.54
Transparency	Average of TI and ICRG measures of corruption (Knack and Keefer 1998; Transparency International 2002)	7	5.39	2.39
Deposit share	Deposits in banks as a share of GDP (Beck, Demirgüç-Kunt and Levine 1999)	3	0.35	0.21
Regional democracy	Mean regional average of Cheibub's contested democracy index (Cheibub and Gandhi 2004)	0	56.90	28.00
Democracy	Indicator of democratic regime (Przeworski and Vreeland 2000)	1	0.60	0.49

MV: Missing values

A.2.3 Sample of Banking Crises, Chapters 5 and 6

"A" stands for non-democratic (authoritarian) government, "D" for democracy, based on the dichotomous indicator of Przeworski et al. (2000):

Argentina 1980 (A), Argentina 1989 (D), Argentina 1995 (D), Australia 1989 (D), Brazil 1994 (D), Bulgaria 1996 (D), Chile 1981 (A), Colombia 1982 (D), Côte d'Ivoire 1988 (A), Czechoslovakia 1989 (A), Ecuador 1996 (D), Egypt 1991 (A), Estonia 1992 (D), Finland 1991 (D), France 1994 (D), Ghana 1982 (A), Hungary 1991 (D), Indonesia 1992 (A), Indonesia 1997 (A), Japan 1992 (D), S. Korea 1997 (D), Latvia 1995 (D), Lithuania 1995 (D), Malaysia 1985 (A), Malaysia 1997 (A), Mexico 1982 (A), Mexico 1994 (A), New Zealand 1987 (D), Norway 1987 (D), Panama 1988 (A), Paraguay 1995 (D), Philippines 1983 (A), Philippines 1998 (D), Poland 1992 (D), Senegal 1988 (A), Slovenia 1992 (A), Spain 1977 (D), Sri Lanka 1989 (A), Sweden 1991 (D), Thailand 1983 (D), Thailand 1997 (D), Turkey 1982 (A), Turkey 1994 (D), United States 1981 (D), Uruguay 1981 (A), Venezuela 1994 (D).

A.2.4 Chapter 7, Hierarchical Ordered Logit Model, Balanced Sample

Argentina, Bangladesh, Bolivia, Botswana, Brazil, Burundi, Cameroon, Chile, China, Colombia, Costa Rica, Dominican Republic, Ecuador, Egypt, El Salvador, Ethiopia, Gambia, Ghana, Greece, Guatemala, Guyana, Honduras, Hungary, India, Indonesia, Ireland, Israel, Italy, Jamaica, Jordan, Kenya, Korea, Laos, Lesotho, Liberia, Madagascar, Malawi, Malaysia, Mauritania, Mauritius, Mexico, Morocco, Mozambique, Nicaragua, Nigeria, Pakistan, Paraguay, Peru, Philippines, Portugal, Senegal, Singapore, South Africa, Spain, Sri Lanka, Sudan, Thailand, Turkey, Uganda, Uruguay, Venezuela, Zambia, Zimbabwe.

A.2.5 Chapter 7, Autocorrelated Distributed Lag Regression, Balanced Sample

Bangladesh, Bolivia, Botswana, Brazil, Bulgaria, Burundi, Cameroon, Chile, Colombia, Costa Rica, Czech Republic, Dominican Republic, Ecuador, Egypt, El Salvador, Gambia, Ghana, Guatemala, Guinea, Hungary, Indonesia, Jamaica, Jordan, Kenya, Laos, Lesotho, Madagascar, Malaysia, Mauritania, Mauritius, Mexico, Morocco, Mozambique, Nicaragua, Nigeria, Panama, Paraguay, Peru, Philippines, Poland, Romania, South Africa, Sri Lanka, Thailand, Trinidad and Tobago, Turkey, Uganda, Uruguay, Venezuela, Zambia, Zimbabwe.

A.3 WinBUGS Code

A.3.1 Hierarchical Weibull Survival Model

```
model{ for (i in 1:I){  t[i] ~ dweib(r, mu[i])I(t.cen[i],)
log(mu[i]) <- alpha[typen[i]] + gamma[1]*gdpchn[qrtr[i]]
 + gamma[2]*cbcredit[qrtr[i]] + beta[1]*car[i] + beta[2]*size[i]
 + beta[3]*herfdahl[i]}
  for (k in 1:3) { alpha[k] ~ dnorm(0, 0.001) }
  for (p in 1:3) { beta[p]  ~ dnorm(0, 0.001) }
  for (j in 1:2) { gamma[j] ~ dnorm(0, 0.001) }
  r ~ dgamma(1, 0.001)}
```

A.3.2 One-dimensional IRT Model

```
model{   for(i in 1:I){        # Loop over countries
    theta[i] ~ dnorm( nu[i], 1 )
    nu[i]   <- delta*democracy[i]
    for(j in 1:J){               # Loop over policies
        y.bis[i,j] ~ dbern( p[i,j] )
        p[i,j]    <- phi( ystar[i,j] )
        ystar[i,j] ~ dnorm( mu[i,j],1 )I(lower[i,j],upper[i,j])
        mu[i,j]   <- beta[j]*theta[i] - alpha[j]}}
# Priors
  for(j in 1:J){ alpha[j] ~ dnorm(0, 0.25)
                beta[j]  ~ dnorm(1, 0.25) }
                delta    ~ dnorm(0, 0.10) }
```

A.3.3 Instrumental Variables Two-Stage Least Squares Model

```
model{ for(i in 1:I){
# yt[,1] holds bailout propensities
# yt[,2] holds Polity IV scores
yt[i,1:2] ~ dmnorm ( yt.hat[i,], Tau.yt[,] )
yt.hat[i,1] <- delta[1]*yt.hat[i,2] + delta[2]*cbi[i] +
               ... + delta[6]*open[i]
yt.hat[i,2] <- eta[1]*neighbor[i] + eta[2]*cbi[i] +
               ... + eta[6]*open[i]  }
delta[1:6] ~ dmnorm(mu.delta[1:6], Tau.delta[1:6,1:6])
eta[1:6]   ~ dmnorm(mu.eta[1:6],   Tau.eta[1:6,1:6])
mu.eta[1] <- 1
for (k in 2:6){ mu.eta[k] <- 0 }
for (k in 1:6){ mu.delta[k] <- 0 }
Tau.yt[1:2,1:2]    ~ dwish(Omega.yt[,], 3)
Tau.eta[1:6,1:6]   ~ dwish(Omega.eta[,], 7)
Tau.delta[1:6,1:6] ~ dwish(Omega.delta[,], 7) }
```

A.3.4 Two-Dimensional IRT Model

```
model{ for(i in 1:I){ theta.1[i] ~ dnorm(nu[i],1)
                      theta.2[i] ~ dnorm(mu[i],1)
nu[i] <- d[1]*regime[i] + d[2]*cbi[i] + d[3]*prop[i]
mu[i] <- e[1]*regime[i] + e[2]*cbi[i] + e[3]*prop[i]
for(j in 1:J){ y.bis[i,j] ~ dbern(p[i,j])
 p[i,j] <- phi(ystar[i,j])
 ystar[i,j] ~ dnorm(xi[i,j],1)I(lower[i,j],upper[i,j])
 xi[i,j] <- b1[j]*theta.1[i] + b2[j]*theta.2[i] -alpha[j]}}
for(j in 1:J){ alpha[j] ~ dnorm(0, 0.25) }
 b1[1] <- 0;              b2[1] ~ dnorm( 1, 0.25)I(0,)
 b1[2] <- 0;              b2[2] ~ dnorm( 1, 0.25)
 b1[3] ~ dnorm(1,0.25)I(0,); b2[3] <- 0
 b1[4] ~ dnorm(1,0.25)I(0,); b2[4] <- 0
 b1[5] ~ dnorm(1,0.25)I(0,); b2[5] <- 0
 b1[6] <- 0;              b2[6] ~ dnorm(-1, 0.25)
 b1[7] ~ dnorm(0,0.25);   b2[7] ~ dnorm( 0, 0.25)
for(k in 1:6){ e[k] ~ dnorm(0, 0.1); d[k] ~ dnorm(0, 0.1)}}
```

A.3.5 Hierarchical Ordered Probit

```
model{ for (i in 1:J){ for (t in 1:T){
# Ordinal logit model
event[i,t] ~ dcat(p[i,t,]); p[i,t,1] <- Q[i,t,1]
p[i,t,2] <- Q[i,t,2]-Q[i,t,1]; p[i,t,3] <- 1-Q[i,t,2]
for(n in 1:2){ logit(Q[i,t,n]) <-  cut[n] - mu[i,t] }}}
# Cutpoints
 cut[1] <- 0; cut[2] ~ dnorm(0, 1)I(cut[1],)
 for (i in 1:J){ for (t in 1:T){
    mu[i,t] ~ dnorm( mu.factor[i,t], 1 )}}
# Linear predictor at t=1
 for (i in 1:J){ f[i] ~ dnorm (0, 1)
    mu.factor[i,1] <- a[1] + b[i] + g[i,1]
    g[i,1] <- g[1]*polity[i,1] +...+ g[3]*growth[i,1] + f[i]
# Linear predictor at t=2 thru T
 for (t in 2:T){ prv[i,t] <- a[t-1] + b[i] + g[i,t]
    g[i,t] <- g[1]*polity[i,t-1] +...+ g[3]*growth[i,t-1]
    mu.factor[i,t] <- phi*(mu[i,t-1] - prv[i,t]) +
                      alpha[t] + b[i] + g[i,t]}}
# Priors
 for (j in 1:3){g[j] ~ dnorm(0, 0.001)}; phi ~ dnorm (0, 0.1)
 for (t in 1:T){a[t] ~ dnorm(0, 0.1)}
 for (j in 1:J){b[j] ~ dnorm(mu.b[j], 0.1)
    mu.b[j] <- d[1] + d[2]*gini[j]}
 for (k in 1:2){d[k] ~ dnorm(0, 0.01)}}
```

A.3.6 Autocorrelated Distributed Lag Regression

```
model{ for (i in 1:I){ for (t in 1:T){
 y[i,t] ~ dnorm ( eta[i,t], tau.y[i] ) }}
# Linear predictor
for (i in 1:I) { for (t in 2:T) {
 eta[i,t] <- a[i] + z[1]*democ[i,t]   +...+ z[4]*rgdp[i,1]
                   + b[1]*democ[i,t-1] +...+ b[4]*rgdp[i,t-1]
                   + b[5]*y[i,t-1]}}
# Modeled random intercepts
for (i in 1:I){ a[i] ~ dnorm( mu.a[i], 0.01)
  mu.a[i] <- d[1] + d[2]*gini[i] + d[3]*trans
# Priors
for (l in 1:3){ d[l] ~ dnorm( 0, 0.01 ) }
for (k in 1:4){ z[k] ~ dnorm( 0, 0.01 ) }
for (h in 1:5){ b[k] ~ dnorm( 0, 0.01 ) }
   tau.y[i] <- pow(sig.y[i],-2)
   sig.y[i]   ~ dunif(0, 100)
```

References

Acemoglu, Daron and James A. Robinson. 2005. *Economic Origins of Dictatorship and Democracy*. Cambridge, MA: Cambridge University Press.

Aghion, Philippe, Patrick Bolton and Steven Fries. 1999. "Optimal Design of Bank Bailouts: The Case of Transition Economies." *Journal of Institutional and Theoretical Economics* 155(1):51–70.

Akerlof, George A. and Paul M. Romer. 1993. "Looting: The Economic Underworld of Bankruptcy for Profit." *Brookings Papers on Economic Activity* 2:1–60.

Albert, James H. and Siddhartha Chib. 1993. "Bayesian Analysis of Binary and Polychotomous Response Data." *Journal of the American Statistical Association* 88(422):669–679.

Allen, Franklin and Douglas Gale. 2000. *Comparing Financial Systems*. Cambridge, MA: Cambridge University Press.

Andrews, David. 1994. "Capital Mobility and State Autonomy: Toward a Structural Theory of International Monetary Relations." *International Studies Quarterly* 38(2):193–218.

Angrist, Joshua D., Guido W. Imbens and Donald B. Rubin. 1996. "Identification of Causal Effects Using Instrumental Variables." *Journal of the American Statistical Association* 91:444–455.

Archer, Candace C., Glen Biglaiser and Karl DeRouen. 2007. "Sovereign Bonds and the 'Democratic Advantage': Does Regime Type Affect Credit Rating Agency Ratings in the Developing World?" *International Organization* 61:341–365.

Arnaudo, Aldo A. 1996. "La crisis mexicana y el sistema financiero argentino." In *La macroeconomía de los mercados emergentes*, ed. Gonzalo Rodríguez Prada. Madrid, España: Universidad de Alcalá.

Ashworth, Scott and Ethan Bueno de Mesquita. 2006. "Monotone Comparative Statics for Models of Politics." *American Journal of Political Science* 50(1):214–231.

Backman, M. 1999. *Asian Eclipse: Exposing the Dark Side of Business in Asia*. John Wiley and Sons.

Bagehot, Walter. 1873. *Lombard Street: A Description of the Money Market*. London: Henry S. King & Co.

Baliño, Tomás. 1990. "La crisis bancaria argentina de 1980." *Ensayos Económicos* 44.

Banco Central de la República Argentina. 1995. "Seminario sobre insolvencia de

187

bancos: Causas y soluciones." Buenos Aires, Argentina.

Barro, Robert. 1973. "The Control of Politicians: An Economic Model." *Public Choice* 14:19–42.

Bartholomew, Philip F. and Nancy A. Wentzler. 1999. "International Bank Lending and the Southeast Asian Financial Crisis." In *International Banking Crises*, ed. Benton E. Gup. Westport, CT: Quorum Books pp. 37–53.

Baum, Christopher F. and Richard Sperling. 2001. "Tests for Stationarity of a Time Series: Update." *Stata Technical Bulletin* 10(58):2–3.

Beck, Thornsten, Asli Demirgüç-Kunt and Ross Levine. 1999. "A New Database on Financial Development and Structure." *World Bank Economic Review* 14:597–605.

Beck, Thorsten, Asli Demirgüç-Kunt and Maria Soledad Martinez Peria. 2008. "Banking Services for Everyone? Barriers to Bank Access and Use Around the World." *World Bank Economic Review* 22(3):397–430.

Beim, David O. 2001. "What Triggers a Systemic Banking Crisis?" In *Banking Crises in Europe: Country Experiences*, ed. Rajshekar N. Subbulakshmi. Hyderabad, India: ICFAI, chapter one.

Beim, David O. and Charles W. Calomiris. 2001. *Emerging Financial Markets*. New York: McGraw-Hill.

Bennett, Randall W. and Christine Loucks. 1994. "Savings and Loans and Finance Industry PAC Contributions to Incumbent Members of the House Banking Committee." *Public Choice* 79(1-2):83–104.

Bernhard, William T. 2002. *Banking on Reform: Political Parties and Central Bank Independence in the Industrial Democracies*. Michigan Studies in International Political Economy. Ann Arbor, MI: University of Michigan Press.

Boix, Carles. 2003. *Democracy and Redistribution*. Cambridge, UK: Cambridge University Press.

Boix, Carles and Susan C. Stokes. 2003. "Endogenous Democratization." *World Politics* 55:517–549.

Bongini, Paola, Stijn Claessens and Giovanni Ferri. 2001. "The Political Economy of Distress in East Asian Financial Institutions." *Journal of Financial Services Research* 19(1):5–25.

Bordo, Michael D. 1986. "Financial Crises, Banking Crises, Stock Market Crashes and the Money Supply: Some International Evidence, 1870–1933." In *Financial Crises and the World Banking System*, ed. F. Capie and G. E. Wood. London, UK: MacMillan.

Bordo, Michael D. 2002. "The Lender of Last Resort: Alternative Views and Historical Experience." In *Financial Crises, Contagion, and the Lender of Last Resort. A Reader*, ed. Charles Goodhart and Gerhard Illing. Oxford, UK: Oxford University Press.

Boylan, Delia M. 2001. *Defusing Democracy: Central Bank Autonomy and the Transition from Authoritarian Rule*. Ann Arbor, MI: University of Michigan Press.

Braessas, Homero and Alejandra G. Naughton. 1997. *La realidad financiera del Banco Central. El antes y después de la Convertibilidad*. Buenos Aires, Argentina: Editorial Belgrano.

Brown, Craig O. and I. Serdar Dinç. 2005. "The Politics of Bank Failures: Evidence from Emerging Markets." *Quarterly Journal of Economics* 120(4):1413–1444.

Broz, J. Lawrence. 2002. "Political System Transparency and Monetary Commitment Regimes." *International Organization* 56(4):861–887.

Bueno de Mesquita, Bruce, Alastair Smith, Randolph M. Siverson and James D. Morrow. 2004. *The Logic of Political Survival*. Boston, MA: MIT Press.

Calderón, César and Lin Liu. 2003. "The Direction of Causality Between Financial Development and Economic Growth." *Journal of Development Economics* 72:321–334.

Calomiris, Charles, Daniela Klingebiel and Luc Laeven. 2005. "Financial Crisis Policies and Resolution Mechanisms. A Taxonomy from Cross-Country Experience." In *Systemic Financial Crises. Containment and Resolution*, ed. Patrick Honohan and Luc Laeven. Cambridge, MA: Cambridge University Press pp. 25–75.

Calomiris, Charles W. 1997. *The Postmodern Bank Safety Net: Lessons from Developed and Developing Economies*. Washington, DC: American Enterprise Institute Press.

Calomiris, Charles W. 2007. "Bank Failures in Theory and History: The Great Depression and Other 'Contagious' Events." NBER Working Paper 13597.

Calomiris, Charles W. 2008. "Banking Crises." *NBER Reporter* 4:10–14.

Calomiris, Charles W. and Joseph R. Mason. 2003. "How to Restructure Failed Banking Systems: Lessons from the US in the 1930s and Japan in the 1990s." NBER Working Paper 9624.

Caprio, Gerard and Daniela Klingebiel. 1997. "Bank Insolvency: Bad Luck, Bad Policy, or Bad Banking?" In *Annual World Bank Conference on Development Economics 1996*. Washington, DC: The World Bank.

Caprio, Gerard, Daniela Klingebiel, Luc Laeven and Guillermo Noguera. 2005. "Appendix. Banking Crisis Database." In *Systemic Financial Crises. Containment and Resolution*, ed. Patrick Honohan and Luc Laeven. Cambridge, UK: Cambridge University Press pp. 309–340.

Chan, Yuk-Shee, Stuart Greenbaum and Anjan Thakor. 1992. "Is Fairly Priced Deposit Insurance Possible?" *Journal of Finance* 47:227–245.

Cheibub, Jose Antonio and Jennifer Gandhi. 2004. "A Six-Fold Measure of Democracies and Dictatorships." Paper presented at the 2004 Annual Meeting of the American Political Science Association.

Chinn, Menzie D. and Hiro Ito. 2002. "Capital Account Liberalization, Institutions and Financial Development: Cross-Country Evidence." University of California–Santa Cruz Center for International Economics Working Paper 02–11.

Clarke, George and Robert Cull. 2002. "Political and Economic Determinants of the Likelihood of Privatizing Argentine Public Banks." *Journal of Law and Economics* 45(1):165–197.

Clementi, Fabio and Mauro Gallegati. 2005. "Pareto's Law of Income Distribution: Evidence for Germany, the United Kingdom, and the United States." In *Econophysics of Wealth Distributions*, ed. Arnab Chatterjee, Sudhakar Yarlagadda and Bikas K. Chakrabarti. Milan, Italy: Springer Verlag pp. 3–14.

Cole, Rebel A. 1993. "When Are Thrift Institutions Closed? An Agency-Theoretic Model." *Journal of Financial Services Research* 7:283–307.

Cole, Rebel A. and Jeffery W. Gunther. 1995. "Separating the Likelihood and Timing of Bank Failure." *Journal of Banking and Finance* 19(6).

Cooper, Richard N. 1968. *The Economics of Interdependence*. New York, NY: Columbia University Press.

Cordella, Tito and Eduardo Levy-Yeyati. 1999. "Bank Bailouts: Moral Hazard vs. Value Effect." *Journal of Financial Intermediation* 12(4):300–330.

Corsetti, Giancarlo, Paolo Pesenti and Nouriel Roubini. 1999. "What Caused the Asian Currency and Financial Crises?" *Japan and the World Economy* 11(3):305–373.

Cox, Gary W. 1990. "Centripetal and Centrifugal Incentives in Electoral Systems." *American Journal of Political Science* 34(4):903–935.

Cukierman, Alex. 1992. *Central Bank Strategy, Credibility, and Independence: Theory and Evidence*. Boston, MA: MIT Press.

Cukierman, Alex, Geoffrey P. Miller and Bilin Neyapti. 2002. "Central Bank Reform, Liberalization and Inflation in Transition Economies. An International Perspective." *Journal of Monetary Economics* 49(2):237–264.

Cukierman, Alex, Steven B. Webb and Bilin Neyapti. 1992. "Measuring the Independence of Central Banks and Its Effect on Policy Outcomes." *World Bank Economic Review* 6(3):353–398.

Dahl, Robert. 1971. *Polyarchy*. New Haven, CT: Yale University Press.

D'Amato, Laura, Elena Grubisic and Andrew Powell. 1997. "Contagion, Bank Fundamentals or Macroeconomic Shock? An Empirical Analysis of the Argentine 1995 Banking Problems." Technical Report, Banco Central de la República Argentina.

Davis, William S. 1913. *Readings in Ancient History II. Rome and the West*. Allyn and Bacon.

De Juan, Aristóbulo. 1999. "Clearing the Decks: Experiences in Banking Crisis Resolution." In *Banks and Capital Markets: Sound Financial Systems for the 21st Century*, ed. Shahid J. Burki and Guillermo E. Perry. Washington, DC: The World Bank.

De Krivoy, Ruth. 1996. "Crisis Avoidance." In *Banking Crises in Latin America*, ed. Ricardo Hausman and Liliana Rojas Suárez. Washington, DC: Inter-American Development Bank.

DeBoef, Suzanna and Luke Keele. 2008. "Taking Time Seriously: Dynamic Regression." *American Journal of Political Science* 52(1):184–200.

DeGroot, Morris and Mark Schervish. 2002. *Probability and Statistics*. Third ed. Boston, MA: Addison-Wesley.

Del Villar, Rafael, Daniel Backal and Juan Treviño. 1997. "Experiencia internacional en la resolución de crisis bancarias." Documento de Investigación 9708, Banco de México.

Dell'Ariccia, Giovanni, Enrica Detragiache and Raghuram Rajan. 2008. "The Real Effect of Banking Crises." *Journal of Financial Intermediation* 17(1):89–112.

Demirgüç-Kunt, Asli and Enrica Detragiache. 2000. "Monitoring Banking Sector Fragility: A Multivariate Logit Approach with an Application to the 1996–1997 Banking Crises." *World Bank Economic Review* 14(3).

Demirgüç-Kunt, Asli, Edward J. Kane and Luc Laeven. 2008. "Determinants of Deposit-Insurance Adoption and Design." *Journal of Financial Intermediation*

17(3):407–438.

Desai, Raj M., Anders Olofsgård and Tarik M. Yousef. 2003. "Democracy, Inequality, and Inflation." *American Political Science Review* 97(3):391–406.

Dewatripont, Mathias and Jean Tirole. 1994. *The Prudential Regulation of Banks.* Cambridge, MA: MIT Press.

Di Bella, Gabriela and Francisco Ciocchini. 1995. "La corrida bancaria de 1995." *Boletín de Lecturas Sociales y Económicas* 7:49–64.

Diamond, Douglas W. and Philip H. Dybvig. 1983. "Bank Runs, Deposit Insurance, and Liquidity." *Journal of Political Economy* 91(3):401–419.

Dinç, I. Serdar. 2005. "Politicians and Banks: Political Influences on Government-Owned Banks in Emerging Markets." *Journal of Financial Economics* 77:453–479.

Downs, Anthony. 1957. *An Economic Theory of Democracy.* Addison-Wesley.

Dziobek, Claudia. 1998. "Market-Based Policy Instruments for Systemic Bank Restructuring." Working Paper 98-113, International Monetary Fund.

Dziobek, Claudia and Celia Pazarbasioglu. 1999. "Lessons from Systemic Bank Restructuring." *Financial Issues* 14.

Eichengreen, Barry and Carlos Arteta. 2002. "Banking Crises in Emerging Markets: Presumptions and Evidence." In *Financial Policies in Emerging Markets*, ed. Mario I. Blejer and Marko Škreb. Cambridge, MA: The MIT Press pp. 47–94.

Elizondo, Carlos. 2001. *La importancia de las reglas. Gobierno y empresarios después de la nacionalización bancaria.* México, DF: Fondo de Cultura Económica.

Enoch, Charles, Gillian Garcia and V. Sundararajan. 1999. "Recapitalizing Banks with Public Funds: Selected Issues." Working Paper 99-139, International Monetary Fund.

Faccio, Mara. 2006. "Politically Connected Firms." *American Economic Review* 96(1):369–386.

Faccio, Mara, Ronald Masulis and John McConnell. 2006. "Political Connections and Government Bailouts." *Journal of Finance* 61(6):2597–2635.

Feijen, Erik and Enrico Perotti. 2005. "The Political Economy of Financial Fragility." Tinbergen Institute Discussion Paper 2005-115.

Ferejohn, John. 1986. "Incumbent Performance and Electoral Control." *Public Choice* 50:5–25.

Fernández, Roque. 1994. *Informe anual sobre las operaciones del Banco Central de la República Argentina al Honorable Congreso de la Nación.* Buenos Aires, Argentina: Banco Central de la República Argentina.

Fernández, Roque. 1995. *Informe anual sobre las operaciones del Banco Central de la República Argentina al Honorable Congreso de la Nación.* Buenos Aires, Argentina: Banco Central de la República Argentina.

Fernández, Roque. 1996. *Informe anual sobre las operaciones del Banco Central de la República Argentina al Honorable Congreso de la Nación.* Buenos Aires, Argentina: Banco Central de la República Argentina.

Franzese, Robert J. 1999. "Partially Independent Central Banks, Politically Responsive Governments, and Inflation." *American Journal of Political Science* 43(3):681–706.

Freixas, Xavier, Curzio Giannini, Glenn Hoggarth and Farouk Soussa. 2000. "Lender of Last Resort: A Review of the Literature." *Journal of Financial Services Research*

18(1):63–87.

Freixas, Xavier and Bruno M. Parigi. 2007. "Banking Regulation and Prompt Corrective Action." Working Paper Series 2136 CESifo.

Freixas, Xavier, Bruno M. Parigi and Jean-Charles Rochet. 2000. "Systemic Risk, Interbank Relations and Liquidity Provision by the Central Bank." *Journal of Money, Credit and Banking* 32(3):611–638.

Freixas, Xavier and Jean-Charles Rochet. 1997. *Microeconomics of Banking.* Cambridge, MA: MIT Press.

Frydl, Edward J. 1999. "The Length and Cost of Banking Crises." Working Paper 99-30. Washington, DC: International Monetary Fund.

Gale, Douglas and Xavier Vives. 2002. "Dollarization, Bailouts, and the Stability of the Banking System." *Quarterly Journal of Economics* 117(2):467–502.

Gavito, Javier and Aaron Silva. 1996. "Mexico's Financial Crisis: Origins, Consequences, and Measures Implemented to Overcome It." Technical Report, Mexican National Banking and Securities Commission.

Gelman, Andrew, John B. Carlin, Hal S. Stern and Donald B. Rubin. 2004. *Bayesian Data Analysis.* Boca Raton, FL: Chapman & Hall/CRC Press.

Gelman, Andrew and Jennifer Hill. 2007. *Data Analysis Using Regression and Multilevel/Hierarchical Models.* Cambridge, MA: Cambridge University Press.

Gerring, John and Strom Thacker. 2004. "Political Institutions and Corruption: The Role of Unitarism and Parliamentarism." *British Journal of Political Science* 34(2):295–330.

Gill, Jeff. 2002. *Bayesian Methods. A Social and Behavioral Sciences Approach.* Boca Raton, FL: Chapman & Hall/CRC Press.

Gleditsch, Kristian S. and Michael D. Ward. 2006. "Diffusion and the International Context of Democratization." *International Organization* 60(4):911–933.

Glick, Reuven and Michael Hutchison. 1999. "Banking and Currency Crises: How Common Are Twins?" Working Paper PB99-07, Federal Reserve Bank of San Francisco, San Francisco, CA.

Goodhart, Charles and Gerhard Illing, eds. 2002. *Financial Crises, Contagion, and the Lender of Last Resort. A Reader.* Oxford, UK: Oxford University Press.

Gorton, Gary and Lixin Huang. 2004. "Liquidity, Efficiency, and Bank Bailouts." *American Economic Review* 94(3):455–483.

Grilli, Vittorio, Donato Masciandaro and Guido Tabellini. 1991. "Political and Monetary Institutions and Public Financial Policies in the Industrial Countries." *Economic Policy* 13:341–392.

Haber, Stephen. 2002*a*. "Introduction: The Political Economy of Crony Capitalism." In *Crony Capitalism and Economic Growth in Latin America. Theory and Evidence*, ed. Stephen Haber. Stanford, CA: Hoover Institution Press.

Haber, Stephen, ed. 2002*b*. *Crony Capitalism and Economic Growth in Latin America. Theory and Evidence.* Stanford, CA: Hoover Institution Press.

Haggard, Stephan. 2000. *The Political Economy of the Asian Financial Crisis.* Washington, DC: Institute for International Economics.

Haggard, Stephan and Andrew MacIntyre. 1998. "The Political Economy of the Asian Economic Crisis." *Review of International Political Economy* 5(3):381–392.

Hall, Maximilian, ed. 2001. *The Regulation and Supervision of Banks.* London, UK: Edward Elgar Publishing.

Hallerberg, Mark. 2002. "Veto players and the choice of monetary institutions." *International Organization* 56(4):775–802.

Hardy, Daniel C. and Celia Pazarbasioglu. 1998. "Leading Indicators of Banking Crises: Was Asia Different?" Working Paper 98-91. Washington, DC: International Monetary Fund.

Haslag, Joseph H. and Rowena Pecchenino. 2005. "Crony Capitalism and Financial System Stability." *Economic Inquiry* 43(1):24–38.

Hawkins, John and Philip Turner. 1998. *Bank Restructuring in Practice: An Overview.* Bank for International Settlements.

Heston, Alan, Robert Summers and Bettina Aten. 2002. "Penn World Table Version 6.1." Philadelphia, PA: Center for International Comparisons at the University of Pennsylvania (CICUP), October.

Ho, Daniel, Kosuke Imai, Gary King and Elizabeth Stuart. 2007a. "Matching as Nonparametric Preprocessing for Improving Parametric Causal Inference." *Political Analysis* 15(3):199–236.

Ho, Daniel, Kosuke Imai, Gary King and Elizabeth Stuart. 2007b. "Matchit: Nonparametric Preprocessing for Parametric Causal Inference." *Journal of Statistical Software.* http://gking.harvard.edu/matchit/.

Holland, Paul. 1986. "Statistics and Causal Inference." *Journal of the American Statistical Association* 81(396):945–960.

Honohan, Patrick and Daniela Klingebiel. 2000. "Controlling the Fiscal Costs of Banking Crises." Working Paper 2441. Washington, DC: The World Bank.

Honohan, Patrick and Luc Laeven, eds. 2005. *Systemic Financial Crises. Containment and Resolution.* New York, NY: Cambridge University Press.

Ishihara, Yoichiro. 2005. "Quantitative Analysis of Crisis: Crisis Identification and Causality." Working Paper WPS-3598. Washington, DC: The World Bank.

Jackman, Simon. 2000. "Estimation and Inference Are Missing Data Problems: Unifying Social Science Statistics via Bayesian Simulation." *Political Analysis* 8(4):307–332.

Jackman, Simon. 2001. "Multidimensional Analysis of Roll Call Data via Bayesian Simulation: Identification, Estimation, Inference, and Model Checking." *Political Analysis* 9(3):227–241.

Jensen, Nathan M. 2006. *Nation-States and the Multinational Corporation: A Political Economy of Foreign Direct Investment.* Princeton, NJ: Princeton University Press.

Johnson, Valen E. and James H. Albert. 1999. *Modeling Ordinal Data.* New York, NY: Springer.

Kahn, Charles and João Santos. 2005. "Allocating Bank Regulatory Powers: Lender of Last Resort, Deposit Insurance and Supervision." *European Economic Review* 49(8): 2107–2136.

Kaminsky, Graciela and Carmen Reinhart. 1999. "The Twin Crises: The Causes of Banking and Balance-of-Payments Problems." *American Economic Review* 89(3).

Kane, Edward J. 2000. "Capital Movements, Banking Insolvency, and Silent Runs in the Asian Financial Crisis." *Pacific Basin Finance Journal* 8(2):153–175.

Kane, Edward J. 2001. "Dynamic Inconsistency of Capital Forbearance: Long-Run vs. Short-Run Effects of Too-Big-To-Fail Policymaking." *Pacific Basin Finance Journal* 9(4):281–299.

Kang, David C. 2002. *Crony Capitalism: Corruption and Development in South Korea and the Philippines.* Cambridge, MA: Cambridge University Press.

Kapstein, Ethan. 1994. *Governing the Global Economy: International Finance and the State.* Cambridge, MA: Harvard University Press.

Keefer, Philip. 2002. "When Do Special Interests Run Rampant? Disentangling the Role of Elections, Incomplete Information and Checks and Balances in Banking Crises." Working Paper 2543. Washington, DC: The World Bank.

Keefer, Philip. 2007. "Elections, Special Interests, and Financial Crisis." *International Organization* 61:607–641.

Keefer, Philip and David Stasavage. 2002. "Checks and Balances, Private Information, and the Credibility of Monetary Commitments." *International Organization* 56(4):751–774.

Keefer, Philip and David Stasavage. 2003. "The Limits of Delegation: Veto Players, Central Bank Independence, and the Credibility of Monetary Policy." *American Political Science Review* 97(3):407–423.

Khwaja, Asim Ijaz and Atif Mian. 2005. "Do Lenders Favor Politically Connected Firms? Rent Provision in an Emerging Financial Market." *Quarterly Journal of Economics* 120(4):1371–1411.

King, Gary and Langche Zeng. 2006. "The Dangers of Extreme Counterfactuals." *Political Analysis* 14(2):131–159.

Knack, Steve and Philip Keefer. 1998. *IRIS-3: File of International Country Risk Guide Data.* 3rd ed. East Syracuse, NY: The PRS Group.

Krugman, Paul. 1998. "What Happened to Asia?" Unpublished manuscript. http://web.mit.edu/krugman/www/.

Kwiatkowski, D., P.C.B. Phillips, P. Schmidt and Y Shin. 1992. "Testing the Null Hypothesis of Stationarity against the Alternative of a Unit Root." *Journal of Econometrics* 54:159–178.

Kydland, Finn E. and Edward C. Prescott. 1977. "Rules Rather than Discretion: The Inconsistency of Optimal Plans." *Journal of Political Economy* 85(3):473–491.

La Porta, Rafael, Florencio López de Silanes and Guillermo Zamarripa. 2003. "Related Lending." *Quarterly Journal of Economics* 118:231–268.

Lindgren, Carl J. 2005. "Pitfalls in Managing Closures of Financial Institutions." In *Systemic Financial Crises. Containment and Resolution*, ed. Patrick Honohan and Luc Laeven. Cambridge UK: Cambridge University Press.

Lindgren, Carl J., Gillian García and Matthew I. Saal. 1996. *Bank Soundness and Macroeconomic Policy.* Washington, DC: International Monetary Fund.

Little, Roderick J. and Donald B. Rubin. 1987. *Statistical Analysis with Missing Data.* John Wiley & Sons.

López Obrador, Andrés Manuel. 1999. *Fobaproa: Expediente abierto.* México, DF:. Editorial Grijalbo.

Mackey, Michael W. 1999. "Informe de la evaluación integral de las operaciones y funciontes del Fondo Bancario de Protección al Ahorro 'FOBAPROA' y la calidad de supervisión de los programas del FOBAPROA de 1995 a 1998." Informe Presentado al H. Congreso de la Unión. México, DF.

Mailath, George and Loretta Mester. 1994. "A Positive Analysis of Bank Closure." *Journal of Financial Intermediation* 3(3):272–299.

Maxfield, Sylvia. 1990. *Governing Capital: International Finance and Mexican Politics.* Ithaca, NY: Cornell University Press.

Maxfield, Sylvia. 1997. *Gatekeepers of Growth: The International Political Economy of Central Banking in Developing Countries.* Princeton, NJ: Princeton University Press.

Maxfield, Sylvia. 2003. "When Do Voters Matter More Than Cronies in Developing Countries? The Politics of Bank Crisis Resolution." In *Critical Issues in International Financial Reform*, ed. Albert Berry and Gustavo Indart. Transaction Publishers pp. 263–294.

Meltzer, Allan H. and Scott F. Richard. 1981. "A Rational Theory of the Size of Government." *Journal of Political Economy* 89:914–927.

Miller, Gary J. 2005. "The Political Evolution of Principal-Agent Models." *Annual Review of Political Science* 8:203–225.

Mishkin, Frederic. 1996. "Understanding Financial Crises: A Developing Country Perspective." In *Annual World Bank Conference on Development Economics*, ed. Michael Bruno and Boris Pleskovic. Washington, DC: The World Bank.

Mishkin, Frederic. 2006. "How Big a Problem is Too Big to Fail? A Review of Gary Stern and Ron Feldman's *Too Big to Fail: The Hazards of Bank Bailouts.*" *Journal of Economic Literature* 44(4):988–1004.

Mitzenmacher, Michael. 2003. "A Brief History of Generative Models for Power Law and Lognormal Distributions." *Internet Mathematics* 1(2):226–251.

Montinola, Gabriella R. and Robert W. Jackman. 2002. "Sources of Corruption: A Cross-Country Study." *British Journal of Political Science* 32(1):147–170.

Moore, Barrington. 1966. *Social Origins of Dictatorship and Democracy: Lord and Peasant in the Making of the Modern World.* Boston, MA: Beacon Press.

Murillo, José Antonio. 2001. "La banca en México: Privatización, crisis y reordenamiento." Unpublished manuscript, División de Estudios Económicos, Banco de México.

Nava-Campos, Gabriela. 2002. "Fiscal Implications of Mexico's 1994 Banking Crisis and Bailout." Documento de Trabajo 109, Centro de Investigación y Docencia Económicas.

Navarrete, Juan. 2000. "Boom, Crisis and Recovery: The Political Economy of Mexican Banking During the 1990s." MSc thesis, Oxford University.

North, Douglas C. and Barry Weingast. 1989. "Constitutions and Commitment: The Evolution of Institutions Governing Public Choice in Seventeenth-Century England." *Journal of Economic History* 49(4):803–832.

Oatley, Thomas. 1999. "How Constraining is Capital Mobility? The Partisan Hypothesis in an Open Economy." *American Journal of Political Science* 43(4):1003–1027.

Oatley, Thomas and Robert Nabors. 1998. "Redistributive Cooperation: Market Failure, Wealth Transfers, and the Basle Accord." *International Organization* 52(1):35–54.

Obstfeld, Maurice. 1998. "The Global Capital Market: Benefactor or Menace?" *Journal of Economic Perspectives* 12(4):9–30.

Olson, Mancur. 1965. *The Logic of Collective Action: Public Goods and the Theory of Groups.* Harvard University Press.

Ortiz Martínez, Guillermo. 1994. *La reforma financiera y la desincorporación bancaria.* México, DF: Fondo de Cultura Económica.

Persson, Torsten and Guido Tabellini. 2003. *The Economic Effects of Constitutions.* Munich Lectures in Economics Cambridge, MA: MIT Press.

Piekarz, Julio A. 1981. *La garantía de los depósitos en los intermediarios financieros.* Number 11 in "Serie de Información Pública" Buenos Aires, Argentina: Centro de Estudios Monetarios y Bancarios del Banco Central de la República de Argentina.

Polillo, Simone and Mauro F. Guillén. 2005. "Globalization Pressures and the State: The Global Spread of Central Bank Independence." *American Journal of Sociology* 110(6):1764–1802.

Przeworski, Adam, Michael E. Alvarez, Jose Antonio Cheibub and Fernando Limongi. 2000. *Democracy and Development. Political Institutions and Well-Being in the World, 1950–1990.* Cambridge, MA: Cambridge University Press.

Przeworski, Adam and James Raymond Vreeland. 2000. "The Effect of IMF Programs on Economic Growth." *Journal of Development Economics* 62(2):385–421.

Rasch, Georg. 1980. *Probabilistic Models for Some Intelligence and Attainment Tests.* Chicago, IL: Meta Press.

Raudenbush, Stephen and Anthony Bryk. 2002. *Hierarchical Linear Models: Applications and Data Analysis Methods.* Advanced Quantitative Techniques in the Social Sciences second ed. Thousand Oaks, CA: Sage Publications.

Repullo, Rafael. 2005a. "Liquidity, Risk Taking, and the Lender of Last Resort." *International Journal of Central Banking* 1(2):47–80.

Repullo, Rafael. 2005b. "Policies for Banking Crises. A Theoretical Framework." In *Systemic Financial Crises. Containment and Resolution*, ed. Patrick Honohan and Luc Laeven. Cambridge University Press. Chapter five, pp. 137–168.

Ribas, Armando. 1998. *Crisis bancarias y convertibilidad. Los sistemas financieros ante los problemas de la globalización.* Buenos Aires, Argentina: Asociación de Banqueros.

Rochet, Jean-Charles. 2003. "Why Are There so Many Banking Crises?" *CESifo Economics Studies* 49(2):141–155.

Rodríguez, Francisco. 2004. "Inequality, Redistribution, and Rent-Seeking." *Economics and Politics* 16(3):287–320.

Rodrik, Dani. 1998. "Who Needs Capital-Account Convertibility?" In *Should the IMF Pursue Capital-Account Convertibility?* ed. Peter B. Kenen. Essays in International Finance No. 207 Princeton, NJ: Princeton University Press pp. 55–65.

Romer, Thomas and Barry Weingast. 1991. "Political Foundations of the Thrift Debacle." In *Politics and Economics in the Eighties*, ed. Alberto Alesina and Geoffrey Carliner. Chicago, IL: University of Chicago Press pp. 175–215.

Rosas, Guillermo. 2002. "Bagehot or Bailout? The Political Economy of Bank Crises, 1975–2000." PhD thesis Duke University.

Rosas, Guillermo. 2006. "Bagehot or Bailout? An Analysis of Government Responses to Banking Crises." *American Journal of Political Science* 50(1).

Rosenbaum, Paul R. and Donald B. Rubin. 1983. "The Central Role of the Propensity Score in Observational Studies for Causal Effects." *Biometrika* 70:41–55.

Rosenbluth, Frances and Ross Schaap. 2003. "The Domestic Politics of Banking Regulation." *International Organization* 57(2):307–336.

Roubini, Nouriel and Brad Setser. 2004. *Bailouts or Bail-ins: Responding to Financial Crises in Emerging Markets*. Washington, DC: Institute for International Economics.

Rozenwurcel, Guillermo and Leonardo Bleger. 1997. "El sistema bancario argentino en los noventa: De la profundización financiera a la crisis sistémica." *Desarrollo Económico. Revista de Ciencias Sociales* 37(3):163–194.

Rubin, Donald B. 1974. "Estimating Causal Effects of Treatments in Randomized and Nonrandomized Studies." *Journal of Educational Psychology* 66(5):688–701.

Rubin, Donald B. 1976. "Inference and Missing Data." *Biometrika* 63(3):581–592.

Rubio, Luis. 1998. "FOBAPROA o las consecuencias de la ineptitud." *Revista Nexos*. México, DF: México pp. 59–67.

Saiegh, Sebastian. 2005. "Do Countries Have a 'Democratic Advantage'? Political Institutions, Multilateral Agencies and Sovereign Borrowing." *Comparative Political Studies* 38(4):366–387.

Sargent, Thomas and Neil Wallace. 1975. "'Rational' Expectations, the Optimal Monetary Instrument, and the Optimal Money Supply Rule." *Journal of Political Economy* 83(2):241–254.

Satyanath, Shanker. 2006. *Globalization, Politics, and Financial Turmoil. Asia's Banking Crisis*. New York, NY: Cambridge University Press.

Schultz, Kenneth and Barry Weingast. 2003. "The Democratic Advantage: Institutional Foundations of Financial Power in International Competition." *International Organization* 57(1):3–42.

Schumpeter, Joseph. 1942. *Capitalism, Socialism and Democracy*. New York, NY: Harper and Bros.

Schwartz, Anne J. 1988. "Financial Stability and the Federal Safety Act." In *Restructuring Banking and Financial Services in America*, ed. William S. Haraf and Rose M. Kushmeider. American Enterprise Institute.

Secretaría de Hacienda y Crédito Público. 1998. *Fobaproa: La verdadera historia*. México, DF: Secretaría de Hacienda y Crédito Público.

Shor, Boris, Joseph Bafumi, Luke Keele and David K. Park. 2007. "A Bayesian Multilevel Modeling Approach to Time-Series Cross-Sectional Data." *Political Analysis* 15:165–181.

Singer, David A. 2007. *Regulating Capital. Setting Standards for the International Financial System*. Cornell Studies in Money Ithaca, NY: Cornell University Press.

Solís, Leopoldo. 1999. *Fobaproa y las recientes reformas financieras*. México, DF: Instituto de Investigación Económica y Social Lucas Alamán.

Soral, H. Bartu, Talan B. İşcan and Gregory Hebb. 2003. "Fraud, Banking Crisis, and Regulatory Enforcement: Evidence from Micro-level Transactions Data." *European Journal of Law and Economics* 21(2):179–197.

Stern, Gary H. and Ron J. Feldman. 2004. *Too Big to Fail: The Hazards of Bank*

Bailouts. Washington, DC: Brookings Institution Press.

Stuckler, David, Christopher M. Meissner and Lawrence P. King. 2008. "Can a Bank Crisis Break Your Heart?" *Globalization and Health* 4(1).

Sundararajan, Vasudevan and Tomás Baliño, eds. 1991. *Banking Crises: Cases and Issues*. International Monetary Fund.

Teichman, Judith A. 1995. *Privatization and Political Change in Mexico*. Pittsburgh, PA: University of Pittsburgh Press.

Thomson, J. B. 1992. "Modeling the Bank Regulator's Closure Option: A Two-Step Logit Regression Approach." *Journal of Financial Services Research* 6:5–23.

Thornton, Henry. 1802. *An Enquiry into the Nature and Effects of the Paper Credit of Great Britain*. London, UK: J. Hatchard.

Transparency International. 2002. "Corruption Perceptions Index." Transparency International Berlin, Germany. http://www.transparency.org/.

Treisman, Daniel. 2000. "The Causes of Corruption: A Cross-National Study." *Journal of Public Economics* 76(3):399–457.

Tsebelis, George. 2002. *Veto Players: How Political Institutions Work*. Princeton, NJ: Princeton University Press.

Vaaler, Paul M. and Gerry McNamara. 2004. "Crisis and Competition in Expert Organizational Decision Making: Credit-Rating Agencies and Their Response to Turbulence in Emerging Economies." *Organization Science* 15(6):687–203.

Van Buuren, Stef and Karin Oudshoorn. 2000. "Multivariate Imputation by Chained Equations: MICE V1.0 User's Manual." Report PG/VGZ/00.038 TNO Prevention and Health Leiden, Netherlands.

Vaugirard, Victor E. 2007. "Bank Bailouts and Political Instability." *European Journal of Political Economy* 23(4):821–837.

The World Bank. 2006. "World Development Indicators." CD-ROM.

Index